EDUCATION, TRAINING, AND THE URBAN GHETTO

THE JOHNS HOPKINS UNIVERSITY PRESS   BALTIMORE AND LONDON

"There is no more cruel punishment
than futile and hopeless labor."

—Albert Camus, *The Myth
of Sisyphus*

BENNETT HARRISON

EDUCATION,
TRAINING,
AND
THE URBAN
GHETTO

The Johns Hopkins University Press, Baltimore, Maryland 21218
The Johns Hopkins University Press Ltd., London

Library of Congress Catalog Card Number 72-4023
ISBN 0-8018-1366-2

Library of Congress Cataloging in Publication data will be found on the last
printed page of this book.

To Barbara

Contents

Tables and Figures

Figures

ABBREVIATIONS

AFDC	Aid to Families with Dependent Children
BES	Bureau of Employment Security
BLS	Bureau of Labor Statistics
CDC	Community Development Corporation
CHIF	Connecticut Housing Investment Fund
CORE	Congress of Racial Equality
CPS	Current Population Survey
EEOC	Equal Employment Opportunity Commission
FHA	Federal Housing Authority
GAO	General Accounting Office
GED	General Educational Development
GNP	Gross National Product
HARYOU	Harlem Youth Opportunities Unlimited
HUD	Department of Housing and Urban Development
IBM	International Business Machines
JOBS	Job Opportunities in the Business Sector
LFPR	Labor Force Participation Rate
MDTA	Manpower Development and Training Act
NAB	National Alliance of Businessmen
NICB	National Industrial Conference Board
NORC	National Opinion Research Corporation
NWRO	National Welfare Rights Organization
OEO	Office of Economic Opportunity
OFCC	Office of Federal Contract Compliance
OJT	On-the-job training
PSC	Public Service Careers Program
SEO	Survey of Economic Opportunity
SIC	Standard Industrial Classification
SMSA	Standard Metropolitan Statistical Area
SSA	Social Security Administration
UES	Urban Employment Survey
USDA	U.S. Department of Agriculture
USDL	U.S. Department of Labor
USES	U.S. Employment Service
VISTA	Volunteers in Service to America
WIN	Work Incentive Program

Foreword

The American dream persists. It promises that opportunities are open to all who seek them and that diligence and toil bring the proper rewards. Our society thus presumably allows upward mobility for all who want to help themselves.

This maxim, however, is increasingly challenged. Doubts have been raised as to whether the rules of the game for the mainstream of American society apply equally to members of minorities. Spurred by the civil rights movement, the research community demonstrated that large sectors of the American population are removed from the opportunities said to be every citizen's birthright. It became clear that America is not the melting pot associated with the Statue of Liberty. Some of those who have been in the pot longest have never been assimilated, including the native Americans who lived on this continent before it was "discovered."

The evidence showed that there are many ghettos in the United States and that their residents are different in many ways from those outside. It was easy to document the deficient education, high crime rates, poor housing, lack of jobs, discrimination, ill health, and other problems.

These disclosures aroused a compassionate society to redress past injustices and halt continuing wrongs. But experience has shown that the problems of the black ghetto are too pervasive to be corrected by a piecemeal approach of improving the education of a few children, training a few adults, and delivering some health services.

Bennett Harrison's *Education, Training, and the Urban Ghetto* is an important contribution to the growing documentation that societal attitudes must be fundamentally changed if blacks and other minorities are to join the mainstream of American society. He has gathered persuasive evidence that education and training are of less help to black ghetto residents than to others in getting a job or, more important, equal pay and the opportunity for advancement. Indeed, Dr. Harrison argues, society has essentially created a separate, and secondary, labor market for blacks and other disadvantaged persons; although no walls enclose this secondary labor market, people with black skin frequently find it difficult to get a passport for travel to the primary labor market.

Education, Training, and the Urban Ghetto is a technical volume. But, unlike many of the numerologists who pervade the dismal science of economics, Bennett Harrison bridges the gap between the gathering and analysis of data and the policy implications of his findings.

His alma mater, the University of Pennsylvania, has already recognized the merits of his contribution by awarding him the William Polk Carey Prize in Economics for the doctoral dissertation which forms the basis for this monograph. It is important that Dr. Harrison's message receive broad and careful attention, for our society cannot long survive if we continue to ignore the ghetto's pressing problems.

Sar A. Levitan

The George Washington University
Washington, D.C.
April, 1972

Author's Preface

In attempting to relieve the underemployment and improve the levels of living of urban minorities, it would seem apparent—especially to an economist—that attention must be addressed to both supply and demand forces in the urban labor market. Yet the professional literature, and a substantial proportion of the policy discussions, have concentrated almost exclusively on attempts to improve the quality of the supply of minority urban labor, through investments in education and training—what Theodore Schultz and Gary Becker have taught us to think of as "human capital."

As a student, I read this literature without questioning the underlying reasons for such a one-sided approach. In the literature, the emphasis on the "productivity" of education and training seemed to be shored up by the statistical results of national studies focusing largely on those very elements in the population—middle class whites—who were least constrained in their efforts to translate education into earnings and improved occupational status, and who were best able to afford to invest in themselves. It was not until analysts began to turn the apparatus toward the examination of minority mobility that any substantial disclaimers were entered. And even here, the samples were always small, and the scope national. Data limitations precluded the study of those geographic concentrations of "hard-core" poverty which have been the scene of the greatest internal disorders in America since the Civil War. The result has been that studies of the payoff to investments in minority workers, while admitting of a "white-nonwhite gap" and occasionally even attributing this to discrimination, have continued to reinforce the policy prescription that a worker—any worker—can succeed in the American economy by "improving himself." Individual action—and investments in one's schooling and/or training are the essence of individualistic action—will, it is argued, continue to provide the key to upward mobility within American society, just as it has always done in the past.

This monograph represents the first microanalytic study of disadvantaged workers in specific urban areas. It is based on my doctoral dissertation for the University of Pennsylvania, which was awarded the William Polk Carey Prize in Economics for 1970-71. I have found that the opportunity costs to ghetto residents of undertaking such individualistic actions as investments in education and training are much higher than has ever been suspected heretofore. Indeed, in many cases, these investments have had no statistically significant payoff at all. To me, these results make it all the more apparent that there are serious faults in the structure of our urban labor markets. Specifically, we must devote much greater attention to stimulating the demand for minority labor. Perhaps we shall require direct governmental action in private markets, already being (gingerly) attempted through the "Philadelphia Plan" and the activities of the Equal Employment Opportunity Commission (EEOC). Perhaps we shall want to expand the kind of public employment program recently begun with Senator Gaylord Nelson's Emergency Employment Act of 1971, a law which—by granting federal wage subsidies to state and local governments—creates wholly new markets in which minorities may compete under ground rules directly subject to public control. Perhaps minorities will find the means (and the concentrated will) to effectively force existing employers to cease their underutilization of lower class workers. Perhaps the residents of the slums will be able to organize ghetto development programs which will themselves provide jobs and incomes for minority families.

But whatever the new agenda, the lesson of this monograph must surely be that our profession and our nation must shift our emphasis away from concentration on the alleged "defects" of the poor themselves toward the investigation of defects in the market system which restrains the poor from realizing their potential.

In researching and writing this book, I am particularly grateful to three groups of colleagues. First, there are those who—in the interest of seeing a more technically complete analysis—have encouraged me both to look beyond the ghetto itself in order to better appreciate the significance of what we find within the ghetto, and to look at other measures of the returns to investments in human capital than income alone, since discrimination occurs at other critical states in the job entry process than solely at the wage-bargaining stage.

A second group of friends are to be thanked for urging me to confront head-on the ideological implications of our society's emphasis on education as an antipoverty instrument.

The third group includes several congressional aides and official antipoverty warriors who patiently guided me through the (often tortuous) course of manpower legislation and program developments of the 1960s, and who never gave up trying to convince me that constructive social change through federal legislation is still possible in America.

For these and other favors, I am grateful to Michael Barth, Barbara Bergmann, Barry Bluestone, Jean Couturier, Matthew Edel, David Gordon, Stephan Michelson, Milton Millon, Harold Sheppard, William Spring, Austin Sullivan, Robert Taggart III, and Howard Wachtel.

Norman Glickman and Mancur Olson gave most thorough readings to various drafts of the dissertation, thereby contributing to whatever improvements are manifest in the present version.

Lawrence Klein was both a helpful and—most of all—patient thesis advisor. Julius Margolis and Paul Taubman offered constructive criticism as the other members of my thesis committee.

This research project involved the processing of over 50,000 interviews conducted by government agencies with workers in sixteen metropolitan areas. For programming assistance—from helpful "hints" to the debugging of initially incompatible data tapes—I am deeply indebted to Marianne Russek and to George Schink. These two friends were also gracious enough to discuss the substance of the research with me on many occasions.

I have always been especially fortunate in having access to superior secretarial assistance. This good luck never failed me throughout the present project, thanks to Rita Dean, Mary Ann Denevan, Frances Phillips, Shirley Pressley, Esther Sager, and Edith Van Ness. Elisabeth McDonnell provided the charts.

Financial support is also to be acknowledged. The Office of Economic Research, Economic Development Administration, U.S. Department of Commerce, provided an initial dissertation fellowship (Grant No. OER-161-G-677). This was later supplemented by a second fellowship from the Manpower Administration, U.S. Department of Labor (Grant No. 91-22-70-19), under the authority of Title I of the Manpower Development and Training Act (MDTA) of 1962, as amended. Researchers undertaking such projects under government sponsorship are encouraged to express freely their professional judgment; therefore, points of view or opinions stated in this document do not necessarily represent the official positions or policies of either the Department of Labor or the Department of Commerce.

Throughout the project, I received additional support from the University of Maryland's Bureau of Business and Economic Research and its former Director, John Dorsey. I am equally grateful to the University's Computer Science Center for successive grants to cover the costs of computer time and ancillary services.

Of the many government officials who consented to and advised on the use of their unpublished data, my greatest debts are to William Milligan, Chief of the Urban Employment Survey (UES) Group in the Bureau of Labor Statistics (BLS), Washington, D.C.; Samuel Ehrenhalt, Deputy Director of the Middle Atlantic Regional Office of the BLS; and Susan Holland, presently of the San Francisco BLS Office. Neither these nor any of the people mentioned above are to be held responsible for the uses to which their suggestions and criticisms have been put.

For the provision of office space and clerical support during a summer in Berkeley, California, I am indebted to Dr. Randy Hamilton, Executive Director of the Institute for Local Self-Government.

Sar Levitan deserves my thanks both for introducing me to my publisher and for agreeing to preface this monograph with his own remarks. He is one of the acknowledged leaders in the manpower research field, and it is an honor to be professionally associated with him.

Last, I must acknowledge the contribution of two very special people. Thomas Vietorisz gave me the opportunity to study urban poverty firsthand, before it became fashionable to do so, and in the finest possible circumstances: as principal investigator on one of the first joint government-black "militant" ghetto development projects implemented in the United States. Since the commencement of the Harlem Project in 1967, Dr. Vietorisz has been my counsellor, my teacher, my co-author, and—best of all—my friend. Were it not for him, it is quite possible that neither the dissertation nor this monograph would ever have been written.

That it would not have been written without the influence of my wife, Barbara, is a certainty. Her contributions as typist, editor, and general critic were invaluable. But far more important was her insistence that the dissertation be completed, in the face of any number of sirens' songs toward which I was drawn on many occasions. Her presence and concern have influenced my attitudes, ideals, and goals beyond my ability to measure.

Bennett Harrison

University of Maryland
College Park
April, 1972

I . . . went sightseeing in downtown Washington. I was
astounded to find in the nation's capital, just a few blocks
from Capitol Hill, thousands of Negroes living worse than
any I'd ever seen in the poorest sections of Roxbury; in
dirt-floor shacks along unspeakably filthy lanes with names
like Pig Alley and Goat Alley. . . .

But I [also] saw other Negroes better off . . . a lot of
"middle-class" Negroes with Howard University degrees, who
were working as laborers, janitors, porters, guards, taxi-
drivers, and the like. For the Negro in Washington, mail-
carrying was a prestige job.

— Malcolm X

If an individual's income is too low, [his] productivity is
too low.

— Lester Thurow

1.

URBAN POVERTY AND HUMAN CAPITAL

POVERTY, PRODUCTIVITY, AND UNDEREMPLOYMENT

Much current concern is being addressed to the issue of minority "economic development," especially in the nation's cities. Many different programs are subsumed under this expression: antidiscrimination efforts in jobs and housing, subsidization of private corporations to increase their employment of the "hard-core unemployed," location of corporate branch plants inside the ghetto, development of atomistic minority-owned commercial enterprises (so-called "black capitalism"), limited renewal of the ghetto's physical plant, expansion of human services in the slums, and—ultimately—comprehensive community development and control of ghetto political institutions by citizen corporations. Even income maintenance is being treated as an antipoverty instrument.

In terms of income alone, the single most important problem of urban minorities is *underemployment.* Minority workers have greater difficulty than whites in finding a job (any job), in being permitted to work full-time, and in obtaining nonpoverty wages when they do work. And most *do* want to work. In 1966, for example, the total number of working-age American males of *all* races who were in the labor force but who did not work at all was probably not more than 86,000, a very small number.[1] In the same year, in ten urban ghettos surveyed by the U.S. Department of Labor (USDL), underemployment was from two to six times as great as simple unemployment (the definition of underemployment underlying this calculation is presented in Chapter Three). The same survey found that those in the ghetto who are employed—even full-time—are unable to earn enough to support a family of four at even a subsistence level.

Job development per se is an integral part of each of the minority economic development programs. But the social objectives of many leaders—especially those in (or of) the ghetto itself—encompass concern for the quality as well as for the quantity of work. And many of the aforementioned programs are decidedly not addressed to raising the quality of minority employment. Thus, for example, two-thirds of the jobs developed by the National Alliance of Businessmen (NAB) in fifteen cities in the first year of the much publicized (and heavily subsidized) Job Opportunities in the Business Sector (JOBS) program paid less than $2.00 an hour.[2] In large cities, these are substandard and seriously inadequate wages, by a number of widely accepted benchmarks. What is more, ghetto dwellers know this, and react accordingly. Newark's NAB developed 800 unskilled job openings for which no candidates appeared over a nine-week period.[3] And a Harvard study of slum dwellers in

1. Bennett Harrison, "Public Service Jobs for Urban Ghetto Residents," *Good Government*, Fall 1969, p. 7; reprinted in *The Political Economy of Public Service Employment*, ed. Harold L. Sheppard, Bennett Harrison, and William Spring (Lexington, Mass.: D. C. Heath–Lexington Books, 1972).

2. National Industrial Conference Board, *Education, Training, and Employment of the Disadvantaged*, Studies in Public Affairs no. 4, 1969, p. 33.

3. *Ibid.*, p. 44.

Boston criticizes local manpower institutions for restricting themselves to "horizontal" (as opposed to "vertical") placements for their ghetto clientele, thereby frustrating instead of promoting occupational mobility for the urban poor.[4]

Underemployment, as a measure of both the quantity and the quality of work, therefore represents the interface between all aspects of urban anti-poverty and minority economic development policy. Although there are many other objectives of political and economic planning in this troubled sector of our society, all approaches seek, at least to some extent, to expand the quality of employment of ghetto residents.

In the classical theories of underemployment, a worker is allocated to a low-paying, low-productivity job because of circumstances quite apart from his own ability. For Marx, the capitalists' quest for acquisition of profits through the employment of labor in technologically progressive industry is more than offset by their desire to hold wages down through the creation of a pool of surplus labor. Ms. Joan Robinson first coined the term "disguised unemployment" to describe those workers in the industrialized countries who were driven during the Great Depression into such occupations as selling matchboxes, where their productivity was much lower than in the occupations they had left. For Sir Arthur Lewis, underemployment in the rural sectors of less developed countries exists because unchecked population increase forces agricultural productivity down effectively to zero, given the scarcity of land. This is fundamentally a Richardian-Malthusian analysis. Laborers may appear to be working but they are so crowded on the land that if some of the labor were removed, total product would remain unchanged. Nevertheless, reallocation of this "surplus labor" into higher-productivity employment is definitely feasible in Lewis's original model. There is no presumption that workers are incapable of performing the new jobs. With respect to the relationship between wages and productivity, the classical analysis indicates that workers must generally be paid a living ("subsistence") wage whether they are marginally productive or not. In the event that labor becomes truly surplus, it would then follow that the wage rate exceeds productivity. But the interrelationship has no normative implications for the classical economists.

The neoclassical concept of underemployment which students of economics learn in today's classes is embodied in the marginal productivity theory of income distribution, and becomes explicit in the theory of "human capital" (whose modern advocates had much to do with the organization and early planning of the War on Poverty). Here, workers are in low productivity jobs because they lack the abilities—without extensive training and complementary capital equipment—to accept higher productivity employment. According to Theodore Schultz, Gary Becker, Burton Weisbrod, and others, low

---

4. Peter B. Doeringer, "Manpower Programs for Ghetto Labor Markets," *Industrial Relations Research Association: Proceedings*, May 1969.

productivity workers being paid any significant wage (and particularly a legal minimum wage) are probably being paid more than they are worth. And their worth will not increase until substantial investments are made in their training and in complementary capital, and until such "investments in human capital" have been "realized." In the neoclassical theory, this is axiomatic; the allocation of resources—in this case, labor, regardless of race, creed or color—is *assumed* to reflect the true underlying productivities of factors. If ghetto and other minority workers are employed as dishwashers and maids, it is because those are the occupations for which the market finds them best suited.

In the current orthodoxy, investments in the human capital of ghetto workers are therefore considered to have the greatest potential for reducing underemployment. Increased (and/or improved) public education and participation in various training programs will, it is believed, improve both the quantity and the quality of employment for ghetto workers, even if they remain in the urban slums.

But another "payoff" to these investments is alleged to lie in their ability to facilitate the "suburbanization" of those presently "trapped" in the ghetto. Education and training will improve the quality of the ghetto labor force. Given their increased productivity, these workers will then be able to command higher quality jobs paying higher wages. Increasingly, "the good jobs are outside the core; the bad jobs are inside." This statement, made by Sam Bass Warner, Jr., at the 1969 convention of the American Economic Association, accurately reflects the (currently) prevailing opinion on this issue.

There are four powerful but implicit sets of assumptions underlying this conventional wisdom. First, it is assumed that the potential productivity of a worker living in the ghetto is enhanced by investments in the education and training of the worker. This proposition is as old as *The Wealth of Nations*,[5] and as recent as the "theory of human capital,"[6] and it is accepted here, although not entirely without question. Ivar Berg, for one, has challenged the popular hypothesis that educational credentials are a good indicator of potential productivity:

> In a comparison of white-collar workers in a major insurance company in the Greater New York area, productivity, as measured by the dollar value of policies sold, varied inversely with years of formal education, and the relationship became stronger when experience was taken into systematic account. This suggests that education, as such, will not guarantee that an employer concerned with the social and psychological intangibles of a

5. Adam Smith, *The Wealth of Nations* (New York: Random House, Modern Library, 1937), pp. 15–16, 100*n*.

6. Cf. Gary S. Becker, *Human Capital* (New York: Columbia University Press, 1964); and Theodore Schultz, "Investment in Human Beings," *Journal of Political Economy*, October 1962 (Supplement).

customer-client relationship can assume benefits from screening requirements based on years of education.[7]

In another case study, a chemical company's executives asserted that "the
'best' technicians in their research laboratory are those with the greatest
educational achievements." But a statistical analysis of personnel records
showed that "turnover was positively associated with educational achievement, and less-educated technicians earned higher performance evaluations
than their better-educated peers. The employer was shocked at these
results. . . ."[8]

Second, it is deduced (from neoclassical axioms about the homogeneity of
labor and the ubiquity of information) that these increases in potential productivity will be proportionately rewarded through the labor market. The
almost metaphysical basis for this logic is illustrated in a recent textbook on
the theory of human capital. According to author Lester Thurow,

> there is practically no direct information on whether or not labor is paid
> its marginal product. Economists take it as an article of faith or else claim
> that it is the best null hypothesis, and economic theory is based on the
> assumption that labor is indeed paid its marginal product. Without this
> assumption, much of economic theory falls apart. The theory of produc-
> tion certainly does. The convenience of the hypothesis for economists,
> however, does not make it correct. . . .
>
> What little evidence [Thurow's techniques] provide does not indicate
> that labor is paid its marginal product. . . . [T]here are at least some funda-
> mental doubts about the validity of the productivity theory of distribu-
> tion. In the rest of this book I shall [nevertheless] assume that labor is
> paid its marginal product unless otherwise stated. The reader, however,
> should at all times keep in mind that this is as yet an unverified assump-
> tion, retained because it is crucial to the concept of human capital and its
> uses.[9]

The central purpose of the present study is to examine whether increases in
the potential productivity (and/or the credential-derived social attractiveness)
of ghetto workers are in fact translated into higher quality employment.

Third, it is assumed that increased educational and/or training experience
facilitates migration from the ghetto to the suburbs. Moreover, this move is
assumed to lead to enhanced freedom of choice for the (former) ghetto
dweller. Both assumptions are subject to question. The little evidence we have
all indicates that, once nonwhites have moved into a central city "poverty

---

7. Ivar Berg, "Education and Work," in *Manpower Strategy for the Metropolis*, ed.
Eli Ginzberg (New York: Columbia University Press, 1968), p. 128.

8. *Ibid.*, p. 131. For the full study, see Ivar Berg, *Education and Jobs: The Great
Training Robbery* (New York: Praeger, 1970).

9. Lester Thurow, *Investment in Human Capital* (Belmont, Cal.: Wadsworth, 1970),
pp. 20–22.

area," virtually all further moves are within the ghetto or to another central city poverty area. This pattern seems to hold regardless of the educational level of the worker. When they are able to move to the suburban ring, non-whites tend to be resegregated into peripheral ghettos, often as remote from the new industrial enclaves and their access routes as were the older, central city slums. Another purpose of the present study is to examine the intra-metropolitan spatial sensitivity of the returns to minority human capital.

Fourth, it is assumed that minority income, earnings and occupational status are higher in the suburban rings of U.S. metropolitan areas than in their cores. This is offered as "evidence" that, to quote a colleague, "the ones who have 'escaped' [from the ghetto to the suburbs] presumably are 'superior' types." Alternatively, it is used to "prove" that suburban jobs are indeed "better"and well worth the social and political costs of suburbanization of urban minorities. I question the assumption that, to make as conservative an interpretation as possible, suburbanization of minorities is associated with an increase in these socioeconomic indicators. I doubt whether nonwhites are more equitably treated by suburban than by central city employers (or fellow employees).

To summarize, public education is widely held to be the form of "human capital" which has served as the principal instrument by which past genera-tions of ghetto dwellers "climbed" out of the urban slums and into the American middle class. Many take it for granted that the "formula" will work again—is working now—for the newest inhabitants of the urban slums. Educa-tion, it is often argued, may in the last analysis be the most effective anti-poverty instrument of all.[10] Job training, both institutional and "on-the-job," is also widely considered to be an effective policy instrument for relieving urban underemployment.

The popularity of these assumptions notwithstanding, a rigorous re-exami-nation of the effectiveness of education and training is surely in order, if only because of the enormous social costs involved. Total expenditures for formal education in 1966–67 amounted to nearly $49 billion, 65 percent of which was allocated to primary and secondary schooling. This comprised nearly 4 percent of the Gross National Product (GNP).[11] Moreover, some studies have concluded that the foregone earnings of those who choose to attend school as an alternative to entering the labor force may amount to as much as three-

10. David Gordon has summarized the logic which seems to underlie this conviction: "To improve the productivity of the low-skilled and the poor—in order to equalize their economic opportunities—we must improve their education; to improve their education in that sense, we must raise their level of cognitive achievement by improving their abilities to read and reason; the schools can effect this increasing equality of opportunity because they have played that role historically; and, in general, it is becoming easier for the schools to fulfill this equalizing function because our society is continuing to become more educationally mobile (and simultaneously more meritocratic) over time." "Educa-tion: Editor's Introduction," in *Problems in Political Economy: An Urban Perspective*, ed. David Gordon (Lexington, Mass.: D. C. Heath, 1971), p. 166.
11. Berg, *Education and Jobs*, pp. 177–78.

fifths of the monetary costs of education.[12] In one state (California), public subsidies for college students amount to as much as $7,000 per student.[13] These are all different ways of expressing the very substantial social cost of education in the United States.

Publicly financed manpower training has also consumed much of the national product during the last decade. Over the period 1963–70, $5.2 billion were expended on a host of job training activities, including institutional (vocational) and on-the-job training under President Kennedy's Manpower Development and Training Act (MDTA), the Neighborhood Youth Corps, Operation Mainstream, Public Service Careers (including the New Careers Program), the Special Impact Program, the Concentrated Employment Program, the JOBS program, the Work Incentive program (WIN), and the Job Corps.[14] In one of the most highly publicized government training programs for the "disadvantaged"—the New Careers Program—costs per trainee per year in 1968 ranged from a low of $4,557 in Harrisburg, Pennsylvania, to a high of $7,695 in Paterson, New Jersey.[15]

Under the (untested) assumption that the potential productivity of a worker living in the ghetto is positively correlated with the number of years of school he has completed, and that participation in formal training programs similarly increases potential productivity, this study examines the magnitude of the job-related returns to these investments in human capital and the sensitivity of these returns to intrametropolitan variations in residential location.[16]

THE MARGINAL EFFICIENCY OF EDUCATION AND TRAINING

It is a matter of some conviction among politicians, managers, economists, sociologists, educators, and citizens that an individual's future employment status improves systematically with the amount of formal education and/or training he acquires. This is held to be true whether employment status

12. *Ibid.*, p. 28.

13. W. Lee Hansen and Burton A. Weisbrod, "The Equality Fiction: California Higher Education," in Gordon, *Problems in Political Economy*, p. 207.

14. U.S. Department of Labor, *1971 Manpower Report of the President* (Washington, D.C.: Govt. Prtg. Off., 1971), p. 299.

15. Harrison, "Public Service Jobs," p. 13.

16. This study does not consider the non-pecuniary benefits of education or training, a fact which should enter into the reader's evaluation of my findings and conclusions. The esthetic and emotional benefits which may accrue to the successful student are probably obvious. More subtle but no less important is the generally positive effect of education on the ability of the residents of urban neighborhoods to cope with the political and economic oligopolies with which they are so often at odds. See David Harvey, "Social Processes, Spatial Form and the Redistribution of Real Income in an Urban System," *Proceedings of the 22nd Symposium of the Colston Research Society* (London: Butterworths, 1970), pp. 290–91. For these reasons alone, it will not be possible in this study to test the hypothesis that education is of *no* value to the urban poor.

(stature in the labor market) is measured by earnings, by infrequency of unemployment "spells," by occupational "prestige," or by low incidence of involuntary part-time employment. Moreover, the relationship is widely believed to hold for nonwhites as well as for whites—albeit less powerfully— even though a number of recent studies have begun to cast some doubt on the latter proposition. Although no one has ever studied the urban ghetto itself, it is thought that the residents of the slums are similarly eligible for the benefits which these investments in "human capital" are said to confer.

The Conventional Wisdom. "In the familiar pattern," writes Daniel P. Moynihan, "wages of white and nonwhite workers tend to increase as the amount of education rises (although) the gain for nonwhite men is much less than for white men."[17] A report by Fordham University's Institute for Urban Studies concludes that, "as with estimates of weekly earnings, the relationship between unemployment and educational achievement attests to the crucial economic significance of education to the individual."[18]

Professor Ivar Berg of Columbia University found that employers are particularly strong advocates of the conventional wisdom:

> Managers, often supported by government leaders and academicians with interests in employment and manpower problems, have well-developed ideologies about the significance of educational achievement. The argument usually begins with a specification of the needs of a highly developed economy and the assertion that with each increment of education—especially increments associated with the receipt of a certificate, diploma, or degree representing a completed course of study or training—attitudes are better, trainability greater, capacities for adaptation more developed, and prospects for promotability enhanced. Simultaneously, those with lesser education, especially those who "drop out" of a course of study in high school, technical school, or college, are held to be less intelligent, adaptable, self-disciplined, personable, attractive, and articulate.[19]

In the Los Angeles Riot Study conducted by scholars from the University of California at Los Angeles (UCLA), businessmen from Watts and other South Los Angeles riot areas were asked: "What one change would you make in Los Angeles or in this area?" Fourteen percent of the merchants answered: "increased education." This was a larger frequency than was recorded for any other policy alternative presented, and nearly twice as great as the number of merchants who thought that "more employment opportunities" were needed.[20]

17. Daniel P. Moynihan, "Employment, Income, and the Ordeal of the Negro Family," *Daedalus*, Fall 1965, p. 756.
18. Institute for Urban Studies, Fordham University, *A Profile of the Bronx Economy* (New York: Fordham University Press, 1967), p. 37.
19. Berg, "Education and Work," pp. 127–28.
20. Nathan Cohen, ed., *The Los Angeles Riot Study* (New York: Praeger, 1969), p. 635.

Not surprisingly (given the absence of interest and lack of data until quite recently), none of the studies showing this strong interrelationship between education and employment status explicitly covered the ghetto labor force. Nevertheless, the findings as to the existence of the relation are frequently generalized to include all American workers. This reinforced the widespread myth according to which public education is viewed as the principal instrument through which past generations of ghetto dwellers climbed out of the urban slums and into the American middle class. Apparently, many take it for granted that the formula will work again—is working now—for the newest inhabitants of the urban ghettos. This argument was made most recently by the U.S. Civil Rights Commission: "Past generations of Americans have escaped from the economic insecurity and meanness of ghetto life by . . . obtaining for themselves or for their children a good education and moving outside the ghetto."[21] Demographer Philip Hauser asserts: "Without question, the major factor in the assimilation of the white immigrant groups who came to this country—their 'Americanization'—was the school."[22] Moreover, "education will undoubtedly continue to help the Negro as it did the white immigrant."[23] Sociologist Everett Hughes also accepts the myth: "Education, as everyone knows, is the American means of climbing out of poverty."[24]

Indeed, some put the case even more strongly. Thus, in studying the "vicious circle of the 'Three E's,' *Education, Employment and Environment*," participants in a recent New Jersey conference on urban problems concluded: "After much research and study of the problem, it is now plain that the real place to begin to break through is in the area of education, because without correcting this problem first, the other two will . . . defy effective solution at all."[25] Hauser firmly believes that "the Negro's major handicap in his efforts to advance in America . . . is undoubtedly to be found in his limited education and skills."[26]

This emphasis on the "supply side" of the problem of minority employment is pervasive in much of the technical literature. Ivar Berg believes that it reflects a deeper bias in our economic philosophy:

> Increasing credence is given the view that the changes in the demand for labor make it imperative to *act* upon the supply of labor unselectively whereas we can only *react*, with appropriate policies, to the demand for labor. Whether we consider textbooks, newspaper editorials, congressional

21. U.S. Commission on Civil Rights, *A Time to Listen . . . A Time to Act* (Washington, D.C.: Govt. Prtg. Off., 1967), p. 41.

22. Philip M. Hauser, "Demographic Factors in the Integration of the Negro," *Daedalus*, Fall 1965, p. 867.

23. *Ibid.*, p. 870.

24. Everett C. Hughes, "Anomalies and Projections," *Daedalus*, Fall 1965, p. 1134.

25. David N. Alloway and Francesco Cordasco, *The Agony of the Cities* (Montclair, N.J.: Montclair State College Press, 1969), p. 23.

26. Hauser, "Demographic Factors," pp. 867-68.

speeches, or the detailed analyses of sundry urban planning commissions . . . we find that the requirements specified by employers are the base around which programs of reform and remedy are designed. . . . Planners have [even] expressed serious doubts about whether educational requirements that go up . . . are in line with the actual demands jobs make. Yet they proceed to see answers only in correcting the "short-comings" in the labor force, however much these short-comings may in fact reflect arbitrary changes in requirements.[27]

Supportive Research: Probably the most exhaustive analyses of the nationwide (aggregate) data have been performed by Herman P. Miller of the Bureau of the Census. Dr. Miller has reported:

> In 1958, [adult] men who started high school but did not graduate received on the average an annual income of about $400 more per year of schooling than men who completed their schooling with graduation from elementary school. High school graduates, however, received about $500 more of annual income per year of schooling than men who started high school but never graduated. Similarly, men who attended college but did not graduate had, on the average, about $700 more per year of schooling than high school graduates. The comparable differential for college graduates was about $900 per year of schooling.[28]

Assuming a forty-year working life following graduation, a rectangular lifetime income distribution, and a discount rate of 6 percent, the present value of the lifetime return to the high school graduate is $13,541 greater than the return to the individual who drops out of school after the eighth grade.[29] The opportunity cost of dropping out of school is clearly very high for the "average" American.

Other studies show similar results. Hirsch and Segelhorst estimated that the present value of the extra male lifetime income attributable to one additional year of school in a St. Louis suburb in 1957 was equal to about $3,100 (interpolated at a 6 percent discount rate).[30] Using the 1950 Census, W. Lee Hansen's calculations (at 6 percent) show a present value of about $2,160 for annual male income per year of school over the range 8–16 years.[31] Finally, Hendrik S. Houthakker has published results (also based on the 1950 Census) showing an incremental male present value of about $2,560 (again at a 6 percent rate) for the range 8–16 years of school completed.[32] The last three

27. Berg, "Education and Work," p. 118.

28. Herman P. Miller, "Annual and Lifetime Income in Relation to Education," *American Economic Review*, December 1960, pp. 956–57.

29. I.e., an additional $900 received annually.

30. Werner Z. Hirsch and Elbert W. Segelhorst, "Incremental Income Benefits of Public Education," *Review of Economics and Statistics*, November 1965, table 2.

31. W. Lee Hansen, "Total and Private Rates of Return on Investment in Schooling," *Journal of Political Economy*, April 1963, table 6.

32. Hendrik S. Houthakker, "Education and Income," *Review of Economics and Statistics*, February 1959, table 3.

estimates are computed on a more or less comparable basis, e.g., all assuming a hill-shaped age-income profile. They indicate an average present value of about $2,600 per year of school, over the period 1949–57.

A strong, positive statistical relation between income or earnings and education is reported in a large number of other studies[33] and reviews of the literature.[34] Still other studies show a significant inverse relationship between education and unemployment.[35] For the literature as a whole, "practically all of the studies arrive at the conclusion that the payoff rate for continued education at all levels is remarkably high—something in excess of ten percent for college education and perhaps as high as fifty percent for increments at lower levels."[36]

Miller, himself, was the first to observe that (as of 1956) nonwhites were not receiving income commensurate with their education. "During all the years [up until 1956] for which figures on income, education, and color are available, the correlation between income and education is much higher for whites than for nonwhites. Among nonwhite men aged 25–44 years . . . elementary school graduates had about the same average income as high school graduates, despite the four year difference in schooling."[37] This conclusion is based upon the following Census data, showing mean 1956 income of males aged 25–44 years:[38]

Years of School Completed	White $	Nonwhite $
0–7	3,222	2,262
8	4,105	3,062
9–11	4,747	3,172
12	5,494	3,050

33. Cf. Gary S. Becker and Barry R. Chiswick, "Education and the Distribution of Earnings," *American Economic Review*, May 1966; Lowell Gallaway, "The Negro and Poverty," *Journal of Business*, January 1967; U.S. Department of Labor, *Statistics on Manpower: A Supplement to the 1969 Manpower Report of the President* (Washington, D.C.: Govt. Prtg. Off., 1969), table B–10; and Elizabeth Waldman, "Educational Attainment of Workers," *Monthly Labor Review*, February 1969.

34. Cf. William G. Bowen, *Economic Aspects of Education* (Princeton, N.J.: Princeton University Press, 1964), pp. 13–33; and Mary Jean Bowman, "Poverty in an Affluent Society," in *Contemporary Economic Issues*, ed. Neil W. Chamberlain (Homewood, Ill.: Irwin, 1969), pp. 69–73.

35. Cf. Harry J. Gilman, "Economic Discrimination and Unemployment," *American Economic Review*, December 1965; and Jeffrey K. Hadden and Edgar F. Borgatta, *American Cities: Their Social Characteristics* (Chicago: Rand McNally, 1965), pp. 138–40.

36. Thomas Ribich, *Education and Poverty* (Washington, D.C.: Brookings Institution, 1968), p. 9.

37. Herman P. Miller, "Does Education Pay Off?," in *Economics of Higher Education*, ed. Selma J. Mushkin (Washington, D.C.: U.S. Department of Health, Education, and Welfare, 1962), p. 130.

38. *Ibid.*, p. 137.

But by the middle of the next decade (1966), all available national nonwhite series were showing a definite payoff to completion of high school. These relationships are displayed in table 1. Nonwhites continue to lag behind whites with equivalent years of school. Moreover, nonwhite joblessness is greater for high school dropouts than for workers who never went beyond the eighth grade. Nevertheless, the overall impression conveyed by these numbers certainly seems to support the conventional wisdom. In fact, the difference in 1966 between the annual mean earnings of a nonwhite adult graduating from high school and a nonwhite adult who never entered high school was $1,479, a figure substantially higher than the aggregate (i.e., white and nonwhite)

Table 1

Income, Education, and Unemployment in the United States: 1965–67

	Whites	Nonwhites
	Individual Mean Earnings in 1965, Both Sexes, Persons Aged 25+ (*dollars*)	
Years of school completed		
0–8	5,433	3,751
9–11	6,722	4,644
12	7,481	5,230
13+	10,367	6,641
	Unemployment Rates in March, 1967, Both Sexes, Persons Aged 18+ (*percent*)	
Years of school completed		
0–4	5.2	6.6
5–7	4.5	5.7
8	4.0	8.7
9–11	4.6	10.6
12	2.9	6.5
13+	1.7	4.1
	Median Education of Males Aged 25–64, by Gross Family Income in 1967 (*years*)	
Gross family income		
$ 0–2,999	9.6	7.8
3,000–5,999	11.1	9.9
6,000–9,999	12.3	12.0
10,000–	12.8	12.6

Sources: U.S. Department of Commerce, Bureau of the Census, *Current Population Reports*, series P–60, no. 59, "Income in 1967 of Families in the United States," Washington, D.C., 18 April 1969, Table F; U.S. Department of Labor, Bureau of Labor Statistics, *Educational Attainment of Workers: March, 1967*, Special Labor Force Report No. 92, 1968, Table L; U.S. Department of Commerce, Bureau of the Census, *Current Population Reports*, series P–60, no. 182, "Educational Attainment: March, 1968," Washington, D.C., 28 April 1969, Table 7.

average reported by Miller for 1958, even after controlling for price changes.[39]

The literature is equally replete with arguments that positive payoffs accrue to the graduates of both public and private job training programs (although there is considerably less agreement on the efficiency with which these programs are operated). A number of studies have supported this contention—although, as with education, few analysts have been able to focus directly on the "hard-core" nonwhite urban poor.

Thus, for example, a 1967 evaluation of the MDTA by the Senate Subcommittee on Employment, Manpower and Poverty found that "on-the-job trainees had a [post-training] employment rate of over 90 percent. The median earnings were 21 percent higher after training than before." A 1967 USDL study comparing 784 trainees to a control group of 825 untrained workers concluded that, "those who completed training had significantly better employment rates, stability of employment, and improvement in income as compared with the control group." A regression analysis of West Virginia retrainees "found retraining to be a major explanatory variable in the improved income of formerly unemployed workers."[40]

Gerald G. Somers, Director of the Ford Foundation Project for Evaluation of Retraining of Unemployed Workers, concludes that his project's studies largely support the conventional wisdom:

> The most significant conclusion to be derived from these studies is that the retraining of unemployed workers is a sound social investment. In almost all of the surveys, at least 75 percent of trainees were employed after their training. With few exceptions, the post-training employment rates of those who completed their government-sponsored courses were substantially higher than the rates experienced by appropriately selected control groups of workers. . . . [T]rainees were found to have a significant employment advantage over non-trainees of the same age and the same education. . . .
>
> The earnings of the [male] trainees provide further evidence. . . . Where these studies draw comparisons between the trainees' earnings and those of non-trainees, the margin enjoyed by the trainees is shown to be appreciable. In most cases the trainees' earnings also rose significantly over their own pre-training income.[41]

However, Somers admits that "the studies . . . show . . . that by and large the trainees . . . were a select group, the cream of the unemployed."[42] So, as with

---

39. The Census Bureau estimates shown in table 1 do not account (or "control") for age differences within the three samples. My analysis, reported in Chapters Two, Three, and Four, shows age to be an important correlate of the returns to schooling.

40. Cited by Gerald Somers, "Introduction," in *Retraining the Unemployed*, ed., Somers (Madison, Wis.: University of Wisconsin, 1968), p. 14.

41. *Ibid.*, pp. 7–11.

42. *Ibid.*, p. 12.

Figure 1

Occupation, Earnings, and Unemployment by Race and Education in the United States

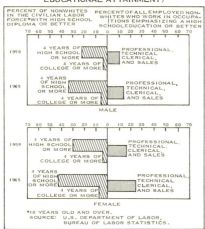

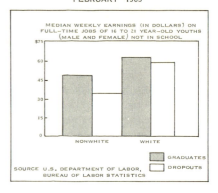

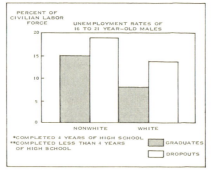

education, we have yet to apply the benefit-cost calculus explicitly to the urban ghetto population.

Critical Research. Many private researchers and at least two government agencies have been dissatisfied with the slow progress of minority groups, despite substantial increases in their education. Much effort, especially in research, has therefore been addressed to more elaborately describing the white-nonwhite "gaps" in employment and income.

The Bureau of Labor Statistics, investigating the payoff to education of black youths, concluded that

> ... the advantages of education to nonwhite youths are barely beginning to make themselves felt in the job market. ... Clearly, nonwhite youths are preparing for today's jobs faster than existing practices are changing to absorb them. ... As matters stand now, many Negro youngsters have more education than they need for the jobs they can get.[43]

The extent of this underutilization described by the BLS is depicted in figure 1, for occupational status, earnings, and unemployment, respectively.

The EEOC recently completed a major survey of 43,000 firms employing some 26 million workers. "This report deals with ... underemployment caused by discrimination ... men and women who perform work which does not fully utilize their education, skills, and talents. ... With very few exceptions, minority group workers are found primarily in the lower paying occupations, and they are under-represented in the higher paying occupations."[44] The study tabulates the median years of school completed by black males and by all males, by 2–digit Standard Industrial Classification industry group.[45] Expressing the former as a percent of the latter, a sample of these statistics on the relative magnitude of the white-black education "gap" in private industry is as follows:

Standard Industrial Classification	Industry	Median Schooling $\dfrac{\text{Black Males}}{\text{Total Males}} \times 100$
25	Furniture	93
31	Leather	101
36	Electrical machinery	86
38	Instruments	89
52	Retail sales	85
62	Brokerages	86
63	Insurance companies	95

In spite of the relative narrowness of the education "gap," nonwhite workers employed in the industries surveyed by the EEOC seem to have failed to

43. U.S. Department of Labor, Bureau of Labor Statistics, *The Negroes in the United States* (Washington, D.C.: Govt. Prtg. Off., June, 1966), bulletin no. 1522, pp. 23–25.
44. U.S. Equal Employment Opportunity Commission, *Job Patterns for Minorities and Women in Private Industry–1966* (Washington, D.C.: Govt. Prtg. Off., 1969), EEO report no. 1, vol. 1, p. 2.
45. *Ibid.*, p. 15.

translate their formal education and years on the job into skills and experience sufficient to guarantee the reward of promotion to better jobs.

Studies by Rashi Fein, Stephan Michelson, Thomas Ribich, Paul Siegel, and Randall Weiss reveal that education is relatively unimportant in explaining the difference between white and nonwhite incomes.[46] Michelson, for example, reports:

> Educating nonwhites equal to whites [through computer simulation] did not prove effective in raising nonwhite income. . . . Full employment at current education and wage levels also did not greatly affect relative incomes [because of high nonwhite underemployment: involuntary part-time employment and low wages]. Perhaps most surprisingly, equating the occupational distribution and years of school did not together close even one-fifth of the [white-nonwhite] income gap.[47]

In his Senior Honors Thesis for Harvard University, Weiss constructed a microeconomic recursive income determination model and fitted it to the 1/1000 sample from the 1960 Census. Education (adjusted for "quality") and location of residence determine occupation, which (in conjunction with the usual demographic variables) determines wages and hours. Weiss summarizes his comparative studies of white and nonwhite performance:

> It was hoped that the analysis of the earnings-determination process would illuminate the forces that affect the earnings of the black. In neither the weeks worked nor the weekly earnings equations, however, were occupation or achievement significant for any age group. Education does not have a significant influence on black earnings . . . because none of the mechanisms of its influence on white earnings are operative for blacks. . . . These results suggest that improving and increasing the education of blacks will not necessarily raise their earnings. Intensive efforts to improve the quality of schools may, in fact, increase inequality by enhancing the economic position of whites while affecting blacks very little. Given a labor market that distributes rewards among blacks without regard to their education, the solution to the black poverty problem seems to be outside the classroom. Although an increase in scholastic achievement coupled with an end of discrimination in the labor market may alleviate the economic condition of blacks, this study offers no support for this contention.[48]

In a recent paper, Howard Wachtel and Charles Betsey regressed individual wage earnings on a composite industry-job title variable, years in the present

46. Rashi Fein, "An Economic and Social Profile of the American Negro," *Daedalus*, Fall 1965; Stephan Michelson, "Incomes of Racial Minorities" (unpublished manuscript; Washington, D.C.: Brookings Institution, 1968); Ribich, *Education and Poverty*; Paul M. Siegel, "On the Cost of Being a Negro," *Sociological Inquiry*, Winter 1965; and Randall D. Weiss, "The Effect of Education on the Earnings of Blacks and Whites," *Review of Economics and Statistics*, May 1970.

47. Michelson, "Incomes of Racial Minorities," p. 8.46.

48. Weiss, "Effect of Education," pp. 29, 33.

job, region, race, union membership, age, city size, sex, education, and marital status. In their regressions, education consistently displays one of the two or three smallest Beta coefficients (an indicator of relative importance).[49] Overall, the authors conclude that

> ... the structural variables associated with the industry and its location are more important determinants of low wages than an individual's personal attributes [including education]. ... Our analysis suggests that the problems of upgrading the low-wage employed involve more than merely more education and training. ... It is not sufficient to simply change the individual; we must also operate on the industrial and geographic environments which affect the low-wage worker in our economy. The latter involves a more politically difficult path to the elimination of wage poverty, but one with potentially greater payoffs.[50]

The Need for Further Research. None of the studies discussed previously was addressed explicitly to the urban ghetto—nor (with one exception) even to specific cities. New microdata sources permit us not only to examine the ghetto, but to engage in intrametropolitan economic analysis for the first time. We know that urban antipoverty and minority economic development policy are critically in need of further information on the costs and benefits of, and the institutional constraints on, alternative strategies. The hitherto untested assumptions underlying these policy discussions—notably the assumption that minority economic opportunity is enhanced by "suburbanization" of nonwhite residences—need no longer go untested.

Several elements of the conventional wisdom—the undereducation of the ghetto labor force, and the possibility of upward (and outward) mobility through education—were questioned repeatedly by those of us associated with the Office of Economic Opportunity (OEO)-Congress of Racial Equality (CORE) "Harlem Development Project" in 1967-68.[51] Many of the people we met in Harlem displayed a literacy considerably beyond the merely

49. Howard M. Wachtel and Charles Betsey, "Employment at Low Wages," *Review of Economics and Statistics*, May 1972. When the observations were stratified by annual earnings, education was found to be a statistically insignificant correlate of wages in all strata below $5,197. For the "working poor," then, education appears to be statistically irrelevant.

50. *Ibid.*

51. The earliest published description of what the Harlem Project was intended to accomplish is Bennett Harrison, "A Pilot Project in Economic Development Planning for American Urban Slums," *International Development Review*, March 1968. An interim report by the black development corporation at the center of the project, the Harlem Commonwealth Council, is available from the OEO, as are the final consulting reports of Columbia University's Development Planning Workshop and the New School for Social Research's Center for Economic Planning. The latter has been expanded into a monograph by the author and a colleague; see Thomas Vietorisz and Bennett Harrison, *The Economic Development of Harlem* (New York: Praeger, 1970). See also Vietorisz and Harrison, "Ghetto Development, Community Corporations, and Public Policy," *Review of Black Political Economy*, Fall 1971.

functional, although they were either unemployed at the time or, if employed, were in clearly inferior job situations, with low wages and too few (or too many) hours, working in what to us seemed intolerable surroundings.[52] Many had graduated from high school, and more than a few had even attended one or another of the city's colleges for a time. There was a general impression of competence which clashed with what we knew (or were beginning to learn) about the employment status of these workers. It is this experience more than any other which has convinced me that the conventional wisdom must be systematically challenged. The new microdata sources permit such a challenge.

The preceding remarks frame a rationale for further study upon the suspected inapplicability of previous (aggregative) results to the urban ghetto. This rationale is independent of whether or not those results are themselves valid or not. But in fact, there *is* reason to doubt their validity, and this creates a second rationale for further study. In much of the previous research on the returns to education, analysts have used *gross family income* as the dependent variable. This is true, for example of the widely quoted work of Miller and Hirsch. I would argue that the use of this variable to measure a compensated increase in productivity constitutes an important specification error. A preferred variable is *individual earnings.* Indeed, if the data would permit it, *wages and salaries* would be even better. While income and earnings are probably sufficiently well correlated for most Americans to permit the use of the former as an indicator of the "payoff" to education and training, it is questionable whether the same can be said for the residents of the ghetto, who have access to so many alternative sources of (sometimes risky) income. Many blocks in the ghetto contain families who, lacking any real alternative, must augment their low wage earnings with income from welfare, prostitution, narcotics distribution, or "running numbers." Moreover, as Oscar Lewis has reminded us, urban slum dwellers all over the world engage in substantial transfers of income among one another.[53]

For these reasons, it may not be possible to attribute the results of studies such as Miller's to the ghetto population, nor (until we better understand the relationship between income and earnings both inside and outside the slums) even to make direct comparisons between the results of these studies and my

52. This absence of a sharp distinction between unemployment and employment—the inadequacy of conventional measures of unemployment to register labor market failure in the ghetto—has also been observed by Peter Doeringer in his work in Roxbury; cf. "Manpower Programs." See also Doeringer, with Penny Feldman, David M. Gordon, Michael J. Piore, and Michael Reich, "Low-Income Labor Markets and Urban Manpower Programs: A Critical Assessment," mimeographed (Washington, D.C.: U.S. Department of Labor, Manpower Administration, January 1969); William Spring, "Underemployment: The Measure We Refuse to Take," *New Generation*, Winter 1971; and *The Political Economy of Public Service Employment*, ed. Sheppard, Harrison, and Spring, esp. chap. 4: "The Measurement of Unemployment and Poverty."

53. Oscar Lewis, *A Study of Slum Culture: Background for La Vida* (New York: Random House, 1968), p. 5.

own analyses of the education-wage relationship in the ghetto, described in the following chapters.

THREE MICROECONOMIC MODELS

The substance of this monograph is an analysis of the returns to investments in the human capital of nonwhite urban workers, taking explicit account of whether they live in a core city ghetto or outside of such a distressed area. Three measures of "payoff" are specified: weekly earnings, whether or not the worker is unemployed, and occupational status (as measured by a scoring procedure which assigns an ordinal rank of 0–100 to each of 308 occupational titles). The policy variables of interest are years of school completed and participation in formal training programs. Control variables include age, sex, race, and industry group in which the person works, as a proxy for the complementary capital with which the person works. Three different residential locations are considered: central city ghettos, the rest of the central city, and the suburban ring.

The first primary sample consists of 21,467 persons aged 14 or more living in the twelve largest Standard Metropolitan Statistical Areas (SMSAs) in March, 1966, drawn from an even more extensive survey conducted in 1966, and again in 1967, by the Bureau of the Census for OEO. This data file is referred to as the *Survey of Economic Opportunity* (SEO). The second sample consists of 37,330 persons aged 14 or more living in one of ten well-defined urban "ghettos" in eight large cities in November, 1966. This data, collected by the USDL, is called the *1966 Urban Employment Survey* (UES). This is the most recent "micro" (i.e., individual person and household) data available for detailed analysis by the academic research community. Moreover, the period covered—1965 and 1966—is ideal for such a cross-section study as this, coming just prior to the height of the Kennedy-Johnson economic "boom". Even had the 1970 Census been available, for example, it would have been difficult to draw useful inferences about minority economic opportunity from observations taken during a recession. This, of course, is only one of several reasons why a truly definitive study of these issues will require the development of longitudinal data: information on the progress of specific individuals and households over time. A few such data bases now exist, but none are as rich as the two cross-section (or "point-in-time") surveys which form the basis for the present monograph.

The Urban Samples. Government leaders, businessmen, private scholars, and particularly the professional antipoverty "warriors" often use the euphemism *disadvantaged* in speaking of the black and the poor. It is probably not unfair to say that, when using this expression, most people have in mind persons, mostly nonwhite, all poor, who have little education, few skills, marginal interest in work, and large families. Another definition, embodying an alternative set of assumptions, is given by Leo Grebler of UCLA. According to Grebler,

> a group of people can be defined as disadvantaged if society-at-large has acted by omission or commission to prevent a disproportionate number of persons in the group from developing individual abilities which make it possible for them to reach or approximate their achievement potentials.[54]

Most—although not all—of the people whose labor force behavior is recorded in the following chapters are, by one or another of these definitions, disadvantaged. Moreover, most—although, again, not all—of the disadvantaged workers in the study live in a core city "ghetto." Actually, "ghetto" is defined in two different ways in the two data sources we are using. In the course of the following discussion, it will be helpful to refer to figure 2, which illustrates the two respective areal definitions of "ghetto."

The SEO permits us to specify, as a proxy for "ghetto," the set of all central city *Census poverty areas* (exemplified by the heavily bordered areas in figure 2). Poverty areas are clusters of census tracts, assembled as follows.[55]

First, all tracts in SMSAs of at least 250,000 population were ranked by the Census Bureau according to the relative presence of each of five equally weighted characteristics as reported in the 1960 Census. These were then combined into an overall "poverty index." The five factors were (a) percent of families with money incomes under $3,000, (b) percent of children under 18 years of age not living with both parents, (c) percent of persons at least 25 years of age with less than eight years of school completed, (d) percent of male laborers and service workers in the labor force, and (e) percent of housing units dilapidated or lacking some or all plumbing facilities. Those census tracts falling in the lowest quartile were then designated as "poverty tracts." Finally, "poverty areas" (as shown in figure 2) were assembled according to three criteria: (a) any region containing five or more contiguous poverty tracts, regardless of the number of families living there in 1960; (b) any region of less than five contiguous poverty tracts, provided the set contained at least 4,000 families in 1960; (c) any *non*poverty tract or set of two (and occasionally four) contiguous tracts which were completely surrounded by poverty tracts. Subsequently, all areal definitions were updated to account for urban renewal activities since 1960. The application of the original criteria

---

54. Quoted by Cohen, *Los Angeles Riot Study*, p. 19.
55. For full technical documentation, see U.S. Department of Commerce, Bureau of the Census, *Current Population Reports*, series P-23, no. 19, "Characteristics of Families Residing in 'Poverty Areas': March, 1966" (Washington, D.C.: Govt. Prtg. Off., 1966); *Current Population Reports*, series P-60, no. 61, "Characteristics of Families and Persons Living in Metropolitan Poverty Areas: 1967" (Washington, D.C.: Govt. Prtg. Off., 1969); and J. R. Wetzel and Susan B. Holland, "Poverty Areas of Our Major Cities," *Monthly Labor Review*, October 1966.

Figure 2

Comparison of Survey of Economic Opportunity and Urban Employment Survey Inner-City Study Areas
(Example: Philadelphia)

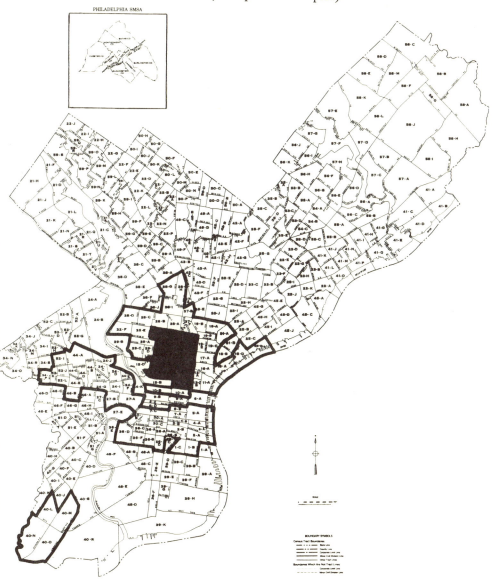

and the urban renewal adjustments resulted in the designation of 193 poverty areas in 100 SMSAs, comprising about 22 percent of the 20,915 tracts in these areas. These 193 poverty areas had an average 1960 population of 106,000 and ranged in size from 6,000 to 992,000. The "ghettos" studied in Chapter Two are the sets of poverty areas in each of twelve SMSAs.

The ten UES study areas are, on the other hand, entirely contiguous, locally defined neighborhoods. The North Philadelphia community—well known to residents of the city—is shown as a heavily shaded rectangle in figure 2. Similarly, such inner-city communities as Central Harlem, East ("Spanish") Harlem, Bedford-Stuyvesant, Roxbury, North Side, and Mission-Fillmore have fairly well-known boundaries. The areas are far from being racially or ethnically homogeneous; in the ten UES "ghettos," the majority group's share of total population ranges from about 44 percent (Mexican-American) in the Salt River Bed section of Phoenix, Arizona, to 92 percent (black) in the North Side section of St. Louis, Missouri. The ten UES "ghettos" analyzed in Chapter Three have an average population (aged 14 or more) of 84,000, ranging in size from 24,000 to 150,000 (see table 7). In any given city—such as Philadelphia—the UES "ghetto" is usually substantially smaller than the SEO "ghetto." Examination of various socioeconomic indices shows that the UES area is, relative to the more dispersed SEO "ghetto," the location of the truly "hard-core" poverty in each city.

For reasons enumerated at the end of this chapter, it became necessary to test the ghetto human capital models on nonghetto urban samples as well. These are drawn exclusively from the SEO file; there is no "outside" data for the eight cities in the 1966 UES.[56] From the SEO, we can distinguish two "outside" areas: the rest of the central city (the remainder of figure 2), and the suburban ring (shown as the unshaded area of the box in the upper left-hand corner of the map). The material in Chapter Four is based upon these "outside" samples.

Measures of the Returns to Education and Training. In Chapters Two and Four (utilizing the SEO data), three different measures of the "payoff" to investments in human capital are specified: individual earnings during the survey week in March, 1966 (w); weeks unemployed in 1965 as a percent of weeks in the labor force in 1965 (u); and occupational status as of March, 1966 ($\emptyset$). In Chapter Three (utilizing the UES data), only two "payoff"

---

56. In a more recent (1968–70) Urban Employment Survey, covering 3,500 households in each of six different central city ghettos, nonghetto control samples were studied in two of the six cities: Atlanta and Detroit. See U.S. Department of Labor, Bureau of Labor Statistics, *Employment Situation in Poverty Areas of Six Cities: July, 1968 to June, 1969*, BLS report no. 370, October 1969, and many subsequent BLS reports on the new UES. The basic data files have just become available to users outside the government, and are the subject of current studies by a number of researchers, including the author and others associated with the University of Maryland Project on the Economics of Discrimination.

variables can be estimated: individual hourly earnings during the survey week in November, 1966 (w); and whether or not the individual was unemployed during the survey week:

$$u = \begin{cases} 1 \text{ if unemployed} \\ 0 \text{ otherwise} \end{cases}$$

The theoretical context within which these variables are assumed to operate will be developed in the following section.

In measuring the monetary return to education and training, it is desirable to use the shortest possible earnings period. Annual earnings may reflect one or more "spells" of nonparticipation in the labor force, which may or may not have been voluntary.[57] Even weekly earnings may reflect absenteeism, the occurrence of holidays during the survey week, and other contingencies. With the SEO data, we are forced to work with weekly earnings because (in the 1966 file used in this study) no hours estimates are available. With the UES data, however, we are able to specify hourly earnings.

Between the two data files, we are studying sixteen different metropolitan areas. In those experiments where the data are pooled, it is desirable to deflate the earnings variable, whose intercity variation reflects differences in the costs of living. Even when (in Chapter Three) we estimate individual city models, comparison of the regression coefficients measuring the marginal effect of education on earnings is facilitated by the use of "real wages." In 1965, Wilbur Thompson remarked on the difficulty of constructing appropriate cross-sectional intercity deflators, in sharp contrast to the wide availability and relative ease of construction of intertemporal cost-of-living indexes:

A firm conclusion on comparative levels of living between cities is thwarted by the utter lack of cost-of-living indexes with which to deflate the money income figures. Nor will the construction of a really useful index be achieved easily or soon, for a host of qualitative and intangible factors must be resolved. To illustrate, the range of choice in consumer goods varies greatly with city size.[58]

This situation has, to some extent, been ameliorated by a new program of the BLS. Each spring, the BLS estimates the cost of a "lower level," "average," and "relatively affluent" annual budget for a family of four in a large number of American cities. As nearly as possible, the three common "market baskets" which are "costed out" for each city are purged of those

57. This is not to suggest that increasing frequency of employment is not an important benefit from educational investment. But it is also a separate effect, to be examined separately.

58. Wilbur R. Thompson, *A Preface to Urban Economics* (Baltimore, Md.: Johns Hopkins Press, 1965), p. 62.

commodities or services whose value and/or quality have particularly high intercity variance.

There are a number of potentially serious flaws in the BLS intercity deflator. Three of these have been identified and analyzed by Roger Wertheimer II of the Urban Institute.[59] First, since tastes and overhead costs (i.e., the costs of taking and holding a job in order to be able to engage in consumption activities) vary from place to place, the BLS ought technically to be pricing baskets of goods yielding constant consumer satisfaction (or "utility") from city to city, rather than baskets containing identical commodities and services. Second, the BLS budgets count state and local taxes as living costs, but the public services which state and local governments routinely supply are not included as consumption items. It follows that jurisdictions with large public service expenditures will show higher computed costs of living than those jurisdictions which do not allocate so much of their revenue to the production and distribution of services. If the level of services is also greater in the former than in the latter jurisdiction, and if the marginal utility of public service consumption is positive, then the cost-of-living difference between these two areas will be overstated. Third, the "standards of experts" are used in place of actual consumption patterns in setting the budget levels for three especially important items: housing, food, and health care. The BLS itself admits that families tend to spend too much on housing, relative to the other two budget categories. Thus, in cities where housing is relatively less expensive than food and health, the BLS index will overstate the cost of living.

"In summary," writes Wertheimer, "the deficiencies of relying on the Bureau of Labor Statistics' cost-of-living figures are severe. They most likely adjust the income differences [between cities] in the right direction but may over-adjust."[60] Nevertheless, the new index is apparently meeting an important need, since it is in exceptionally great demand. In fact, many political organizations (such as Dr. George Wiley's National Welfare Rights Organization) have proposed the BLS "lower level" budget ($6,000/year for New York City in 1967) as a far more realistic poverty threshold than that of the OEO–Social Security Administration (SSA)–Mollie Orshansky "poverty line" (about $3,300 in 1967).

The lower level BLS budgets for the sixteen cities studied in this monograph are listed in table 2. Using Boston as numeraire, relative cost indexes were constructed. These were then used to deflate all earnings data in Chapters Two, Three, and Four. At a minimum, this methodology assumes that relative costs varied proportionately among the cities between January, 1965, and March, 1967, the range which includes all earnings periods reported in the SEO and UES and the month of the 1967 BLS cost-of-living survey (the earliest survey available).

59. Roger F. Wertheimer II, *The Monetary Rewards of Migration Within the U.S.* (Washington, D.C.: Urban Institute, 1970), pp. 45–56.

60. *Ibid.*, p. 51.

Table 2

BLS Lower Level Budget for a Family of Four in
Sixteen Metropolitan Areas, Spring, 1967

SMSA	Annual Money Cost of the Lower Level Budget	Relative Cost (Boston = 1.00)
Boston	$6,251	1.00
Baltimore	5,820	0.93
Chicago	6,104	0.98
Cleveland	5,915	0.95
Detroit	5,873	0.94
Houston	5,542	0.88
Los Angeles	6,305	1.01
New Orleans[a]	5,597	0.90
New York	6,021	0.96
Philadelphia	5,898	0.94
Phoenix[b]	5,237	0.84
Pittsburgh	5,841	0.93
St. Louis	6,002	0.96
San Antonio[b]	5,237	0.84
San Francisco	6,571	1.05
Washington, D.C.	6,133	0.98

Source: U.S. Department of Labor, Bureau of Labor Statistics, *Three Standards of Living for an Urban Family of Four Persons, Spring, 1967*, Washington, D.C., bulletin 1570-75, 1969.

[a]New Orleans was not included in the BLS budget study; I am therefore using Atlanta (another southern metropolis) as a proxy.

[b]Phoenix and San Antonio were not included in the BLS budget study; I am therefore using Austin (another southwestern metropolis) as a proxy.

Increased education is assumed to reduce the incidence of unemployment. Since the SEO file contains annual (or annualized) data, the unemployment variable in Chapters Two and Four will be weeks unemployed as a percent of weeks in the labor force during the year prior to the interview. This specification may be thought of as a normalization of the variable *weeks worked in 1965*, which displays substantial interpersonal variation. This transformation of the variable serves to distinguish the act of seeking work (i.e., entering the labor force) from that of finding work. As argued in note 57, it is desirable to separate out these distinct effects.

Since the UES data refer to the week preceding a single survey week in November, 1966, the unemployment variable in Chapter Three must be dichotomous; either a worker (in the labor force) is unemployed, or he is not.[61]

61. The specification of a dummy dependant variable in a multiple regression model introduces a statistical problem known as "heteroskedasticity," the correction of which requires the consumption of substantial amounts of computer time. The procedure is described in Appendix C.

The third "payoff" variable examined in the monograph is occupational status. The SEO contains 308 occupational categories, one of which is assigned to each person in the sample. The UES identifies only eight, too few to be of much use. Thus, our interest in this variable is developed in Chapters Two and Four, but not in Three. Using a technique developed by the National Opinion Research Corporation (NORC) and sociologist Otis Dudley Duncan (described in Appendix A), it has been possible to transform (or "map") each occupation data point in the SEO into an ordinal prestige score varying between 0 and 100. This is how the occupational status variable is measured in the regressions of Chapters Two and Four.

Control Variables. The two policy variables analyzed in the following chapters are years of school completed (E) (Chapters Two, Three, and Four) and participation in one or more of five training programs (T_i) (Chapter Two).

The partial relationships between the policy variables and the payoff variables may be assumed to vary among workers with different family and personal characteristics, different industrial attachments, and different residential addresses. It is therefore necessary to "control" for these influences on the parameters which express the marginal impact of education and training on wages, unemployment, and occupational status. Variables introduced for this purpose in the chapters that follow include intermetropolitan location (i.e., name of city of residence), intrametropolitan location (ghetto, rest of central city, or suburban ring), age, race, sex, and current industrial attachment. Two frequently used control variables which were not included in my analyses are relationship to head of household and family size. The former is highly correlated with sex, while the latter and age are strongly collinear. On the argument that sex and age are the theoretically more satisfactory variables,[62] the other two are excluded from consideration. One final control variable which is included in the analyses of the SEO data (Chapters Two and Four) is a dummy variable indicating whether or not the individual was employed at least 35 hours per week for at least half of the weeks he or she worked in 1965. The SEO data (i.e., the 1966 file) will not permit us to identify hours worked per week. With no further control, substantial interpersonal variation in weekly earnings may possibly be attributable to differences in hours worked per week. With the SEO, the best we can do to remove this source of variation is to specify a full-time/part-time dummy variable.[63] We have no such problem with the UES (Chapter Three), where the earnings variable can be adjusted for hours worked per week.

For most workers, seniority is an extremely important determinant of employment status. Earnings generally rise with years on the (same) job,

---

62. Insofar as their interaction with education in determining earnings, unemployment and occupational status is concerned.

63. This variable was indeed highly significant in all regressions in which it was included.

and—particularly in unionized industries—probabilities of unemployment generally vary inversely with tenure. This is confirmed by the Wachtel-Betsey study, in which job tenure consistently displayed one of the largest Beta coefficients. In fact, the job tenure Beta coefficient was always greater than the indicator of relative importance of education. Unfortunately, job tenure data are unavailable in either the SEO or the 1966 UES.

Three General Models. The work of Duncan, Duncan and Peter Blau, and Weiss on the education-occupation-income nexus[64] has convinced me of the desirability of organizing these variables into a model of the employment process which is essentially sequential in nature. Workers use their educational and training credentials to gain entry into an occupation, after which they "bargain" for (or are assigned an administered) wage. With such a model, it is possible to allow race, sex, and class discrimination to enter the process at each stage.

The model is developed in detail in Appendix A. It is also shown there that the model is recursive, so that each "payoff" variable may be studied separately. The three general regression models to be estimated in subsequent chapters are coded as equations (8), (9), and (10) in Appendix A. In the first, individual wages are assumed to vary with years of schooling, participation in training programs, race, sex, age, SMSA of residence, area within the SMSA, and industry in which the worker is employed. The second equation relates individual unemployment to the same "explanatory" variables as the first equation. In the third equation, occupational status is related to the same set of variables, with the exception of industry (since a person is assumed to "enter" an occupation prior to actually beginning a job).

EDUCATIONAL QUALITY, JOB REQUIREMENTS, AND THE ON-THE-JOB PERFORMANCE OF THE "HARD-CORE" UNEMPLOYED

No attempt is made in this study to make an adjustment for the quality of education, even though it is widely believed that the education received by ghetto dwellers is inferior to that of other urban residents, and that this inferior quality contributes in an important way to the allegedly lower productivity of ghetto workers.

Most analysts have surrendered before the formidable problem of measuring educational quality. For example, in one of the earliest economic treatments of racial discrimination, Becker explicitly assumed whites and non-

64. Otis Dudley Duncan, "Measuring the Trend in Social Stratification," paper delivered to the Annual Meeting of the American Statistical Association, December 31, 1967; Duncan, "A Socioeconomic Index for All Occupations," in *Occupations and Social Status*, ed., Albert J. Reiss, Jr. (Glencoe, N.Y.: Free Press, 1961); Peter M. Blau and Otis Dudley Duncan, *The American Occupational Structure* (New York: Wiley, 1967); and Weiss, "Effect of Education."

whites with the same amount of education (and of similar ages and sex) to be perfect substitutes in production.[65]

Most of those analysts who *have* attempted to "adjust" their estimates of the relationship between interracial differences in education and income for differences in the quality of schooling have used the so-called Coleman scores.

> Using achievement test scores from over 60,000 American students, the federally sponsored survey, *Equality of Educational Opportunity*[66] (widely known as the "Coleman Report" after its principal author), reported that black students had lower achievement scores than white students at every grade level, that only a portion of this difference could be explained by the poorer socioeconomic backgrounds of black students, and that the gaps in achievement scores tended to grow larger at higher educational levels. The report concluded from these separate results that white students received much higher quality education while in school than did black students.[67]

James Coleman translated these racial differences in achievement scores into roughly equivalent differences in years of schooling. For example, for students living in Northeastern cities, blacks at grade six were approximately 1.6 years behind whites in achievement. At grade nine, the gap had grown to 2.4 years. By the end of the twelfth grade, it was 3.3 years.[68]

In his microanalytic study of the 1960 Census, Weiss found that the Coleman scores were statistically related to earnings for whites (whites with higher achievement test scores tended to enjoy higher earnings), but not for nonwhites. Moreover, the effect of interracial differences in schooling on interracial differences in income (itself quite weak to begin with) was not affected at all by substituting the Coleman equivalents for actual black years of school (e.g., replacing a Census value of 12 for a Northeastern urban black with the "adjusted" figure of 12 − 3.3 = 8.7).[69]

In another study utilizing the Coleman scores, Barbara Bergmann and Jerolyn Lyle used EEOC and Census data to explain variations in the white-nonwhite "occupational status gap" across 67 industries and 46 cities. The

65. Gary S. Becker, *The Economics of Discrimination* (Chicago: University of Chicago Press, 1957), p. 95.

66. James S. Coleman et al., *Equality of Educational Opportunity* (Washington, D.C.: Govt. Prtg. Off., 1966).

67. Gordon, *Problems in Political Economy*, p. 164. The unstated logic by which Coleman and his colleagues drew this conclusion is explicated by Gordon: "The analyses assume that cognitive achievement tests accurately reflect the skill dimension through which education affects increased productivity. Those with more education are more productive, they presume, especially because they have learned how to read and reason more skillfully." *Ibid.*, p. 165.

68. It is a tenable hypothesis that differences in the quality of the schooling received by whites and nonwhites, even when significant, are themselves the result of racial discrimination at least as much as they are attributable to "personal defects" of the nonwhite poor.

69. Weiss, "Effect of Education."

authors conclude that "explanations . . . of the differences which run in terms of differences in circumstances having little or nothing to do with discrimination do not seem to be valid. Variables bearing on the quantity and quality of education come out particularly badly . . .[E]fforts to encourage non-discriminatory behavior of employers will have a bigger pay-off than efforts to improve education, transportation, and all the rest."[70]

Within racial groups, the implications of not adjusting the data for educational quality are fairly easy to assess. Following Weiss, we may assume that the "quality of schooling, grades, individual ability and motivation, and *parents'* income, education and occupation [are] probably . . . correlated positively with years of school [such that] estimates of the increase in earnings associated with an additional year of school will [in the absence of controls for the above factors] be biased upward."[71] It follows that my intraracial estimates of the marginal returns to education are, if anything, overstated. A similar inference may be drawn from an observation by Ivar Berg, i.e., that the "basic assumption of the theory of human capital" (that education and productivity are positively correlated) usually goes untested in most human capital studies—including my own. If earnings *are* roughly proportional to productivity, then any model which *assumes* a positive correlation between education and productivity may impart an upward bias to the estimates of the monetary returns to that education. Berg himself has identified industries in which (he estimates) education and productivity are, if anything, *inversely* related.[72]

Thus, I would argue that any biases associated with the omission of educational quality measures from this study probably do not vitiate the results. My already low estimates of the returns to education are, if anything, *overstated.*

"Controlling" for quality differentials through the use of test scores is itself a rather crude way of trying to equalize educational *experiences*, which is the real objective of such statistical exercises. In the present study, we are in a position to obtain some degree of control with respect to such experiences. We know that the whites and nonwhites in our sample are neighbors; it is therefore plausible that at least the youngest ones attended the same schools (although many poor whites, it must be admitted, are known to attend parochial schools, where discipline at least is greater than in the inner-city public schools). We also know that many of these whites have lived in the urban slums for several generations, under secularly deteriorating educational conditions. Finally, we know that many of the whites in the ghetto—or their parents and grandparents—migrated from rural Southern communities with unquestionably inferior schools.

70. Barbara R. Bergmann and Jerolyn R. Lyle, "The Occupational Standing of Negroes by Areas and Industries," *Journal of Human Resources*, Fall 1971.
71. Weiss, "Effect of Education," p. 152.
72. Berg, *Education and Jobs*, chap. 5.

In short, there is every reason to believe that whites and nonwhites living in the same small, urban poverty neighborhoods studied in subsequent chapters have received education of rather similar (or rather of similarly poor) quality.

In any case, there is important new evidence that—even if minority (and particularly ghetto) education is inferior in quality to the schooling received by most urban whites—the mechanism by which this contributes to nonwhite poverty and unemployment is not inadequate skills or low potential productivity, but rather the growing infatuation of private and public employers with educational credentials. The practice of "credentialism"—the use of educational credentials as a quick and allegedly inexpensive device for screening out socially undesirable individuals—appears to be an increasingly important explanation of the correlation between completion of high school or college on the one hand, and income on the other.[73] Whether or not such concern reflects wilful discrimination, the result is to "screen out" minority workers who may well be capable of performing the requisite job tasks. I am arguing that the inferior quality of the education received by many minority youth—particularly in city schools—in itself probably contributes little to the explanation of nonwhite poverty. Rather, I deduce that it is the behavior of employers, using the alleged inferior quality of minority education to rationalize rejection of nonwhite job applicants, which is the principal explanatory factor. If this deduction is valid, then the analytical benefits from "correctly" measuring educational quality would probably not be worth the costs of attempting such a difficult project.

My hypothesis is deduced from two kinds of evidence. The first has to do with the myth and reality of skill requirements. In one of the earliest urban antipoverty programs, Dr. Kenneth Clark's Harlem Youth Opportunities Unlimited (HARYOU) staff asserted that

> clearly, the projected trends in employment point to the necessity for a thorough and comprehensive education for a place in tomorrow's world. These jobs which are due to expand within the next decade are those which will require considerable mathematical and verbal skills, plus a

73. S. M. Miller, *Breaking the Credentials Barrier* (New York: Ford Foundation, 1967); S. M. Miller and Marsha Kroll, "Strategies for Reducing Credentialism," *Good Government*, Summer 1970; *The Political Economy of Public Service Employment*, ed. Sheppard Harrison, and Spring, chap. 5: "Barriers to the Public Employment of the Disadvantaged." In a study of West Coast cities during the summer of 1970 for an OEO–National Civil Service League project designed to identify those civil service rules and procedures which most often "screen-out" the black, brown, and poor from jobs in local government, I found the practice of credentialism to be indeed ubiquitous. Civil service examiners asked future janitors to "select antonyms to the word 'alleviate' "! Meter maid candidates were required to have high school diplomas and to solve complex algebra problems involving cars passing one another on superhighways. See Bennett Harrison, "Government Employment and the Disadvantaged," in U.S. Department of Labor, *1971 Manpower Report of the President* (Washington, D.C.: Govt. Prtg. Off., 1971), pp. 171–75; and Harrison, *Public Employment and Urban Poverty* (Washington, D.C.: Urban Institute, June, 1971), paper no. 113–43.

broad knowledge of science, literature, history, and social science. Concomitantly, those jobs requiring few of these skills are rapidly disappearing as machines and automation take over.[74]

This prognostication reflects a belief in what Charles Killingsworth calls the "skill twist" resulting from the progressive elimination of simple, repetitive production processes in American industry.[75]

It is difficult to accept such a forecast. The automation or mechanization of certain work activities does not imply that the remaining (or newly developing) job tasks will be more technical. The rapid postwar substitution of white-collar for blue-collar (or of service for production) workers in our economy has not been accompanied by an equivalent substitution of skilled for semi-skilled labor—if by "skilled" we mean the acquisition of special capabilities beyond those for which general education is sufficient preparation. In fact, a powerful case can be made (and is being made in the "new careers" literature) that the growing dominance of the service industries, especially government at all levels, *reduces* the technical composition of many jobs. There is no compelling evidence that it is more difficult to operate a computer than to operate a lathe. Contrary to popular opinion, individuals with less than a college education are now and will probably continue to be the most sought after of all groups in the economy.

> While the number of jobs for which people with low educational achievement are "qualified" is shrinking, there is not as great an increase in the number of higher-level jobs (e.g., for college graduates) as might be supposed from the frequency with which higher education is stressed. The big increase is in middle-level jobs. . . . The story with respect to the achievement of the work force is that there is a "shortage" of high school graduates and a "surplus" of college graduates.[76]

The simplicity of a broad range of jobs (relative to the inflated requirements often assumed in the literature) is perhaps best illustrated by reference to "job task analyses." Studies of this kind decompose a "job" into its various functional "tasks," and assess the kind and the extent of preparatory training necessary to perform each task at an "average" level of competence. Many task analyses have been prepared in recent years, especially in connection with the New Careers and other paraprofessional job development programs.[77] The most impressive (and certainly the most comprehensive) of

74. Harlem Youth Opportunities Unlimited, Inc., *Youth in the Ghetto* (New York: HARYOU-ACT, 1964).

75. Charles Killingsworth, *Jobs and Income for Negroes* (Ann Arbor: Institute for Labor and Industrial Relations, University of Michigan–Wayne State University, 1968).

76. Berg, "Education and Work," p. 125.

77. Cf. Sidney A. Fine, *Guidelines for the Design of New Careers* (Kalamazoo, Mich.: W. E. Upjohn Institute, September, 1967); Arthur Pearl and Frank Riessman, *New Careers for the Poor* (New York: Free Press, 1965); U.S. Department of Commerce, Bureau of the Census, *Job Qualification System for Trades and Labor Occupations*

these are the two studies by the Bureau of Employment Security (BES) of the USDL, entitled *Estimates of Worker Traits Requirements for 4,000 Jobs* and published in 1956 and 1966. The purpose of the BES studies was to prescribe—through the use of panels of technical experts and personnel officials—both "general education" and "vocational education" requirements for each job title. Table 3 shows the educational requirements in terms of years of schooling needed to permit average performance in a selected number of jobs of increasing importance in urban areas, drawn from a much more extensive set developed by James Scoville.[78] This sample (and the entire set of 4,000 titles from which it is drawn) displays an average general educational requirement of considerably less than twelve years of school. Moreover, two years of experience are sufficient to enable a worker to achieve an average level of competence on the job. These are far more modest requirements than those currently implicit in the credentials without which workers are frequently excluded from these very same jobs.

Hirsch Ruchlin has compared employers' educational requirements (EER) with GED scores expressed (as in table 3) in school year equivalents, for the period 1959–69. He found that the differences were most often positive (EER > GED) for clerical and service occupations, and invariably negative (EER < GED) for skilled and semiskilled occupations. Relative excess supplies of the former classes of labor, and excess demand for the latter category, may help to explain why employers' educational demands systematically exceed or fall short of real technical requirements. In other words, when screening techniques are needed, educational credentials are often used—regardless of the technical requirements of the tasks to be performed.[79]

I referred earlier to the theory of the alleged "skill twist." The "general educational development" (GED) scores developed by the BES have been used to test the "twist" hypothesis explicitly. Morris Horowitz and Irwin Herrnstadt have compared the 1956 and 1966 trait requirements "as well as the detailed job descriptions for five industries. They concluded that the overall or net change in the skill requirements was remarkably small, especially considering that their study covered a quarter-century (1940–66).

(Washington, D.C.: Govt. Prtg. Off., 1969); and U.S. Department of Labor, *A Handbook for Job Restructuring* (Washington, D.C.: Govt. Prtg. Off., 1970).

78. James G. Scoville, "Education and Training Requirements for Occupations," *Review of Economics and Statistics*, November 1966. See also Berg, *Education and Jobs*, chap. 3, and Richard S. Eckaus, "Economic Criteria for Education and Training," *Review of Economics and Statistics*, May 1964. The reader should note that the translations of the job task requirements into equivalent required years of schooling was conducted by the above-cited academic researchers, *not* by the BES, which has never endorsed these translations. For a good discussion of the methodological issues and problems, see Berg, *Education and Jobs*, chap. 3.

79. Hirsch S. Ruchlin, "Education as a Labor Market Variable," *Industrial Relations*, October 1971. Since the urban poor are disproportionately crowded into the clerical and service occupations, they are therefore especially troubled by the practice of credentialism.

Table 3

General Education and Vocational Education
Requirements for Selected Jobs

Job Title	General Education Requirements (Equivalent Years)[a]	Vocational Education Requirements (Equivalent Years)[b]
Draftsmen	12.68	2.68
Nurses, professional	12.00	2.50
Technicians, testing	12.27	1.65
Inspectors, public	11.46	2.16
Purchasing agents and buyers	12.00	7.00
Bookkeepers	10.33	0.44
Cashiers	10.67	0.53
Mail carriers	8.50	0.10
Office machine operators	8.42	0.23
Stenos, typists, secretaries	10.91	0.58
Advertising agents and salesmen	10.00	0.04
Compositors and typesetters	12.00	4.38
Electricians	11.14	1.73
Job setters, metal	10.67	3.00
Mechanics:		
Automobile	10.80	1.66
Office machine	11.00	3.00
Attendants, hospitals	9.50	0.10
Policemen	11.33	0.19

Source: James G. Scoville, "Education and Training Requirements for Occupations",
Review of Economics and Statistics, November, 1966.

[a]These are index numbers based upon actual and prescribed educational attainment
of workers in detailed categories which have been aggregated to produce the job
titles appearing in the table. See Scoville.

[b]The amount of time required to learn the techniques, acquire the information, and
develop the facility needed for average performance.

'There was considerable change in occupational requirements and content,
but on balance, it was inconsequential or inconclusive with respect to overall
skill levels.' "[80]

Media commercials (so-called public service announcements) increasingly
assert that a high school diploma is a minimum prerequisite for employment
in the United States. As an institutional (cultural) prerequisite, this appears to
be only too accurate. As a functional (technical) prerequisite, however, it is
simply not true. And this misplaced emphasis on the "sheepskin" places an
intolerable burden on the poor. Thus, in one public jurisdiction, a laundry

80. Quoted by Berg, *Education ʾd Jobs*, pp. 81-82. A number of other studies
have shown that "the advent of automation and mechanization has not increased the
aggregate level of educational requirements for satisfactory job performance [either] in
the manufacturing or service sector." Ruchlin, "Education as a Labor Market Variable,"
p. 288, and the references cited in n. 3.

section supervisor must have five years' experience and a high school diploma—for a $6,000 job. In the same jurisdiction, a beginning inexperienced laundry worker must have completed high school—for a $3,600 job.[81] Surely, a laundry worker need be no more than functionally literate. According to the National Industrial Conference Board (NICB), "a functional literate is an individual with not more than a fourth grade education."[82]

Probably the best evidence that the determinants of inflated skill requirements are institutional or cultural rather than technical is that, in tight labor markets, these barriers to employment of the poor are usually lowered to some extent. Professor Edwin Harwood, in his studies of the recent migration of white Appalachian families to Chicago, found that they had little trouble obtaining work—at wages of $90 to $130 a week. Moreover,

> inadequate formal education was no handicap to the Appalachians, though most had less than ten years of formal schooling in the rural border states. Nobody at the [Chicago] plants had cared whether they had a high school diploma, [probably] because, in a tight labor market, employers have no choice.[83]

In his January, 1968, manpower message, President Lyndon Johnson announced a Job Opportunities in the Business Sector (JOBS) program, to be promoted by a volunteer National Alliance of Businessmen (NAB) whose first chairman was Henry Ford, II. The USDL would provide subsidies[84] (ultimately averaging about $3,000 per worker) to large, NAB-affiliated private corporations to pay for "the added costs of hiring, training, and retaining low productivity workers."[85] The NAB, as promoter of the scheme, would seek "job creation pledges" from private corporations across the country.

81. Robert H. Dicks, "A Close, Hard Look at Testing," *Good Government*, Winter 1969.

82. National Industrial Conference Board, *Education, Training, and Employment*, p. 28.

83. "Many Youths Jobless by Choice," *Washington Post*, December 17, 1969, p. C5.

84. Under the most recent JOBS contract, the following "incentives" are made available to private firms: "one-half of a trainee's salary for a period of from 10 to 40 weeks, depending on the complexity of the job . . . the entire wage during periods when the trainee is receiving job-related basic education, counseling, and orientation . . . the full cost (up to certain established ceilings) of providing those services (job-related basic education, counseling, and orientation) plus the cost of transportation assistance, child care assistance, medical and dental treatment (if necessary), 'human relations' training for the employer's supervisory personnel, plus an allowance for administrative costs. For these items, a firm with a JOBS contract could receive up to $5,213 per trainee." U.S. Senate, Subcommittee on Employment, Manpower, and Poverty, *The JOBS Program*, 91st Cong., 2d sess., April 1970, p. 110.

85. Sar A. Levitan, Garth L. Mangum, and Robert Taggart III, *Economic Opportunity in the Ghetto: The Partnership of Government and Business* (Baltimore, Md.: Johns Hopkins Press, 1970), p. 20. The formal criteria for inclusion in the class of "low productivity workers" are a family income below the official poverty line (currently about $4,000 for a family of four), lack of a high school diploma, age under 22 or over 44 years, possession of a physical, mental or emotional handicap, or some "special obstacle" to employment, a criterion which is "somewhat of a catchall." U.S. Senate, Subcommittee on Employment, *JOBS Program*, p. 108.

There is considerable evidence that the NAB-JOBS program has been something less than successful (see Chapter Six). The actual (as opposed to the pledged) number of hires has been smaller than anticipated, the jobs have often been of a marginal character for which $3,000 "worth" of training is difficulty to justify, and upgrading has been virtually nonexistent. Moreover, as expected by most labor economists, the new JOBS hires were the first to be laid off in the post-1968 national economic decline. For example, early in 1970, Chrysler withdrew from its JOBS contract to train 4,450 hard-core unemployed. This followed a series of layoffs of 11,000 workers previously trained in the JOBS program. Chrysler's withdrawal occurred at about the same time Lynn Townsend, Chairman of the Board of Chrysler, became chairman of the NAB, and Byron Nichols, a Chrysler vice president, became president of NAB.[86]

Nevertheless, during the period between the riots of 1965–67 and the 1970 recession, many disadvantaged workers who had previously been unacceptable to employers because of their alleged lack of skill (widely attributed to the poor quality of their education) were at least temporarily given an opportunity to demonstrate their capabilities.

Edward Chave, second vice president of the Equitable Life Assurance Society, reports on the "surprising" results of his company's experiments with new examination procedures designed to "screen-in rather than screen-out the hard-core":

> It is not merely that they are found to be "street-wise." Experiments with the so-called culture-fair tests suggest that among the disadvantaged there are many highly intelligent people. [In Equitable, the] tests showed that one-fifth of our hard-core hires had IQ's of 120 or more, a percentage higher than found among the normal [*sic*] U.S. population.[87]

In Western Electric's two "mini-plants" located in the Newark ghetto in 1968, entrance requirements were substantially altered, to eliminate (1) all "educational requirements beyond functional literacy," (2) "preemployment psychological and physical dexterity tests," (3) binding "company health standards," and (4) "automatic disqualification for reasons of conviction of any crime." The "hard-core" were then given on-the-job (OJT) and institutional training. The Western Electric officials discovered that "the teaching of technical skills constitutes only about 25% of the effort of the shops' supervisory personnel," much to their "great surprise."[88]

During the first year of the Ford Motor Company's "Inner City Recruiting Program" in 1967, which served as the pilot project for the subsequent JOBS

86. Testimony of Mr. Nathaniel Goldfinger, Director of Research, AFL-CIO, in U.S. Senate, Subcommittee on Employment, Manpower and Poverty, *Hearings*, 91st Cong., 2d sess., 1 April 1970, pp. 1404–5.

87. National Industrial Conference Board, *Education, Training, and Employment*, p. 4.

88. *Ibid.*, pp. 56–57.

program, more than 5,000 poor workers were placed in Ford jobs. In a sample of 2,000, about 75 percent were high school dropouts. These new workers, 84 percent of whom were nonwhite, were evaluated by Ford at the end of their first year with the company:

> The retention rate compares favorably with that of other applicants who applied directly at the same plants during the same period.
> Their absenteeism has been only slightly higher than that noted for other employees with similar seniority.
> Overall reaction of plant management has been one of satisfaction with the attitudes of these employees and their ability to adjust to the industrial environment. Their performance compares favorably with applicants hired in the Detroit area during recent years.[89]

A 1970 survey of the overall JOBS program conducted by the USDL and reported in testimony before the U.S. Senate revealed that "turnover . . . appears to be about on a par with the usual experience in entry-level jobs" in these companies.[90] (Then) Assistant Labor Secretary for Manpower, Arnold Weber, told the Senators that the retention rate for JOBS trainees during the program's first year averaged 56.4 percent (a figure which includes the nearly 9 percent who dropped out of the program to take other jobs). "Compared to the 54 percent turnover of American industry as a whole, it would appear that the program is at least retaining the chronically unemployed on a par with the general mainstream of the nation's work force."[91] An independent study of the JOBS program in ten metropolitan areas, conducted by Greenleigh Associates, Inc., found that "71 percent of those willing to hire JOBS employees indicated that there was no difference between the work habits of this group and those of regular employees of the same level."[92] Jules Cohn's interviews with 247 corporations engaged in hiring the disadvantaged led him to a similar conclusion:

> [T]he notion that the disadvantaged cannot be reached by normal techniques of manpower management has been popularized. A new technology of training is necessary, it is argued, and sizable investments are required to pay counselors, teachers, and sensitivity trainers. The government's own JOBS program legitimates (and stimulates) substantial training expenditures by providing subsidies for them, and for other services. . . . But perhaps the training task is not as onerous or as costly as the literature and the sales talks of the consultants suggest. . . . It would appear from the data that it is not as difficult to motivate and train the disadvantaged as many people think. . . . [I]ndustry's programs prove that the performance of the hard-core of the poor in entry-level is not markedly inferior to that

89. *Ibid.*, p. 59.
90. U.S. Senate, Subcommittee on Employment, *JOBS Program*, p. 10.
91. *Ibid.*, p. 173.
92. Cited in General Accounting Office, *Comptroller General's Report to the Congress: Evaluation of Results and Administration of the Job Opportunities in the Business Sector (JOBS) Program in Five Cities* (Washington, D.C.: Govt. Prtg. Off., 1971), p. 82.

of other new employees. Many corporate leaders and line department heads, including personnel directors, feel that they were led to expect more severe training problems than they actually encountered.[93]

Edward Banfield reports on the hiring procedures used in the International Business Machines (IBM) Bedford-Stuyvesant plant. "In evaluating applications, no importance was attached to lack of . . . a grade school education." With regard to previous employment, police and credit records, "the personnel officers stopped looking at the investigation reports. Soon afterward, the company gave up the use of investigating agencies altogether." In place of the conventional credentials, IBM required applicants to take a physical dexterity test which, if successfully passed, was followed by an oral interview. In the latter, "a manager's judgment was enough." The result of these special procedures was that "sixty-seven percent passed the dexterity test. This was exactly the percentage that passed in the other plants."[94]

The workers so hired displayed what the IBM executives called "surprising" performance characteristics. "In the first six months of operation, the absenteeism rate was about normal for an IBM plant." Turnover rates were also low. Neither was there the expected vandalism or insubordination. In fact, IBM's chief engineer

> soon saw that the assumptions on which he had based his planning were unduly pessimistic. The workers did more and better work than anyone had expected. To be sure, some of them had to be taught to use soldering irons; none, however, had to be taught the elements of personal hygiene. What held production back was lack of supplies. Expecting very little of the workers, the planners had not scheduled a large enough flow of material from the Poughkeepsie supply base.[95]

The public sector has also learned a great deal over the past several years about the capabilities of the poor. Since 1967, the Oak Ridge plant of the Atomic Energy Commission has given OJT in industrial work to 834 previously underemployed Tennessee workers. These individuals had, prior to their hire at Oak Ridge, worked as service station attendants, grocery clerks, bus boys, janitors, and farm laborers, averaging $3,577 a year. By late 1969, "more than 95 percent of them were still employed [at Oak Ridge] and earning an average of $6,333 a year," working in mechanical drafting, industrial electronics, metal machinery, combination welding, glass blowing, and general mechanics. This upgrading required on the average only six months.[96]

93. Jules Cohn, *The Conscience of the Corporations* (Baltimore, Md.: Johns Hopkins Press, 1971), pp. 58–59.

94. Edward C. Banfield, "The I.B.M. Plant in Bedford-Stuyvesant," in *Programs to Employ the Disadvantaged*, ed. Peter B. Doeringer (Englewood Cliffs, N.J.: Prentice-Hall, 1969), pp. 43–44.

95. *Ibid.*, pp. 48–50.

96. James L. Echols, "Technicians: How to Grow Your Own," *Manpower*, January 1970, pp. 8–9.

Under its widely publicized "Project 100,000," the Department of Defense began in the Fall of 1966 to induct "men who would not have met earlier mental or educational standards." These men received regular training. Analyses of the performance of these individuals "confirm the judgment that when conventional screening standards are lowered, even substantially, no dire implications for performance ensue."[97]

Finally, in a two and one-half year study of their examination procedures, the California State Personnel Board found that

> minority group members competed successfully in promotional examinations [which do test skill and achievement] for technical or professional classes. [But] they were at particular disadvantage in the lower entry examinations requiring relatively little (public) education.[98]

From this, Nancy Rapoport of New York University concludes that OJT and other "hire first" programs should completely discontinue any use of competitive entrance examinations, and indeed defer the examination process altogether until after the worker has acquired on-the-job experience which is objectively testable.[99]

OTHER POSSIBLE SOURCES OF BIAS IN THE ESTIMATES REPORTED IN THIS STUDY

We have already examined the argument that the absence of adjustments for racial differences in the quality of education may bias the results of this study. Several other possible sources of bias will now be considered briefly.

The Possibility of Selective Outmigration of the Most Educated Workers. Readers of early drafts of the dissertation observed that only the "ghetto" itself was at that time the object of study. A ghetto sample, it was argued, is inherently biased since those for whom education has "paid off" will presumably have moved out, leaving us wih a sample heavily skewed toward thc "failures."[100] This criticism motivated the extension of the thesis

97. Berg, *Education and Jobs*, p. 158.
98. Dicks, "A Close, Hard Look," p. 13.
99. In a landmark 8-0 decision delivered on March 8, 1971, the U.S. Supreme Court (in *Griggs* v. *Duke Power Co.*) interpreted Title VII of the 1964 Civil Rights Act as prohibiting employers from "screening Negroes out of desirable jobs on the basis of general aptitude tests and educational requirements that are not related to job performance." The decision requires employers to "validate" any test or credential requirement used in selecting workers. "Job Tests Held in Violation of Rights Act," *Washington Post*, March 9, 1971, p. A-1. The Griggs case is discussed further in Chapter Seven.
100. Professor Paul Taubman observes, however, that the whites who remain in urban slum neighborhoods are less constrained in their residential choices by discrimination, with the result that the white "stayers" might be expected to be even more biased downward in terms of motivation and achievement than the black "stayers." Yet, as the results of Chapter Two will show, blacks in the ghetto still lag behind ghetto whites in economic welfare.

to urban workers living outside of the central city ghettos. The models developed previously reflect this broader concern. One finding of this study may be previewed at this point. The structure of returns to investments in nonwhite human capital is highly insensitive to intrametropolitan location. But the structure of white returns is quite sensitive to variations in residential location. Moreover, the nonwhite-white earnings, unemployment and occupational status "gaps" grow wider as we move out from the central city ghetto to the suburbs. All of this constitutes powerful indirect evidence that the relative insensitivity of the ghetto "payoff" variables to investments in the human capital of ghetto workers—which is the major finding of this study—is not the result of an inherent bias in the ghetto samples.[101]

A very recent (and decidedly unofficial) finding of the BLS-UES group provides some remarkable direct evidence that the conventional wisdom on selective outmigration from the ghetto must be modified. Of 7,200 ghetto families who were to be reinterviewed by the BLS over a twelve-month period in 1968–69 (a period of exceptionally high mobility nationally), only 900 had moved from one residence to another. And of these 900 families, only sixty had moved out of the ghetto; all of the rest were either intraghetto moves (750) or involuntary relocation, e.g., into the armed forces or to jail (90).

In other words, the rate of outmigration from the urban ghetto in 1968–69 was less than 1 percent. According to Anthony Downs, "normal population turnover causes about twenty percent of the residents of the average U.S. neighborhood to move out each year."[102]

Cross-Section vs. Time-Series Estimates. Reasoning suggested by Barbara Bergmann indicates that my results are probably biased upward vis-à-vis appropriate time-series estimates. The difference in pay between a well-educated black professional and less educated blacks may depend a good deal on the relative scarcity of educated blacks. Increasing the number of black professionals by increasing the number of educated blacks—over time— might reduce the differential between the pay of blacks with different amounts of education. The result is that a cross-section model predicting income from schooling exaggerates the effect of improving black educational achievement on black income. This, of course, reinforces the upward bias associated with the absence of "controls" for educational quality. It confirms that the already very low nonwhite human capital returns estimated in the subsequent chapters are, if anything, too large.

101. It is also strongly indicative of a major flaw in the popular argument that "suburbanization" of minority groups will significantly improve their employment status. See Chapter Four.

102. Anthony Downs, "Alternative Futures for the American Ghetto," *Daedalus*, Fall 1968, p. 36. In 1969–70, 25 percent of all black households in America changed residence. In the UES sample, as indicated in the text, only 900 of 7,200 households (13 percent) changed residences in 1968–69.

Voluntary Versus Involuntary Unemployment. During the sample period of January 1, 1965, to March, 1966, the national unemployment rate fell from 5 percent to a little under 4 percent. As the economy approaches "full employment," we normally expect voluntary quit rates to increase, since the opportunities for upgrading through acquisition of a new job will have risen. Thus, it is possible that any cross-sectional measurement of unemployment during such a period of economic expansion will overstate the magnitude of involuntary unemployment.

Our data do not permit any distinction between this kind of "frictional" unemployment and the usual involuntary joblessness. We can only observe that our particular samples display average unemployment rates far in excess of the national average (6.7%–10.8% in table 4; 6.3%–12.5% in table 7; 3.5%–10.4% in figure 18). At these considerably less than "full" employment levels, quit rates are unlikely to be very large.

FORMAT OF THE MONOGRAPH

The next two chapters present estimates of models (8) through (10), using exclusively ghetto data. In Chapter Two, the twelve sets of central city poverty areas in the SEO are examined. Chapter Three covers the ten ghettos surveyed in the UES.

In order to place the findings of Chapter Two in context, and to study additional questions associated with the concept of "suburbanization," returns to the human capital of workers living outside the ghetto (in the rest of the central city and in the suburban ring) are estimated in Chapter Four. This chapter concludes with systematic comparisons of the marginal returns by race and intraurban location.

Chapter Five places these findings within the structure of a new labor market theory presently being developed by several young economists. Chapter Six summarizes the statistical findings, and draws upon these in a critical evaluation of the "current orthodoxy" concerning urban minority manpower policy. Finally, new directions in employment policy are recommended in Chapter Seven.

West Indian Archie had the kind of photographic memory that put him among the elite of numbers runners. He never wrote down your number; even in the case of combination plays, he would just nod. He was able to file all the numbers in his head, and write them down for the banker only when he turned in his money. This made him the ideal runner because cops could never catch him with any betting slips.

— Malcolm X

Several studies commissioned by the Government in recent years have shown that the major reasons the income of Negroes lags far behind that of whites continues to be discrimination, not education or training. But government has increasingly been emphasizing the latter in preference to the former, presumably because the policy makers consider discrimination too difficult to combat.

— John Herbers, in
The New York Times

2.

CENTRAL CITY POVERTY AREAS IN TWELVE STANDARD METROPOLITAN STATISTICAL AREAS

INTRODUCTION

In March, 1966, the Bureau of the Census conducted a special *Survey of Economic Opportunity* for the Office of Economic Opportunity. The purpose of the SEO was to supplement the regular Current Population Survey (CPS) with additional information on the structure of poverty. In order to obtain a limited but useful longitudinal profile, most (but unfortunately not all) of the questions were asked again in a reinterview conducted one year later, in March, 1967. Changes in address and other sampling problems resulted in a 75 percent reinterview rate.

The SEO sample of about 30,000 occupied households (initially nearly 40,000 total households) consists of two parts. The first is a national random sample of 18,000 households, drawn in the same way as the CPS sample. An additional 12,000 households were drawn from areas with large nonwhite populations. The OEO then contracted the Brookings Institution to edit and prepare two user-oriented data files (1966 and 1967). Because it contains information on job training, I have chosen to use the 1966 file in this study.

In the 1966 SEO, 37,280 "households"—physically distinct addresses—were visited. Physical and economic characteristics, e.g., the availability of sanitation facilities, rental rates, etc., were recorded on nearly 30,000 of these. At these inhabited addresses, the Census enumerators interviewed 27,340 families (or "interview units") containing 89,925 persons, of whom 61,517 were "adults," i.e., fourteen years of age or older. Personal data were recorded on all individuals, but labor force characteristics were recorded only for the latter group.

The twelve largest Standard Metropolitan Statistical Areas—identified by name on the data tapes—contain 21,467 of the 61,517 "adults" in the file: better than a third of the sample. Of these, 11,454 were no longer in school in March, 1966, and had been in the labor force for at least thirteen weeks in 1965. This is the subsample which I have chosen to study, here and in Chapter Four. Some two-thirds of all the blacks living outside the South reside in these twelve largest cities.

This subsample is distributed as follows:

SMSA	No. of Observations
Baltimore	652
Chicago	1,220
Cleveland	317
Detroit	827
Houston	506
Los Angeles	1,680
New York	2,640
Philadelphia	941
Pittsburgh	277

St. Louis	328
San Francisco	977
Washington, D.C.	1,089

An alternative distribution of the sample is:

Whites

– in central city poverty areas	821
– in the remainder of the twelve central cities	2,125
– in the suburban rings	3,163

Nonwhites

– in central city poverty areas	2,935
– in the remainder of the twelve central cities	1,565
– in the suburban rings	845

Although the SEO identifies the individual areas, some of the SMSA sample sizes are quite small relative to the number of variables in the more intricate regression models which follow. Inferences from such small samples would be highly unreliable, if not actually infeasible.[1] Therefore, I have chosen to experiment with the pool of twelve SMSAs, rather than with the individual areas. Intercity variations in earnings, unemployment and occupational status will be captured (at least partially) through the specification of dummy variables representing each SMSA.

In modifying the 1966 SEO file, I created a new file in which each logical record completely describes the physical quarters, family, personal characteristics, and work experience of each "adult"; well over 200 variables. In this study, however, only a fraction of this wealth of microdata is utilized—just enough to estimate regression models (8), (9) and (10).

UNDEREMPLOYMENT AND HUMAN CAPITAL IN CENTRAL CITY POVERTY AREAS

While straightforward joblessness is not the only element of underemployment, it is still the most dramatic. Figure 3 displays quarterly white and nonwhite unemployment rates in the poverty areas of the one hundred largest metropolitan areas in the country, since mid-1967. It is apparent that race "counts" significantly—even within the "ghetto"—as a factor in explaining unemployment. The white-nonwhite "gap" is smaller for primary working age males than for the poverty area population as a whole, reflecting the espe-

---

1. Relative to the size and structure of the regression models, specification of individual SMSA's would lead to high probabilities of matrix singularity resulting from the presence of many empty cells.

Figure 3

Unemployment Rates in Urban Poverty Areas and the United States—Third Quarter, 1967, to Second Quarter, 1971[a]

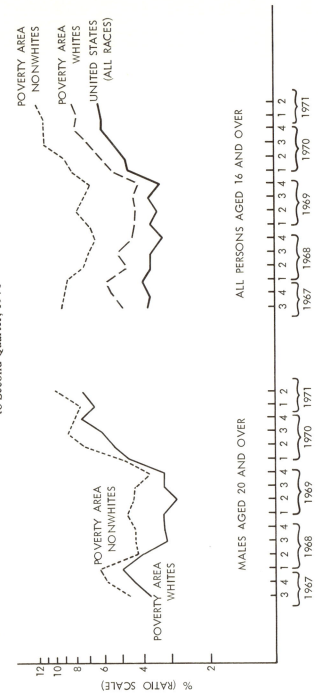

Source: U.S. Department of Labor, News Releases Nos. 10–017, 10–175, 10–388, 10–560, 71–207, and 71–391.

[a]Includes poverty areas in the 100 SMSAs with populations of at least 250,000. Data for the first six quarters are not seasonally adjusted. In 1971, these 100 sets of poverty areas accounted for about 7.5 percent of the country's population and labor force.

cially serious unemployment among nonwhite ghetto teenagers (nearly 25 percent in 1968). Throughout the period, the relative gap between poverty area and U.S. unemployment has remained virtually constant for both races, with nonwhite "ghetto" unemployment averaging twice the national rate. Notice that poverty area nonwhite men took considerably longer to benefit from the national expansion of 1967-69, and suffered relatively more quickly from the recession of 1970-71, than did their white neighbors. This finding, of course, supports the popular hypothesis that blacks—or at least ghetto blacks—are the "last hired and first fired."

For all races, poverty area underemployment is also manifested in fewer hours of work per week. "A greater proportion of poverty neighborhood residents continued to work on 'economic part-time'—due to slack work, material shortages, and so on—compared with workers in other parts of the cities, and a smaller proportion worked on overtime."[2] The gap in 1968 was greatest between nonwhite poverty area workers and whites residing elsewhere in the one hundred SMSAs. Over three times as many ghetto nonwhites were involuntarily part-time employed as nonghetto whites, while over a quarter of the latter enjoyed access to overtime as opposed to less than a sixth of the former.[3]

A major cause of nonparticipation among working-age people is discouragement over lack of job opportunities, previous unhappy experiences in job search, and so forth. In 1968, the labor force participation rate (LFPR) in the one hundred sets of poverty areas was four percentage points below the "outside" rate; for men aged 25-54, the difference was 5.3 percent.[4] The uniformly lower LFPR for the ghetto is most pronounced in a comparison between nonwhite ghetto men aged 25-54 and white nonghetto urban men in the same age group; 7 percent fewer of the former than of the latter were in the labor force in 1968.[5]

In our sample of 3,756 workers living in the central city poverty areas of the twelve largest SMSAs (referring now to the sample period of 1965 and early 1966), underemployment is reflected in additional ways. For both racial groups, table 4 indicates that, over a full year, substantial numbers of ghetto residents who sought work were unable to find it. Five-sixths of the nonwhite ghetto men sought year-round employment in 1965, but only about 66 percent found it. At the opposite extreme of the distribution, only 5 percent of the nonwhite ghetto males voluntarily sought fewer than 33 weeks of work in 1965, but over 13 percent—nearly three times as many—actually worked that seldom, indicating substantial involuntary part-time employment. For whites, the respective gaps between intended and actual employment were much

2. Paul M. Ryscavage, "Employment Developments in Urban Poverty Neighborhoods," *Monthly Labor Review*, June 1969, p. 53.
3. *Ibid.*, table 5.
4. *Ibid.*, table 8.
5. *Ibid.*, table 9.

smaller, as table 4 reveals. Overall "micro" unemployment rates, defined as

$$u = \left\{ 1 - \frac{\text{weeks worked in 1965}}{\text{weeks in the labor force in 1965}} \right\} \times 100$$

again display the racial pattern identified above. In table 4, we see that the white-nonwhite unemployment gap within the ghetto is even greater for women than for men.

Table 4

Profile of the Labor Force in the Central City Poverty
Areas of Twelve SMSAs, 1965-66[a]

(in percent)

Variable	Whites		Nonwhites	
	Women	Men	Women	Men
Sample size	306	515	1,331	1,604
Age (range = 14-84)				
14-19 years	7.5	3.1	4.7	3.4
20-27 years	22.2	16.9	17.2	15.6
28-35 years	14.7	18.6	16.6	18.4
36-43 years	19.3	15.3	20.9	21.1
44-51 years	12.1	16.9	18.0	17.0
52-59 years	12.1	14.4	13.4	15.5
60-67 years	8.1	11.3	7.8	7.5
68-75 years	3.3	2.9	1.3	1.2
76- years	0.7	0.6	0.2	0.2
Median years	38.3	42.0	40.4	40.7
Weeks worked in 1965				
(range = 14-52)				
14-20 weeks	4.9	3.5	7.5	5.5
21-32 weeks	11.4	4.0	15.0	7.9
33-44 weeks	21.6	15.6	20.2	17.5
45-50 weeks	4.6	5.0	3.9	3.6
51-52 weeks	57.5	71.9	53.3	65.5
Median weeks	51.1	51.4	51.0	51.3
Weeks in the labor force in 1965				
(range = 14-52)				
14-20 weeks	11.8	4.9	13.1	5.1
21-32 weeks	0.0	0.0	0.0	0.0
33-44 weeks	18.3	8.5	17.6	9.8
45-50 weeks	3.9	2.7	2.4	1.8
51-52 weeks	66.0	83.9	66.9	83.3
Median weeks	51.4	51.7	51.4	51.7
Occupational status[b]				
(range = 0-96)				
0-9 rank	14.1	19.2	17.0	32.0
10-19 rank	30.4	32.8	53.0	38.2
20-29 rank	2.9	9.5	4.6	9.1

Table 4 (Continued)

(in percent)

Variable	Whites		Nonwhites	
	Women	Men	Women	Men
Occupational status (cont.)				
30–39 rank	3.6	8.2	8.5	4.8
40–49 rank	21.9	12.8	8.2	8.0
50–59 rank	3.6	2.3	1.3	2.6
60–69 rank	19.0	10.9	5.3	3.7
70–79 rank	3.6	1.4	1.9	1.0
80–89 rank	1.0	1.9	0.1	0.4
90–96 rank	0.0	1.0	0.2	0.1
Median rank	31.2	19.4	16.2	14.7
Weekly earnings				
(range = $0– $ 635)				
0–39 $ week	29.70	15.30	42.70	18.30
40–79 $ week	43.80	24.10	42.90	33.20
80–119 $ week	20.90	31.80	10.70	29.40
120–159 $ week	4.20	16.70	3.00	14.70
160–199 $ week	0.70	6.60	0.50	3.00
200– $ week	0.70	5.40	0.20	1.50
Median earnings	58.54	98.33	46.81	78.19
Unemployment rates in 1965[c]				
(range = 0–98)				
0–14	88.9	84.7	83.9	83.7
15–29	0.3	1.2	0.2	0.2
30–44	4.2	7.0	4.7	6.2
45–59	0.7	0.0	0.2	0.1
60–74	226	4.1	5.2	5.2
75–89	2.0	2.1	2.5	2.4
90–	1.3	1.0	3.2	2.3
Mean rate	6.7	8.8	10.8	10.4

Source: Author's calculations from the *1966 Survey of Economic Opportunity*

[a]Includes all persons in the sample who were aged 14 or more in March, 1966, no longer in school as of the same month, in the labor force for at least 14 weeks in 1965, and living in one of the twelve largest SMSAs (see text).

[b]Duncan-NORC occupational prestige ordinal ranking; see Appendix A.

[c]$(1 - \dfrac{\text{weeks worked in 1965}}{\text{weeks in the labor force in 1965}}) \times 100.$

Underemployment is also manifested in low occupational status. For both racial groups in the twelve sets of poverty areas, women attain relatively higher status occupations than men. Although cardinal comparisons between the status score distributions in table 4 are not strictly permissible since the scale on which they are measured is purely ordinal, it is highly probable that the white-nonwhite "status gap" is greater for women than for men, as was the case with unemployment. The median white female score of 31 is exemplified by such occupations as theatrical entertainer, building manager, and housekeeper. Female-intensive occupations with a Duncan-NORC status score of 16 (the nonwhite female median) include waitresses, kitchen workers, laundry operatives, and hairdressers. The typically male occupations associated with the two male medians in table 4 are very similar to one another: watchmen, barbers, truck drivers, parking attendants, roofers, maintenance men, and concrete finishers. These are all occupations in which relatively little skill is required, and for which training entails the initial learning of a very small number of simple tasks.

Finally, ghetto workers are underemployed in terms of earnings. The weekly equivalent of the 1966 "poverty line" was about $60. This is, of course, only one of a number of benchmarks we might use in gauging the "adequacy" of ghetto earnings. In order to establish an appropriate benchmark, we must turn for a few moments to the problem of defining poverty. In the United States, we generally define poverty as a condition in which a person or his family receives less than some normatively determined "critical minimum" level of income. The important—and frequently forgotten—thing about the use of money income as the poverty criterion is that income represents command over goods and services. A person is poor if he is unable to purchase an adequate standard of living. Thus, defining poverty really comes down to defining an "adequate standard of living."

It is for this reason that relative income definitions of poverty are sometimes ambiguous. Some analysts, using the "Lorenz curve approach," define as poor those in the lowest fifth of the U.S. income distribution.[6] This is an especially undesirable definition; under such a concept, the poor will indeed always be with us. Similarly, the gap between any individual income and some national average (such as the median) is sometimes advocated as a measure of poverty; for example, by Victor Fuchs. We must be careful here; as a measure of equity in the society, the dispersion (or "spread") of the income distribution is quite relevant. But it is not correct to infer (as is sometimes done) that *poverty*—the inability to purchase an "adequate standard of living"—has necessarily been reduced when the income distribution becomes more compact.[7]

The most well-known absolute income definition of poverty was first published by the Council of Economic Advisors in 1964, based upon Mollie Orshansky's work at the Social Security Administration (SSA) on the income requirements of a nonfarm family of four.[8] The story behind the construction of the poverty index is interesting, both because it illustrates my earlier point

6. This definition is stated—and roundly criticized—in Mary Jean Bowman, "Poverty in an Affluent Society," in *Contemporary Economic Issues*, ed. Neil W. Chamberlain (Homewood, Ill.: Irwin, 1969), p. 53.
7. See *Problems in Political Economy: An Urban Perspective*, ed. David M. Gordon (Lexington, Mass.: D.C. Heath, 1971), p. 227, for some arguments in favor of relative as opposed to absolute definitions of poverty.
8. Cf. Mollie Orshansky, "Recounting the Poor: A Five-Year Review," *Social Security Bulletin*, 29 (1966).

that the definition of an "adequate standard of living" is at the heart of the matter, and also because it shows rather bluntly how marginal has been our national commitment to eliminating poverty.

Based upon Department of Agriculture (USDA) diet studies, the SSA first recommended an allowance of 28 cents per person per meal, or $3.36 per day for a family of four. In 1955, the USDA had found that about 35 percent of the expenditures of low-income families went for food. Using this as a benchmark, SSA multiplied the $3.36 food allowance by a factor of three, to obtain their so-called low cost budget allowance of $10.08 per day or (with some upward adjustment for "occasional holidays" and "special purchases") an annual budget of $3,955.

This, however, was a far higher level of expenditure than welfare agencies were allowing for families on relief. The SSA was therefore forced to construct a new, lower budget standard, set this time at the rate of 23 cents per person per meal, or $2.74 per family of four per day. Multiplying by the factor of three again, and eliminating the "special purchases" and "occasional holidays," the resulting so-called economy budget was fixed at about $3,000 per year. Under this standard, it was found that about a fifth of the nation—some 35 million people—were in poverty at the beginning of the decade.

This official "economy budget" was not, contrary to popular belief, designed to reflect a minimum subsistence standard of living. Rather, it was quite explicitly a deficiency standard "built on the foundation of a diet that was deemed appropriate only for temporary use in an emergency. It assumed that foods would be bought more economically, handled less wastefully, and prepared more skillfully than would in fact be the case."[9] Moreover, according to a 1961 USDA study, the fraction of total expenditures then going for food was no longer a third but a quarter.

The SSA has periodically revised its poverty standard to account for inflation, differences in the size and composition of families, and differences in location. Yet the 1967 standard was only $3,553, and was still "based on a deficiency diet designed for temporary or emergency use."

Since World War II, the USDL has periodically published its "City Worker's Family budget," providing for the goods and services needed for a "healthful, self-respecting mode of living, for the nurture of children, and for normal participation in the life of the community." Detailed examination of the items it contains reveals none that appear to be luxurious or extravagant. The 1966 recommended USDL budget was $9,000.

A considerably more detailed budget breakdown for an urban family of four, on a city-by-city basis, was constructed by the USDL for the first time in March, 1967 (see the discussion in Chapter One). Three standards of living were computed. The middle (or average) standard corresponds to the previous "City Worker's Family budget." But the new "lower level" budget

9. Clair Wilcox, *Toward Social Welfare* (Homewood, Ill.: Irwin, 1969), p. 28.

is the most important for our purposes. For thirty-nine cities, the average level of the subsistence (i.e., minimally adequate) budget was $5,994. For Washington, D.C., it was $6,133; for Nashville, $5,677. These budget levels are based on a family consisting of a 38-year-old employed husband, a wife not employed outside the home, an 8-year-old girl, and a 13-year-old boy. This family is assumed to spend less than $100 a month for rent, less than $100 a year for recreation, less than $50 a year for education—including books and supplies—and less than $100 a year for visits to a physician.[10]

It is to these new USDL subsistence income standards, which are twice as high as the conventional "poverty line," that Dr. George Wiley and the National Welfare Rights organization (NWRO) have called our attention recently. Wiley advocates the use of these standards as an alternative to President Nixon's proposed welfare reform legislation. As of September, 1971, the latter would guarantee only $2,400 a year for a family of four.

I have dwelt at length on these budgetary definitions of poverty because it is the components of these budgets, or rather the inability of poor people to consume these various budget elements, which constitute the private costs of poverty. And it is the long-term effects of continual malconsumption of certain of these elements which create the social costs of poverty. Food, housing, health, and education are some of the principal budget elements which are underconsumed by the poor.

Poverty, then, is defined as the inability to purchase minimum adequate supplies of these major budget elements. Normative definitions of adequacy vary greatly. If, with George Wiley, we employ as a standard the $6,000 minimum subsistence budget computed by the USDL for 1967, then 24 million American families—30 percent of the whites and 61 percent of the blacks—were still poor in 1967, even after four years of continuous national economic growth.[11]

From the Orshansky standard (1960=$3,000) to the USDL lower standard (1967=$6,000), we may therefore want to refer to weekly incomes which fall below a threshold of from $60 to $120 as inadequate. Assuming one wage-earner per family, the median weekly earnings in table 4 all fall well below these thresholds. Even more striking is the very small proportion of workers whose earnings exceed the benchmarks. Fewer than half of the nonwhite men earned more than $60 per week in March, 1966, and only a fifth earned $120 per week or more. White men in the ghetto did little better: only 68 percent earned more than $60 per week, and fewer than 30 percent earned above $120 per week.

10. U.S. Department of Labor, Bureau of Labor Statistics, *Three Standards of Living for an Urban Family of Four Persons: Spring, 1967* (Washington, D.C.: Govt. Prtg. Off., 1969), bulletin no. 1570-5.
11. Computed from statistics in U.S. Department of Commerce, Bureau of the Census, *Current Population Reports*, series P-60, no. 59, "Income in 1967 of Families in the United States" (Washington, D.C.: Govt. Prtg. Off., 1969), table 9.

Across the country, "forty-five percent of all poor families in 1966 had two or more wage-earners."[12] In the same year, 90 percent of all the adults in the United States received up to $2,500 from sources other than earnings.[13] Taken together, these statistics suggest that a larger proportion of families will have received nonpoverty incomes than is implied by the previous discussion of individual earnings. According to my calculations from the SEO data file, 72 percent of the families in the twelve sets of poverty areas—81 percent of the whites and 65 percent of the nonwhites—received incomes in excess of $3,000 in 1965 (but only 50 percent of the families—59 percent of the whites and 41 percent of the nonwhites—received as much as $6,000). In the absence of these non-wage incomes, urban poverty would therefore be substantially greater than our wage distributions indicate.

It is often argued that urban nonwhites suffer greater underemployment as a group than their white neighbors because of the relative youth of the former. In areas where the nonwhite age distribution is either skewed left or strongly bimodal,[14] this may well be a contributing factor. In his study of seventy-five metropolitan areas, Edward Kalachek has explained how non-white youths invariably find themselves at the back of the hiring queue and, because of their low opportunity wage, at the bottom of the pay scale.[15] The nonwhite age distribution for the twelve-city poverty area labor force is, however, neither skewed nor bimodal, as indicated by table 4 and figure 4.[16] Young, nonwhite workers do indeed fare especially poorly in big city labor markets. But overall nonwhite underemployment in the core areas of the twelve largest SMSAs cannot be explained by a skewed age distribution.

The question, of course, is the extent to which it can be explained by inadequate human capital. Table 5 shows educational attainment, distributed by race and area of residence within the metropolis. About a third of the poverty area nonwhites had completed at least twelve years of school by March of 1966, as compared with 42 percent of the poverty area whites. Several benchmarks are available by which to assess these relative accomplishments. By 1966, in the United States as a whole, fewer than 28 percent of the blacks (who constitute 91 percent of the "nonwhites" in our sample) had acquired at least a high school diploma (see table B-1 in Appendix B). Even three years later, in 1969, the national black average had risen to only 32.3

---

12. Bennett Harrison, "Public Service Jobs for Urban Ghetto Residents," *Good Government*, Fall 1969, p. 7.

13. U.S. Office of Economic Opportunity, "Survey of Economic Opportunity: 1966 Unweighted Counts" (mimeographed, 1969), p. 2.37.

14. As, for example, in Central Harlem; see Thomas Vietorisz and Bennett Harrison, *The Economic Development of Harlem* (New York: Praeger, 1970), p. 17.

15. Edward Kalachek, "Determinants of Teenage Employment," *Journal of Human Resources*, Winter 1969. A discussion of the employment policy implications of Kalachek's analysis is contained in Harrison, "Public Service Jobs," p. 9.

16. This applies to the ghetto labor force only. The total ghetto population is definitely skewed toward the young.

Figure 4

Central City Poverty Area Age Distributions, by Race

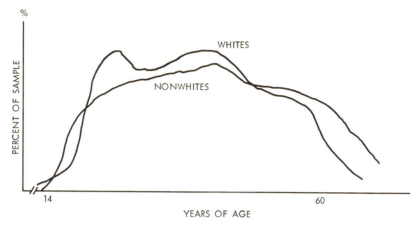

percent. National whites, on the other hand, completed more years of school than the twelve city poverty area subset. According to table B-1, over half of the whites in America had completed at least twelve years of school. Thus, relative to their national counterparts, the poverty area whites are less educated, while the poverty area nonwhites are relatively more educated.

Table 5

Percentage Distribution of Years of School Completed, by Race and Residential Location within the Twelve Largest SMSAs, March, 1966[a]

(in percent)

Race and Location	Years Completed					
	8	9–11	12	13–15	16+	12+
Whites						
Central city poverty areas	15.8	20.0	24.5	8.5	9.3	42.3
Rest of central city	10.2	20.0	34.1	13.8	13.6	61.6
SMSA ring	9.1	20.1	37.6	12.0	15.0	64.6
Nonwhites						
Central city poverty areas	12.4	30.4	23.9	6.8	2.5	33.2
Rest of central city	8.6	24.5	33.0	11.0	10.0	54.0
SMSA ring	10.1	27.1	28.4	10.1	4.6	43.1

Source: Author's calculations from the *1966 Survey of Economic Opportunity*. N = 11,454.

[a]Sample includes all individuals aged 14 or more who were in the labor force for at least 14 weeks in 1965, and were no longer in school in March, 1966.

A more appropriate set of benchmarks are the statistics for the 212 SMSAs in the country. If we interpolate between the 1960 and 1969 statistics in table B-1, we arrive at high school completion estimates of about 33 percent for nonwhites and 54 percent for whites in 1966. "Ghetto" nonwhites have, therefore, acquired critical educational credentials such as the high school diploma in about the same proportions as all metropolitan area nonwhites across the country. But—again—white workers in the ghetto have not done as well as their peers living in the nonghetto neighborhoods of the nation's large urban centers.

Table B-2 in Appendix B permits still another comparison. The average 1960 level of nonwhite high school completion throughout the same twelve SMSAs which we are studying (albeit six years later) was only 32 percent, ranging from a low of 20 percent in Baltimore, to a high of 45 percent in Los Angeles.

In these twelve SMSAs, however, the educational level of nonwhites has risen extremely rapidly during the 1960s. We see from table 5 that, by 1966, about 50 percent of the nonghetto nonwhites in the twelve SMSAs had at least graduated from high school, an increase of 56 percent in just six years. We cannot identify the sources of this growth—immigration of well-educated persons, outmigration of dropouts, or rapid upgrading of permanent residents—from the available data. But we can observe that, as a result of this growth, ghetto nonwhites in these twelve areas now lag behind nonwhites who live outside of the poverty areas in the same twelve SMSAs.

We may conclude that nonwhites in the poverty areas of our twelve largest cities lag behind whites (including their white neighbors in the ghetto), but that their educational attainment in terms of acquisition of credentials crucial to job seeking is probably quite similar to that of any nonghetto nonwhite group in the nation except for those living in the same twelve SMSAs, whose high school completion rate is known to be greater. There is, in other words, a human capital "shortage" among nonwhites in the ghetto, although it is not nearly so pronounced as has been imagined. The consequences of this "capital scarcity" will be examined in what follows.

Another important form of investment in human capital is job training. Five categories of training are identified in the SEO. *Institutional* training includes programs in business colleges or technical institutes, usually in preparation for jobs in drafting, electronics, secretarial work, or nursing. *Apprenticeship* training is usually conducted by unions, and intended to lead to journeyman status, e.g., in the building trades. In the SEO, *on-the-job* training is defined as a "full-time program in a company (or public agency) training school, lasting six weeks or more."[17] *Army vocational* training is conducted for selected enlisted men by each of the armed services. Finally, *government* training is defined to include "programs conducted by social or government

17. U.S. Office of Economic Opportunity, "Survey of Economic Opportunity: Codebooks and Technical Documentation," August 1969, p. 253.

Table 6

Percentage Distribution of Training Program Participants,
by Type of Program, Race, and Residential Location within
the Twelve Largest SMSAs, March, 1966

(in percent)

Race and Location	Training									
	Institu- tional		Appren- tice		Private OJT		Army Voca- tional		Govern- ment Program	
	A	B	A	B	A	B	A	B	A	B
Whites										
Central city poverty										
areas	4.5	2.9	C	C	1.8	C	1.6	C	4.1	1.1
Rest of central city	7.2	2.5	1.6	C	4.0	C	2.2	C	6.0	1.5
SMSA ring	7.4	2.9	1.7	C	4.7	C	2.9	C	5.6	1.3
Nonwhites										
Central city poverty										
areas	5.5	3.8	C	C	2.2	C	1.5	C	3.1	2.2
Rest of central city	8.3	5.6	C	C	2.8	C	2.0	C	5.0	2.4
SMSA ring	6.7	3.4	C	C	2.2	C	1.8	C	3.2	2.7

Source: Author's calculations from the *1966 Survey of Economic Opportunity*. See text
for definitions of training programs. N = 11,454.

A = training program completed.
B = training program not completed.
C = frequency was less than 1 percent.

agencies . . . such as vocational rehabilitation programs, government programs such as those under the Manpower Development and Training Act, and Job Corps, etc."[18]

Table 6 displays training program participation by workers in the twelve SMSAs, distributed by race, residential location, and whether or not the program was completed. In no cell of the table does participation exceed 8.3 percent, and in twenty-two of the sixty cells, participation was less than 1 percent. Although the frequencies may be too small to permit fully confident inference, it does appear that relatively greater institutional training has been invested in nonwhites than in whites, while whites have received more attention from the government—both the armed forces and the civilian agencies— than nonwhites. In general, workers of both races living outside the ghetto do display somewhat higher rates of participation—and especially of completion (and certification)—than workers living "inside." The impact of these differences (and the differences in education previously described) on employment status is the subject to which we now turn our attention.

18. *Ibid.*, p. 256.

THE MARGINAL EFFECT OF EDUCATION AND
TRAINING ON EARNINGS

We begin by fitting model (8) to the data for the central city poverty areas of the twelve largest SMSAs. Actually, on the (subsequently confirmed) hypothesis that the samples are heterogeneous with respect to race, we fit separate regressions for whites and nonwhites. First, a linear (i.e., constant proportional) relationship between education and earnings is investigated (the model is coded as equation [13] in Appendix B). Then a nonlinear, discontinuous "step"-functional relationship between education and earnings is estimated (see equation [14] in Appendix B). In both models (as is explained in the appendix), other variables include training program participation, sex, age, industry group, city of residence, and full- versus part-time employment status. As indicated earlier, it was decided to deflate the wage data to control (at least crudely) for differences in purchasing power in the twelve SMSAs, using the deflators in table 2.

The linear-E and the nonlinear-E models each explained about 28 percent of the variation in the weekly earnings of central city poverty whites. The nonlinearities were highly significant, as will be seen in a moment. For non-whites, about 35 percent of the wage variation was explained by these models.[19] For both races, the control variables age, sex, and full-time/part-time employment were highly significant and positively related to earnings, as expected. The industry and location coefficients, however, differed substantially between the races. Four of the eleven remaining city dummies and nine of the fourteen remaining industry dummies were significant in the nonwhite regressions.[20] But none of the city dummies and only five of the industry dummies were significant for poverty area whites. This suggests that the white urban poverty population is relatively more homogeneous than the nonwhite poor, both across cities and across industries. So consistently does this appear in all the regressions estimated in this study that one is forced to conclude that any national (i.e., highly standardized) antipoverty program would seem likely to have a more predictable impact on the white poor than on the nonwhite population for whom such programs are generally designed. Sensitivity of nonwhite weekly earnings to variations in industrial attachment and city of location suggests that in order to project the results of urban anti-poverty policies, the government must take into account such city-specific

---

19. Complete statistical results for all the regressions described in this monograph are contained in the doctoral dissertation, which is available under the same title from the Clearinghouse for Federal, Scientific and Technical Information, 5285 Port Royal Road, Springfield, Virginia, 22151. The CFSTI file number is PB–196–454.

20. Certain dummy variables must be excluded in order to ensure valid statistical results (see Appendix B). The excluded dummies included New York (C_7) and the construction industry (I_1). Since New York is a relatively high-wage city and since construction is a very high-wage industry, many of the estimated coefficients had negative signs. Indeed, this served as a useful check on the reliability of the results.

characteristics as the local industry mix. This is especially important for equal employment opportunity policy.

But our principal interest in this study is not in the complete explanation of variation in the several dependent variables. We are interested primarily in the payoffs to investments in education and training. The first four columns of table B-3 in Appendix B display the full set of estimated policy parameters. Since the nonlinear education parameters correspond to mutually exclusive dummy variables, these parameters represent the *cumulative* effects of education on earnings. White and nonwhite education step-functions constructed from these parameters are displayed in figure 5. Only those successive differences which are statistically significant are shown. Thus, for example, the difference between the marginal white return to "some college" ($16.99) and "high school" ($24.88) is not significant at the 0.10 level, and is

Figure 5

Incremental Weekly Earnings Associated with Education—
Central City Poverty Areas in Twelve SMSAs, March, 1966

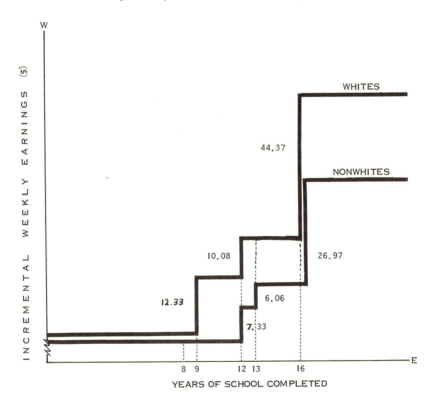

therefore not displayed in figure 5. These calculations are explained in Appendix B (table B-4).

Education is much more efficient for ghetto whites than for ghetto nonwhites. According to the continuous model, whites in central city poverty areas earn on the average well over twice as much per extra year of schooling as nonwhites. With the (institutionally determined) discontinuities taken into account, we find that the weekly wage of white high school graduates is nearly $25 higher than that of whites not attending high school at all; for the nonwhites, the difference is only slightly above $8. High school, therefore, has three times as high a marginal payoff for ghetto whites as for ghetto nonwhites.[21] This is frankly remarkable, since so many of the popularly proposed "causes" of ghetto underemployment—such as the physical isolation of the slums from new, suburban blue-collar-oriented industrial complexes and the alleged inadequacy of job information flows linking the ghetto with the rest of the city—will presumably affect all the residents of the ghetto: black and white. These results would therefore seem to constitute a valid estimate of the earnings involuntarily foregone by nonwhites in the urban ghetto because of racial discrimination.

To make these results comparable to those reported in the literature and summarized in Chapter One (pp. 10–13), I have computed the following present values, on the assumptions of a 40-year working life, a "rectangular" (i.e., constant annual) lifetime earnings distribution, and a 6 percent discount rate:[22]

	Whites	Nonwhites
Present value of the extra lifetime earnings attributable to one additional year of school	$ 3,047	$1,362
Present value of the lifetime return to high school relative to the grade school graduate	18,717	6,267

21. This white-nonwhite earnings "gap" at E=12 is significant at the 0.10 level (see table B-2 in Appendix B).

22. These are highly unrealistic assumptions. First, by assuming equivalent (and *continuous*) earnings periods for both races, I am surely understating the racial earnings "gap" since nonwhite employment and labor force participation rates are well known to be significantly lower over time than the rates for white workers. Second, age-earnings profiles over a lifetime are known to be hill-shaped. How, then, can these assumptions be employed? Since identical assumptions were made in computing the present value associated with Miller's annual estimates on page 10, while the Hirsch-Hansen-Houthakker estimates were based on different assumptions, the only strictly valid comparison I can draw is between my ghetto findings and the national returns published by Miller. However, a comparison of the Miller and Hirsch estimates (both based on approximately the same time period—the mid-50s) shows them to be nearly identical, in spite of the different assumptions employed in the calculations. I therefore conclude that the admittedly simplistic (but computationally convenient) assumption of a "rectangular lifetime earnings distribution" probably gives a fair approximation. If so, then the Hirsch-Hansen-Houthakker estimates—suitably inflated to adjust for the up to seventeen year difference in sample dates—are suitable benchmarks after all.

The results for whites are similar to the (adjusted) results from previous studies; indeed, they are virtually identical to the estimates of Miller and Hirsch. In contrast, the nonwhite ghetto returns are less than half as large as the benchmark national rates reported earlier. Moreover, my ghetto calculations assume a 50-week year. Since ghetto nonwhite unemployment rates exceed those of any other group in America, the racial earnings "gap" indicated in these figures is undoubtedly understated.

This discussion has emphasized returns to the high school years, since fewer than 20 percent of the ghetto whites and 9 percent of the ghetto nonwhites—or, for that matter, 27 percent of suburban whites—go on to college. Table B-3 and figure 5 show that returns do indeed increase as ghetto workers acquire a college education, although the white-nonwhite gap is even larger for college graduates than for those with less schooling.

Very few of the training variables were significant. Columns 1–4 of table B-3 show largely empty training cells. An equal proportion of ghetto whites and nonwhites completed vocational training in the armed forces (table 6), but only the nonwhites benefited. Conversely, although a larger proportion of nonwhites than whites completed on-the-job training, only the latter benefited. Finally, there is some (not very strong) evidence for the "credentials" hypothesis in the last row of table B-3. Ghetto nonwhites who began a government training program (usually MDTA-sponsored) but who dropped out before receiving "diplomas" earned nearly $12 per week less than workers similar in every respect except that they had never even entered the training program in the first place. Perhaps those who try for but fail to win the appropriate credentials become discouraged and/or rejected by potential employers.

A priori reasoning and examination of variations among the estimated parameters of models (13) and (14) suggest that a number of the control variables probably interact with education (and with training as well). In other words, the marginal effects of (E) and (T) on (w) are themselves sensitive to the levels of the other variables. There are, for example, at least two ways in which age (A) might interact with education. On the one hand, secular increases in real wages mean that individuals educated recently might be expected to exhibit a relatively stronger earnings effect than persons educated farther back in time. On the other hand, an opposite effect may also be present. If age acts as a proxy for experience (or is correlated with job tenure, as seems almost certain), if the latter helps to determine seniority (which in turn improves earnings), and if tenure and education are correlated,[23] then

---

23. Which, however, is not at all certain. See Peter B. Doeringer, "Manpower Programs for Ghetto Labor Markets," *Industrial Relations Research Association: Proceedings*, May 1969; and Chapter Three of this volume for evidence that tenure and education are *not* well correlated for ghetto workers.

we might expect to find that the marginal effect of, say, education on earnings itself increases with age.[24]

As indicated previously, location apparently "counts" in explaining real wage variation, even after removing the influence of the racial mix and relative cost of living obtained in each city. Does location also affect the structure of the partial w–E relation itself? Is a high school education "worth" more in the San Francisco labor market, say, than in the New York labor market—at least to a worker from the ghetto? We may get at this question by specifying education-city interaction terms.

Similarly, we may ask whether education is "worth" more in one industry than another, e.g., because of differing availabilities of complementary capital among industries.

Finally, since employers discriminate against women as well as against nonwhites, the w–E relation cannot be assumed to be independent of sex. Education-sex interaction terms are therefore called for.

It is plausible to posit interactions among the control variables themselves. For example, given the widespread belief that "the smart kids get out," and given the relatively high proportion of young mothers in the ghetto, we should not assume that age and sex are distributed independently of one another in these neighborhoods. And it is surely the case that the sexes are not distributed equally among all industries. Thus, we may specify age-sex and industry-sex interaction terms.

Since education and training are not well correlated, and since (from table B-3) training appears to be poorly correlated with earnings, the training variables are deleted in the interaction model (15) described in Appendix B. The detailed results of fitting these nonwhite and white regression models are given in the dissertation (see note 19 to this chapter). As expected, age and sex interact in the determination of earnings; the older the worker (regardless of race), the greater his or her earnings, with the strength of the relationship itself greater for men than for women.[25] For men—but not for women— earnings are relatively higher in the manufacture of durable goods than in other industries. The effect is just the reverse for retail sales, business services, and personal services; in these industries, expected earnings are greater for women than for men. Finally, the additive control variable for "full-time/ part-time" is highly significant, as it should be.

The purpose of the terms in model (15) which interact with education is to test for the sensitivity of the slope ($\Delta w/\Delta E$) to variations in city of resi-

24. I.e., $\dfrac{d(\Delta w/\Delta E)}{dA} > 0.$

25. A more precise, e.g., quadratic, specification of the age variable would no doubt produce somewhat different results, although probably not by very much. Certainly, most empirical research on human capital has employed the simple linear specification of age as an approximation.

dence, industry of employment, age, and sex. For whites, education does interact with age and sex, but not at all with city or industry. For nonwhites, on the other hand, in addition to the [ES] and [AS] terms, eight of the city terms interactive with education are significant. Only the government-education and personal services-education interactions "count."

It is convenient to summarize these sensitivities by evaluating all possible combinations of the variables [ES, EA, EC, EI] and identifying the maximum and minimum slopes. For 20-year-old white ghetto dwellers, the minimum effect is $0.60 per week in extra earnings per year of school completed, for women. The maximum effect is $2.64 per week per year of schooling, for men. There is no industry or city effect. These maxima and minima increase by $0.03 per week for each additional year of age. Recall the earlier finding (shown in table B-3) that the *average* effect (derived from the simple linear model) was $4.05 per week per year of school.

For 20-year-old nonwhites, the minimum effect is $-$1.77 per week per year of school for Houston women employed in personal services, e.g., beauticians. The maximum effect is +$6.26 per week per year for Detroit men employed by the federal government. These maxima and minima increase by $0.02 per week for each additional year of age. The *average* effect (from table B-3) is $1.81.

These results reinforce our earlier impressions from the additive earnings model, concerning the substantially greater intercity and interindustry variation for ghetto nonwhites than for ghetto whites. We saw in columns 1 and 3 of table B-3 that the average incremental payoff to each additional year of school is $1.81 per week for nonwhites and $4.05 per week for whites. The interaction model provides us with more precise estimates and with ranges of variation: -$1.77 to $6.16 and $0.60 to $2.64, respectively (for 20-year-olds). In other words, the most successful nonwhite men in the sample earn more (per week per year of school) than the most successful white men. But considerably more whites than nonwhites are "successful," so that the average white return is much higher than the average nonwhite return.

THE MARGINAL EFFECT OF EDUCATION AND TRAINING
ON UNEMPLOYMENT

In this section, we turn our attention to general model (9) in which unemployment is the dependent variable. As in the previous section, we start with two additive specifications, linear and nonlinear in E. Then we proceed to the evaluation of a model with interaction terms.

Equations (16) and (17) in Appendix B are the same as equations (13) and (14), with (u) as the dependent variable instead of (w). We should expect to find a *negative* relationship between education and unemployment. For example, in a cross-section analysis of U.S. cities, using the 1960 Census, Hadden and Borgatta consistently found a strong inverse correlation between median education and unemployment, regardless of intraurban location or city size. Their estimated correlation coefficients for median years of school and the local unemployment rate vary from −0.40 for central cities to −0.59 for suburban rings, and from −0.39 for large cities to −0.54 for small towns.[26] None of my models explained as much variation in unemployment as they had for wages. Table B-3 shows coefficients of determination of 0.221, 0.129, 0.231, and 0.135, respectively. Of the control variables, full-time/part-time was significant and negative in all four runs, indicating that those who tend to work full-time when they do work also tend to work relatively more often. This is perfectly sensible; the demand for part-time workers surely fluctuates more than the demand for full-time workers. Sex, on the other hand, was statistically insignificant in all four regressions. Since the sexes are not distributed equally among the fifteen industry groups in the model—since there are well-known "male-intensive" (e.g., durable goods manufacture) and "female-intensive" (e.g., personal services, state and local government) industries—we had best reserve our judgment on this matter until we have had the opportunity of examining the industry-sex interaction terms which follow. With respect to the age variable, unemployment diminishes with age for both races, but this relationship is statistically significant only for nonwhites. As expected, the acquisition of tenure and experience with age reduces the proportion of weeks per year during which (at least nonwhite) workers seek jobs but cannot find them. As with earnings, the nonwhite unemployment rates are much more sensitive to location than are the white rates. Eight of the eleven city dummies in the nonwhite regressions were significant at the 95 percent level of confidence or better.[27] For whites, only two cities in model (16) and four cities in model (17) were significant. With respect to the relationship between unemployment and the industry "mix" associated with the poverty area population, however, both races displayed exceptionally great sensitivity. All of the industry dummies were significant in the two nonwhite and in the two white models. This helps us to narrow down the policy inference drawn in the preceding section of this chapter. National aggregative economic policies can perhaps improve white earnings by predictable amounts, but are likely to be far less predictable in terms of their impact on inner-city unemployment for either race. Knowledge and manipulation of the local industry mix would seem to be crucial—policy, that is, which is explicitly addressed to the structure of local demand for poverty area labor.

The cumulative marginal impacts of education and training on unemployment are displayed in columns 5-8 of table B-3; the white and nonwhite

26. Jeffrey K. Hadden and Edgar F. Borgatta, *American Cities: Their Social Characteristics* (Chicago: Rand McNally, 1965), pp. 138–40.

27. The sign of $(\Delta u/\Delta C)$ provided another reliability check. New York City had one of the lowest unemployment rates in the country in the 1960s. Thus, with New York as the "benchmark" city in the regression analysis, we should expect $(\Delta u/\Delta C) > 0$. This was indeed the estimated sign on every C-coefficient but one.

education-unemployment step-functions (whose construction is described in table B-4 in Appendix B) are graphed in figure 6. These results are simply striking. Education has virtually no effect whatever on nonwhite unemployment. Moreover, no training experience pays off in a reduced probability of nonwhite joblessness. In fact, in the government programs, participation short of certification *increases* expected unemployment by nearly 8 percent. For whites, on the other hand, the model displays results which are fully consistent with the conventional wisdom. In the linear specification, each additional year of schooling reduces expected unemployment by 0.6 percent. In the nonlinear model, the return to completion of high school, relative to the white worker who never went beyond the eighth grade, is a 3.5 percent reduction in the chances of being unemployed over the course of a year. Assuming full-time labor force participation (52 weeks per year), a white college graduate from the slums can expect to be unemployed nearly two months less per year than a white high school dropout from the same ghetto. But the nonwhite high school graduate can expect only a 0.7 percent smaller

Figure 6

Incremental Unemployment Rates Associated with Education—
Central City Povery Areas in Twelve SMSAs, March, 1966

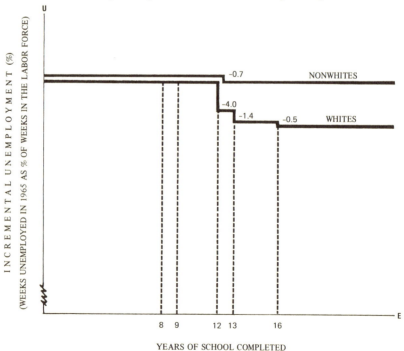

YEARS OF SCHOOL COMPLETED

chance of unemployment than his neighbor who never entered high school. Moreover, college does not further reduce his risk of joblessness at all. Whites—even in the ghetto—benefit from education (although apparently not from training; see table B-3) not only in terms of higher wages, but also in terms of reduced unemployment. But nonwhite wage benefits are much smaller than those of whites, and nonwhite employment "benefits" are, on the average, virtually nonexistent.

Following the discussion in the previous section, it would seem useful to ask whether the presence of interactions among the variables significantly affects our conclusions about the effect of education on unemployment (again, we may delete the training variables, which seem to be of little consequence). Model (18) was therefore fit to the white and nonwhite "ghetto" data (this equation is the same as [15], with [u] as the dependent variable instead of [w]).

The only interaction terms which are significant in the "white" regression are (ES) and (EA). Each additional year of school reduces expected unemployment by 0.01 percent per year of age. Thus, for example, white 20-year-old men who have graduated from high school can expect to be unemployed 0.4 percent fewer weeks per year than young, white male workers who did not remain in school beyond the eighth grade. By age forty, the differential has risen to only 0.8 percent. At any age and level of schooling, women face a 0.1 percent lower risk of unemployment than men.

For nonwhites, on the other hand, there is—again—substantial variation. Unemployment "rates" are highly sensitive to the interaction between sex and industry. For nonwhite men, expected unemployment is higher in communications, wholesale trade, business and personal services than in manufacturing, transportation, utilities, retail trade, or government service. The nonwhite unemployment-education slope is also highly sensitive to variations in the other variables. Whereas only 0.1 percent separates the extreme values for white ghetto men and women, 2.0 percent separates the nonwhite extremes of Los Angeles men employed in durable goods manufacturing (whose chances of unemployment actually *increase* with education) and St. Louis women employed in personal services. Compare these ranges of variation with the white and nonwhite average payoff coefficients of −0.6 percent and 0.0 percent, respectively (table B-3, columns 7 and 5).

THE MARGINAL EFFECT OF EDUCATION AND TRAINING ON OCCUPATIONAL STATUS

In general model (10), the dependent variable is occupational status, measured by the Duncan-NORC ordinal prestige ranks which vary from 0 to 100. As developed in Chapter One, the correct interpretation to be placed upon the "policy" coefficients in this model, e.g., ($\Delta\phi/\Delta E$), is that education, etc., does (or does not) contribute to interoccupational mobility, and that these, e.g., education-induced movements are—in terms of national tastes and attitudes—movements into occupations of relatively greater or lesser status. With this interpretation firmly fixed, we may proceed to estimate the additive models with equations (19) and (20) in Appendix B.

The models did a better job of explaining white occupational status than nonwhite status, as indicated by the respective values of R^2 in table B-3: 0.260 and 0.309 for the whites; 0.149 and 0.203 for the nonwhites. The by now familiar result of relatively greater intercity homogeneity among poverty area whites than among poverty area nonwhites appears once again. In the nonwhite regressions, up to nine of the eleven city dummy variables were significant, as compared with only two cities in each of the white regressions. In the summary to this chapter, we shall hazard a guess at the cause of this remarkably persistent phenomenon.

Age was significant in both of the white regressions, and had the correct (positive) sign. If the probability of making an occupational change after entering the labor force through some initial occupation is positive—no matter how small—then it follows that $(\Delta\phi/\Delta A) > 0$. For the nonwhites, however, this term was not significant, even though—as we shall see in a moment—nonwhite occupational status was sensitive to variations in education. In the context of the preceding remarks, this can only mean that poverty area nonwhites do not have (or have not had) any significant chance to move beyond the occupation through which they first enter the labor market.

Sex was significant and negative for whites. The negative sign means that white ghetto women enjoy somewhat greater status than white ghetto men, *ceteris paribus*. This is undoubtedly because of the high density of inner city white working class women in the medium range ($40 \leqslant \phi \leqslant 60$) clerical occupations, relative to the concentration of white men in the low-status service and laboring occupations. For the nonwhites, however, the sex variable was not significant. This, too, makes sense. Nonwhite ghetto women are much more likely than their white counterparts to be working as waitresses ($\phi=16$), usherettes or hostesses ($\phi=25$), and maids ($\phi=10$). Since many of the nonwhite ghetto men tend to report occupations similar to those held by white men in the slums, there is less intersex status variation among nonwhites than among whites. Finally, since we know that there are a number of ghetto workers who are engaged in relatively high-status occupations, we must infer that, for poor whites, women have a greater opportunity than men to achieve these "heights," while, for nonwhites, both sexes are more or less equally represented. The prototypes are the black male minister ($\phi=75$) and the black female social worker ($\phi=64$).

The last four columns of table B-3 display the education and training coefficients. It is easily seen that these investments in human capital induce comparable variations in occupational status among *both* whites *and* nonwhites in the ghetto. By national standards of taste, moreover, this variation is toward more prestigious occupations, since the coefficients all have a positive sign. Table B-4 in Appendix B shows that the differences between the white and nonwhite "steps" from E=12 on are statistically significant but not very large. Training (as an explanatory variable) is generally as ineffectual here as it has been elsewhere in the analysis thus far.

This would be a good place to sum up what we have learned thus far. Overall, whites in the ghetto benefit substantially from education, by all three measures of "payoff" (in Chapter Four, we shall see that the returns enjoyed by suburban whites—but not by suburban nonwhites—are even greater). Education contributes significantly (but nominally) to nonwhite access to what are supposed to be relatively higher status occupations. But—once having entered these occupations—the nonwhites find themselves systematically underemployed, regardless of their educational background. Even the acquisition of precious credentials—the high school diploma, the certificate of completion of training, even a Bachelor's degree—does not reduce the risk or duration of their unemployment. Moreover, the nonwhite workers receive substantially lower wages and salaries than white workers of the same age, sex, residential location, and industrial attachment. These substandard earnings are improved only nominally by the acquisition of educational credentials, at least up to college entrance. The monetary returns to collegiate experience for nonwhites begin to become substantial. But of course it would be the epitome of racism to argue from this that "everything would be fine if only 'they' would get a college degree." As demonstrated earlier, most Americans—white as well as black—do *not* go on to college. Why should we then establish the B.A. as a new minimum acceptable performance threshold for blacks?

When interactions in the occupational-determination process are modeled (equation [21] in Appendix B), the effects just discussed are unambiguously reinforced. Only three of the eleven "white" city interaction terms but all of the "nonwhite" city interaction terms are significant. Sex is not significant for white ghetto workers; for nonwhites, men attain slightly "higher" occupational status than women at every level of age and city.

The findings on the sensitivity of $(\Delta\phi/\Delta E)$ to intercity, intergenerational and intersex variations are summarized—as before—by identifying the "mix" of factors which yield the maximum and minimum educational "payoff" for each race. Comparisons here must be made cautiously, since we are measuring occupational status on an ordinal scale. We really cannot say that a status score which is numerically twice as large as another indicates the attainment of "twice as prestigious" an occupation. We can only observe that the range of variation of white status scores runs from 1.31 extra status "points" per year of school for 20-year-old Pittsburgh workers of either sex to 2.39 "points" for 20-year-old District of Columbia workers of either sex. For nonwhites, the minimum effect is 0.77 "points" for 20-year-old Los Angeles women; the maximum effect is 1.34 "points" for 20-year-old San Francisco men. All of these "payoffs" increase with age.

In summary, there is no question that—even in the ghetto—education helps members of both races to move into what are nationally considered to be "better" (i.e., more prestigious) occupations, although the magnitude of the "push" is significantly greater for whites than for nonwhites (at least for those with less than sixteen years of school—which is the vast majority). What awaits them when they have attained these new positions again varies substantially according to race. For nonwhite ghetto workers, in terms of expected earnings and the risk of unemployment, the "new" occupations are not much better than the "old" ones.

CONCLUSIONS ON THE RETURNS TO HUMAN CAPITAL IN THE GHETTO

In this section, we shall summarize the statistical evidence on the marginal impacts of investments in human capital on each of the three measures of employment status in the set of areas selected as a proxy for the "urban ghetto." First, however, it would be well to review some of the secondary results of the research described in this chapter.

First, why does training show up so poorly in every regression? Gerald Somers reports that

> . . . in a regression analysis of . . . West Virginia data . . . completion of a retraining course was found to be a more significant influence on employment success than such variables as age, education, sex, race, regular occupation, and labor market area. Regression analysis of the Tennessee program led to similarly favorable results for the value of retraining.[28]

Of course, Somers is speaking exclusively of people who have worked before and are now being retrained, whereas our sample includes substantial numbers of workers whose training preceded their entry into the labor force. Nevertheless, the ineffectiveness of training as a policy instrument for ghetto dwellers of either major racial group is a profoundly disquieting discovery, to the extent that it is a sound finding. Unfortunately, the results on training are probably not sound. We cannot attribute the general insignificance of the (T)s to multicollinearity. But there are just too few observations (particularly of persons having completed training) for us to be very confident about the results. Conclusive statements about the efficacy of training will have to await the availability of different samples.[29]

---

28. Gerald Somers, "Introduction," in Somers, ed., *Retraining the Unemployed* (Madison, Wis.: University of Wisconsin, 1968), p. 8.

29. A growing number of evaluations of federal manpower training programs have concluded that the marginal returns to training are (a) minimal and (b) apparently totally unrelated to program inputs. For a further discussion of these evaluations and what may well be the true role of manpower training programs in urban labor markets, see Chapter Five.

In the regression experiments, we found that poverty area whites displayed substantially greater intercity homogeneity with respect to both the level of payoff and the responsiveness of payoff to variations in education than did the nonwhites. The Census category "white" includes many Puerto Ricans and all Mexican-Americans. Thus, it seems quite surprising that populations as distinctive in character as white Americans of various national or ethnic origins and the two large minority groups just cited should display such homogeneity, while the nonwhites (about 92 percent of whom are Negroes) should show such cross-sectional heterogeneity.

One possible explanation is as follows: Whites in all large American cities enjoy roughly equal (and more or less full) access to a wide range of jobs. The non-Negro minorities enjoy similarly uniform (but uniformly limited) access across the country. The blacks, on the other hand, have been challenging "the system" for a longer period of time than have the other minorities, and have acquired substantial experience as political organizers. As a result, they have begun to achieve breakthroughs in employment. These, however, have occurred at different tempos in different places, according to the relative strength of black political power (overt or latent), the strength and conviction of opponents to social change, and the relative tightness of the labor market in each place.[30] The result is that, in order to predict black (but not white or other minority) employment status at any given time, we must first know which city or region we are talking about.

As suggested earlier, this pervasive result of our experiments implies that, if we judge the tempo of upward black mobility to be too slow, then corrective policies must be city-specific if they are to be predictable. This makes the design of an effective national urban policy for blacks much more difficult.

Let us now attempt to summarize the education results reported in detail earlier in this chapter.

Earnings. In central city poverty areas, whites earn on the average well over twice as much per extra year of schooling as nonwhites. The nonwhite payoff varies very much more than the white payoff from city to city, across the sexes, and by age. For nonwhite Houston women working in personal services, increased education actually reduces expected weekly earnings. And the older the woman, the greater the deficit. In the nonlinear additive model which isolates the effects of passage of important institutional milestones, the weekly wage of white high school graduates is nearly $25 higher than that of whites who never entered high school. For nonwhites, the difference is only $8. High school, therefore, has three times as high a marginal payoff for ghetto whites as for ghetto nonwhites. Finally, on the assumptions of a

---

30. For some quantitative evidence of the relationship between overt or latent "black power" and the relative success of at least one important minority job development program, see Bennett Harrison, "The Participation of Ghetto Residents in the Model Cities Program," *Journal of the American Institute of Planners*, January 1973.

forty-year working life, a rectangular lifetime earnings distribution, and a 6 percent rate of time preference, the present value of the lifetime return to completion of four full years of high school is nearly $19,000 for whites, as compared with about $6,000 for nonwhites. Clearly, education has a very high opportunity cost for nonwhites living in the urban ghetto. There are any number of (albeit illegal) activities out "on the street" which are capable of returning at least $6,000 in a single year.

Unemployment. For whites, the risk of unemployment falls with years of school completed. Over the interval 8-12 years, the expectation of jobless-ness falls by 3.5 percent (the average payoff per year of school over the entire range of 0–18 years is a 0.6 percent reduction). Across all twelve cities, fifteen industries, sex and age, this payoff varies by no more than 0.1 percent. For nonwhites, on the other hand, the average effect of education on unem-ployment, as well as the effect in the 8–12 year interval, is virtually zero. A white college graduate from the slums can expect to be involuntarily out of work nearly two months less per year than a white high school dropout who also lives in one of the urban ghettos in the sample. But the nonwhite college graduate faces nearly the same risk of unemployment as the nonwhite high school dropout. There is, however, some intercity and interindustry variation around the nonwhite average "slope," which attains a maximum payoff of – 1.1 percent per year of school for 20-year-old St. Louis women employed in personal services.

Occupational Status. Education facilitates the entry of both white and nonwhite ghetto workers into new occupations, and (at least for whites) interoccupational mobility. Moreover, by national standards, these variations represent a move "up" into higher status occupations. On the average over the entire range 0–18 years of school, each additional year is associated with an upward movement for whites of 2.7 "points" along the Duncan-NORC ordinal prestige scale, and 2.0 "points" for nonwhites. The relative payoffs for the nonlinear 8–12 interval are 15.8 "points" for whites and 10.2 "points" for nonwhites.

These findings show clearly that the effects of racial discrimination per-vade even the poorest neighborhoods in the urban economy. Even though they share many similar problems, such as spatial isolation from new indus-trial growth centers and poor access to job information, ghetto residents diverge significantly by race insofar as their labor force status is concerned. Education helps members of both races to move into what are nationally considered to be more prestigious occupations. But, once there, the non-whites are systematically underemployed, receiving earnings which are hardly above the levels enjoyed in the previous position, and facing almost exactly the same expectations of unemployment as before. For ghetto whites, on the other hand, the occupational mobility induced (at least to some extent) by education is translated into substantially higher earnings and significantly lower risks of joblessness. The contrast is dramatic.

REJOICE

REJOICE CHILDREN, LITTLE BROTHER, HE'S DEAD.
WHY, THAT'S THE BEST THING THAT COULD HAPPEN TO
   HIM
'MEMBER HOW DARK HE WAS WHY, HE'D NEVER'VE GOTTEN
FURTHER THAN HIGH SCHOOL.
HE COULDN'T PASS LIKE YOU DO RODNEY. . . .
   SO WHAT, HE WAS ONLY TWO YEARS OLD.
   NOW HE'S GONE,
   THERE'S MORE FOOD TO GO ROUND.
   RATS GOT TO HIM IN HIS CRIB AND THEY HAD A FEAST
   NOW I CAN GO BACK TO SCHOOL AND PLAY IN THE
   AFTERNOON.
   'CAUSE I DON'T HAVE TO BABYSIT.
   DON'T HAVE TO PAY NO MORE DOCTOR AND CLINIC
   BILLS: CAN PAY MR. GOLDBERG ALL THE BACK RENT
   ON THE APARTMENT.
   MAYBE NOW HE'LL FIX THE FALLING PLASTER,
   LEAKING TOILET BOWL, AND GIVE US A NEW STOVE
   AND ICE BOX.
YEAH BROTHERS AND SISTERS, I'M SO GLAD LITTLE
BROTHER IS DEAD.
HE DON'T HAVE TO GO THROUGH WHAT WE HAVE.

Clorox   Age 17

— The Me Nobody Knows

3.

TEN INDIVIDUAL CORE-CITY GHETTOS IN EIGHT STANDARD METROPOLITAN STATISTICAL AREAS

INTRODUCTION

In November, 1966, the U.S. Department of Labor conducted interviews in ten low-income communities in eight American cities.[1] Unlike the "poverty areas" which served as our proxy for "ghetto" in the previous chapter, each of these ten areas is a single, well-defined urban neighborhood. The operational distinction between Census poverty areas, which are sets of depressed census tracts, and the Urban Employment Survey ghettos, which are also sets of depressed tracts, is the contiguity or clustering of the tracts in the latter (refer back to figure 2 in Chapter One).

In the 1966 UES, a total of 37,330 usable records on ghetto individuals aged fourteen and over were generated, with each record containing up to sixty-five variables. This represents a 4.5 percent sample of the approximately 836,000 persons over age fourteen believed to be living in the ten urban ghettos in that year.

The most prominent government statisticians have long recognized that "response errors . . . abound in the reporting of income and education in household surveys and censuses."[2] The UES enumerators reported special problems ("Do the questions and concepts used in the surveys mean the same to these groups [in the ghetto] as to the general population?").[3]

Many of the variables in the UES data base have extremely high nonresponse rates. Others display unacceptably large numbers of meaningless outliers. I have spent a considerable amount of time, both alone and in consultation with USDL officials, identifying and separating out the "soft" from the "hard" variables in the 1966 UES.

---

1. Most of the information collected in this first of the Department of Labor's Urban Employment Surveys has remained unpublished, except for brief summaries in the 1967 and 1968 *Manpower Reports of the President* (Washington, D.C.: Govt. Prtg. Off.), and a set of individual city pamphlets (known in official Washington as the "UES comic books") with the common title "A Sharper Look at Unemployment in U.S. Cities and Slums." For a discussion of the political circumstances surrounding the implementation of these ghetto surveys, see William Spring, "Underemployment: The Measure We Refuse to Take," *New Generation*, Winter 1971.

A limited (three-city) survey was conducted in 1967 by the Bureau of Labor Statistics for the purpose of "debugging" the UES questionnaire and otherwise gaining experience in inner-city interviewing, e.g., in dealing with the notorious male undercount. See U.S. Department of Labor, Bureau of Labor Statistics, *Pilot and Experimental Program on Urban Employment Surveys*, report no. 354, March 1969.

A six-city UES was conducted in fiscal 1969 and fiscal 1970 (see note 56, Chapter One), some of the results of which have been published in the 1970 and 1971 U.S. Department of Labor's *Manpower Reports*. During 1970, the UES questionnaire was appended to the regular Decennial Census survey package in 51 cities and 8 rural counties. The results of this "Census Employment Survey" have been published as U.S. Department of Commerce, Bureau of the Census, *Employment Profiles of Selected Low-Income Areas*, 1970 Census Series PHC (3) (Washington, D.C.: Govt. Prtg. Off., 1972), 76 vols.

2. Herman P. Miller, "Annual and Lifetime Income in Relation to Education," *American Economic Review*, December 1960, p. 963.

3. U.S. Department of Labor, *Pilot and Experimental Program*, p. 1.

Those UES variables which are used in this chapter appear to be relatively satisfactory. For the subset of the sample who were employed during the survey week, the nonresponse rate for the variable "wages" is virtually zero. For the entire sample, the nonresponse rate for the variable "education" is about 20 percent.

The relatively "hard" variables display substantial dispersion with relatively few large outliers. Consider, for example, the following representative 95 percent confidence intervals and standard deviations (σ), computed from the Roxbury file:

Mean weekly wage = $74.78 ± $1.12 ($\sigma$ = $20.06)
Mean hourly wage = $ 1.92 ± $0.02 ($\sigma$ = $0.40)
Mean education = 10.3 years ± 1.6 years (σ = 3.0 years)

There is more than sufficient variation in the data to permit the estimation of the posited models. The ranges of four variables used in the study of education and employment status in Mission-Fillmore, for example, are:

Weekly wage:	$2.00 to $99.00
Hourly wage:	$0.60 to $ 5.00
Education:	1 year to 18 years
Family size:	1 to 9 persons

The individuals in our sample are sufficiently homogeneous in their relation to the labor force so that, even though the UES regressions contain at most five variables, the coefficients of determination attain values as high as 0.42. Relative to other cross-section, social science models, this is a very high order of explanatory power.[4]

There are, nevertheless, major limitations in the UES. For one thing, the important variable "age" is already categorized on the data tape, and the class intervals are wider than we should prefer, particularly in the primary working age range. These categories are 14-15, 16-19, 20-24, 25-44, 45-54, 55-64, and 65+ years of age.

Similarly, the occupational classifications in the UES are already aggregated. With this variable, however, the degree of aggregation is so great—professional, craftsman, clerical, operative, laborer, domestic, farm worker, and "other"—as to preclude altogether the specification of occupation as a measure of the payoff to investments in human capital.

4. For example, Malcolm Cohen's model for explaining the labor force participation decision of women interviewed in the Current Population Survey—a model containing seven classes of variables and ten interaction terms—yielded an R^2 of only 0.168. See Malcolm S. Cohen, "The Micro Approach to Manpower Research," *Industrial Relations Research Association: Proceedings*, May 1969. Peter Doeringer estimated cross-section regressions of Boston slum area workers' length of tenure in their last job on seven variables. His most successful equation (for adult males) explained only 13 percent of the variation in the dependent variable. See "Manpower Programs for Ghetto Labor Markets," *Industrial Relations Research Association: Proceedings*, May 1969.

While the UES does contain data on educational attainment, the USDL interviewers did not question ghetto workers about their participation in training programs. Thus, the only policy (or "social investment") variable which we can evaluate here is education.

In the discontinuous specifications of education studied in Chapter Two, we were able to decompose the category "thirteen or more years of school completed" into two subsets: E_{13-15} and E_{16+}. In the 1966 UES, however, there are insufficient numbers of ghetto residents with college degrees to permit such a decomposition.

At least one colleague has suggested that this "left skewness" of the ghetto education distributions in the UES biases the regression results. "If only 'those people' will go on to college, then they'll be able to succeed in our urban labor markets." Nonwhite college graduates are indisputably in great demand now, and—given their relative scarcity—command substantial salaries.[5] Nevertheless, according to table B-1, nearly half the adults (44 percent of the whites) in the United States in 1969 had entered the "world of work" without the benefit of a high school diploma. Moreover, "nearly two-thirds of the youth in the United States still go directly from our high schools in search of some type of employment."[6] For the bulk of American workers, the high school diploma is therefore still the terminal academic credential. Completion or near-completion of high school is also the modal behavior of blacks in the UES sample, as documented in tables C-1 through C-10 in Appendix C.

In the previous chapter, industry attachment served as an important control variable. Variations among industries (reflecting, for example, variations in the complementary capital with which employees work) were seen there to significantly affect not only wage and unemployment variation, but also to interact with the marginal payoffs to education and training. Unfortunately, while industry attachment was recorded on the UES questionnaires, it was never transcribed to the data tapes. I have not, therefore, been able to include this variable in the models in this chapter.

Finally, the unemployment variable in the UES differs from the one studied previously in an important way. Although there is no difference in the basic concept, the time-frames differ substantially. In the UES, the individual is asked about his activity during the previous week; in the SEO, an annual perspective is taken. This means that, with the UES, a person either is or is not unemployed during the week preceding his or her interview; the variable is dichotomous rather than continuous. And the regression coefficients (as well as the predictions generated by the estimated regressions) are now to be interpreted as conditional probabilities of individual unemployment.

5. This may, however, already be changing. See the summary in Chapter Six of Jules Cohn's interviews with 247 employers.
6. August C. Bolino, *Manpower and the City* (Cambridge, Mass.: Schenkman, 1969), p. 62.

Thus, while the UES allows us to engage in additional experiments along the lines begun in Chapter Two, these will have to be substantially more modest than the earlier studies.

The UES is superior to the 1966 SEO file in at least one respect. The former contains figures on the hours worked by each worker during the survey week. Thus, we can estimate hourly earnings, and use this as one of the measures of the payoff to investments in education.

In this chapter, we shall therefore investigate the properties of two, rather than three, general models. Two measures of payoff will be specified: hourly earnings (w), and the 0-1 variable unemployed/employed (u). The policy variable of interest is years of school completed (E). The control variables are age (A), race (R), and sex (S). Symbolically, the general models are:

$$w = f(E, A, R, S)$$
$$u = f(E, A, R, S); \hat{u} = p[u| (E, A, R, S)]$$

A PROFILE OF THE GHETTO ECONOMY

The ten urban ghettos surveyed by the USDL in the fall of 1966, are identified and described in table 7. The smallest community surveyed was the predominantly Mexican-American Salt River Bed section of Phoenix, Arizona, with a population (aged fourteen and over) of 24,000. The largest ghetto, with an "adult" population of 150,000 (and a total population of about 200,000), was the nearly all black Central Harlem area of New York City.

All of these areas tend to have at least two things in common (besides the high incidence of minority population): (1) critically deteriorated physical capital stock and/or absence of basic infrastructure; and (2) relative isolation from the rest of the city and particularly from suburban "growth centers." As an example of the second problem:

> At its huge plant seventeen miles from the North Side [of St. Louis], McDonnell Douglas, by far the biggest employer in the metropolitan area, has actively recruited and trained St Louis Negroes. But though McDonnell's work force has swelled from 22,000 to 42,000 since 1960, the company still employs fewer than 5,000 St. Louisans. The proportion of city residents on the payroll has actually slumped since 1960, from seventeen to twelve percent.
>
> One employment obstacle for North Side people is the lack of direct public transportation to where the jobs are. It takes as much as two hours and three buses to get from the North Side to the McDonnell plant.[7]

7. William S. Rukeyser, "The St. Louis Economic Blues," in *The Negro and the City* (New York: Time-Life Books, 1968), p. 99. Many writers have attributed the "special" employment problems of ghetto dwellers to this physical isolation. For a critique of this argument, see Chapters Four and Six; and Bennett Harrison, *Metropolitan Suburbanization and Minority Economic Opportunity* (Washington, D.C.: Urban Institute, 1973).

Table 7

Socioeconomic Profiles of Ten Urban Ghettos, November, 1966

Characteristic	Roxbury (Boston)	Central Harlem (NYC)	East Harlem (NYC)	Bedford-Stuyvesant (NYC)	North Philadelphia (Phila)	North Side (St. Louis)	Slums of San Antonio	Mission-Fillmore (San Francisco)	Salt River Bed (Phoenix)	Slums of New Orleans
Estimated population (aged 14+)[a] (000)	43.3	150.4	84.3	147.7	67.5	112.3	77.4	41.9	24.2	87.0
Males (percent)	47.0	43.4	44.4	44.1	43.9	43.4	46.0	51.5	46.8	43.7
Females (percent)	53.0	56.6	55.6	55.9	56.1	56.6	54.0	48.5	53.2	56.3
UES sample size (number)	3,945	3,581	4,217	4,220	3,969	4,068	3,770	2,617	3,314	3,629
Unemployment rates (aged 16+)	*(— — — — — — — — — — — — — — — — — — — percent — — — — — — — — — — — — — — — — — — —)*									
Ghetto	6.5	8.3	9.1	6.3	9.1	12.5	7.8	11.4	12.5	9.5
SMSA	2.9[a]	3.7[a]			3.7[a]	4.4[a]	4.2[b]	5.4[a]	3.3[a]	3.3[b]
Ghetto subemployment rate[a]	24.2	28.6	33.1	27.6	34.2	38.9	47.4	24.6	41.7	45.3
Labor force participation rates	58.9	62.4	51.3	58.8	53.1	56.4	53.3	61.7	50.2	54.4
Earnings	*(— — — — — — — — — — — — — — — — — — — dollars — — — — — — — — — — — — — — — — — — —)*									
Mean hourly wage rate during the survey week	1.92	1.82	1.82	1.89	1.79	1.67	1.44	1.98	1.62	1.54
Median individual wage during the survey week	74	73	67	73	65	66	55	74	57	58
Median monthly earnings of workers in households										
With male head[c]	324	300	288	320	284	296	236	328	256	264
With female head[c]	240	264	220	268	188	200	140	772	160	140
Mean hourly mfg. wage rate in the SMSA[d]	2.76	2.71			2.87	3.02	1.98	3.42	2.82	2.83

74

Family income, previous year										
Median annual family income	4,224	3,566	3,641	4,736	3,392	3,544	2,876	4,200	2,520	3,045
Percentage of families receiving some form of public assistance					*----- percent -----*					
Families with male head	11.8	10.1	16.1	10.6	11.0	9.8	6.7	14.9	12.6	12.0
Families with female head	62.9	40.1	64.5	58.5	56.8	57.5	41.4	48.6	59.6	46.5
BLS lower level family budget[e] ($)	6,251	6,021			5,898	6,002	6,571			
Occupational distribution					*----- percent -----*					
Professional	13.7	9.3	7.5	8.8	8.0	6.7	7.5	14.4	6.9	6.2
Clerical	13.1	16.9	15.9	14.6	11.3	11.1	17.1	19.0	6.9	9.4
Craftsman	10.6	5.8	4.8	4.8	9.2	4.7	17.0	10.8	6.9	9.2
Operative	21.8	17.8	14.7	28.5	22.6	19.8	17.1	12.8	17.7	16.9
Laborer	14.3	13.8	27.8	16.9	19.5	19.2	14.1	13.7	17.0	19.9
Of those unemployed during the survey week										
Never worked	14.8	10.6	17.7	23.0	22.5	21.7	27.9	16.2	20.7	19.9
Previously employed as white collar or craftsman	23.0	23.4	20.2	15.1	17.4	7.9	21.1	32.3	12.3	19.7
Willing to take on-the-job training	79.3	76.5	75.5	83.6	76.7	81.3	75.2	76.3	80.3	80.1
Racial composition					*----- number -----*					
Black	68.2	84.8	22.4	82.0	86.4	92.0	10.6	45.4	32.6	79.1
Spanish-surname	3.0	10.4	54.1	11.0	6.6	–	84.6	13.5	43.6	–
White	26.3	4.3	22.8	5.6	6.1	6.9	4.7	36.9	21.5	19.3
Median age										
Black	34.3	41.2	34.8	33.0	25.8	25.6	54.0	33.9	27.3	32.6
Spanish-surname	38.8	35.2	46.3	49.0	48.0	–	62.0	54.0	50.2	–
White	51.0	46.8	25.5	37.0	39.0	25.0	33.1	34.9	36.0	29.7
Median family size										
Black	3.1	2.9	3.0	3.2	3.0	4.7	3.4	2.1	3.2	4.7
Spanish-surname	4.5	4.0	2.0	3.8	2.0	–	2.2	2.7	2.1	–
White	2.0	2.7	4.6	4.1	4.5	3.5	7.9	4.6	4.1	3.6

(For table notes, see page 76.)

Table 7 (Continued)

	Ghetto and City									
Characteristic	Roxbury (Boston)	Central Harlem (NYC)	East Harlem (NYC)	Bedford-Stuyvesant (NYC)	North Philadelphia (Phila.)	North Side (St. Louis)	Slums of San Antonio	Mission-Fillmore (San Francisco)	Salt River Bed (Phoenix)	Slums of New Orleans
Median years of school completed (aged 20+)										
Black	11.5	11.4	10.7	11.7	10.5	9.7	11.1	12.1	9.0	8.8
Spanish-surname	8.5	8.9	8.3	8.7	8.1	–	6.1	10.1	8.3	–
White	11.1	10.8	10.3	11.4	11.7	8.8	11.5	12.1	9.2	9.4
SMSA average, 1960 (all races)[f]	12.1		10.7		10.5	9.7	10.5	12.2	11.6	9.7

Source: Author's calculations from unpublished 1966 Urban Employment Survey Data Files, unless otherwise noted.
[a]Calculated by the U.S. Department of Labor; distributed to UES users on unpublished summary sheets.
[b]March, 1967.
[c]Based on reported weekly wage during the survey week.
[d]See table 8.
[e]U.S. Department of Labor, Bureau of Labor Statistics, *Three Standards of Living for an Urban Family of Four Persons: Spring, 1967* (Washington, D.C.: Govt. Prtg. Off., 1967), bulletin no. 1570-5.
[f]U.S. Department of Commerce, Bureau of the Census, *Statistical Abstract of the United States, 1967* (Washington, D.C.: Govt. Prtg. Off., 1967), pp. 908–35 ("Persons Aged 25 and Over").

Even in New York City, with its extensive subway and bus network, a trip from Bedford-Stuyvesant to the industrial complex on Staten Island requires two (or sometimes three) buses, at a round-trip fare of $1.20 (as of 1968).[8] Thus, in Harlem,

> ... William Taylor walked into a large liquor store to buy a half-pint of whiskey. "I'm a porter," he said. "I haven't been to work all week. There's no point to it. Cost you $4 or $5 a day just for the taxi. My wife does housework out on Long Island. She can't get there. We got $100 laid by. When that is gone, we going ta just have to rough it. The whiskey? That takes the sting out."[9]

The deterioration of ghetto infrastructure is exemplified by the case of the Lower Ninth Ward of New Orleans, another of the UES study areas. This neighborhood of some 18,000 people, most of them black is

> ... cut off from the rest of the city by an industrial canal, and there are only two bus lines into the area. Sixty-five percent of the homes are classified as "having deficiencies." The neighborhood was built before underground transmission lines were developed, and enormous high-tension poles line the streets. They are not only ugly and block drivers' vision, but they are dangerous during hurricanes. The area does not have sub-surface drainage, and the main drainage system is an open ditch [which is also] used for garbage disposal, and ... serves as the playground for children in the area. ... The narrow, two-way streets are dirt or topped with shell. There are no curbs and gutters. There are no sidewalks.[10]

Even Harlem, located in the richest city in the world, suffers from shortages of vital services and adequate infrastructure. In a major report to Mayor John V. Lindsay, written over a two-year period by a group of Harlem businessmen led by Freedom National Bank president, William R. Hudgins, it was asserted that the New York City Sanitation, Health, and Markets Departments systematically neglect the Harlem community, and the "bus service [is] deliberately curtailed during rush hours so as to better service the more vocal areas of the city."[11]

Prior to the implementation of the UES, the unemployment rate of any nonwhite area in the country was frequently "estimated" by a rule of thumb according to which one multiplied the overall city or SMSA rate by a factor of two. This "guesstimate" was widely accepted and well known among professional statisticians and antipoverty planners. From the UES samples, we see that it substantially understates the magnitude of the unemployment

8. Oscar A. Ornati, *Transportation Needs of the Poor* (New York: Praeger, 1969), p. 56.

9. Allen Schoener, ed., *Harlem on My Mind* (New York: Random House, for the Metropolitan Museum of Art, 1968), p. 236.

10. Genevieve Ray, "Big Easy," *Vista Volunteer*, Fall 1969, p. 10.

11. Charles G. Bennett, "Three-Year Aid Plan in Harlem Urged by Businessmen," *New York Times* (July 5, 1968), p. A-1.

problem in the ghetto. In table 7, the ratio of the ghetto unemployment rate to the rate associated with the corresponding SMSA ranges from a low of 1.70 in the black Brooklyn slum of Bedford-Stuyvesant to a high of 3.80 in Salt River Bed (the highest ratio for a black ghetto is 2.84 in St. Louis's North Side). The weighted average ratio for the ten-ghetto sample is about 2.5. In planning a job development program (say, for Central Harlem), use of the "rule of two" to set the program target would lead to a shortage of nearly 2,000 jobs.

The ten unemployment rates in table 7 average 8.3 percent. In 1966, the national rate averaged only 3.7 percent. For whites, the national rate was even smaller: 3.3 percent. Even the national nonwhite unemployment figure was less than the ghetto average; in 1966, the U.S. nonwhite rate was 7.3 percent.

In conducting the 1966 UES, the USDL recognized the inability of the conventional measure of unemployment to capture the full force of labor market failure in the ghetto. They observed:

> The traditional unemployment measure counts as working the person who is working only part-time, although he is trying to find full-time work; gives no consideration to the amount of earnings; omits those who are not "actively looking for work"—even though the reason for this is their conviction (whether right or wrong) that they can't find a job, at least one they want; and omits the "undercount" factor—those who are known to be present in the community, but who do not show up at all under the present survey methods.[12]

As the first step toward a remedy, the USDL therefore constructed a new index number called the "subemployment rate." It consists of the sum of those who are actually unemployed, those working part-time, but seeking full-time work, heads of households under 65 years of age earning less than $60 a week full-time, non-heads under 65 years of age earning less than $56 a week full-time, half the number of male nonparticipants aged 20–64 (on the grounds that they have given up looking not because they do not want to work but because of the "conviction—whether right or wrong—that they can't find a job"), and half of the "unfound males."[13]

The components of the subemployment rate are illustrated in figure 7. Highly imperfect as yet, and subject to arbitrary choices of weights in its

12. U.S. Department of Labor, "A Sharper Look at Unemployment", p. 5.
13. The male ghetto undercount $\overline{M}$ is estimated according to the formula

$$\overline{M}_{\text{ghetto}} = \left[F_{\text{ghetto}} \times \left(\frac{M}{F} \right)_{\text{city}} \right] - M_{\text{ghetto}}$$

where F = measured female population and M = measured male population. *Ibid.*, p. 6.

Figure 7

"Subemployment" Rates in Selected Urban Employment
Survey Areas, November, 1966

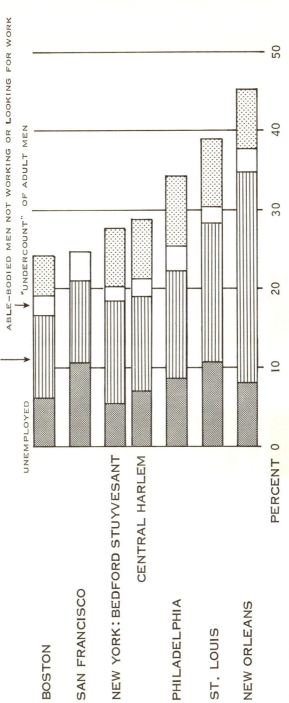

Source: U.S. Department of Labor, *A Sharper Look at Unemployment in U.S. Cities and Slums* (Washington, D.C.: Govt. Prtg. Off., 1967).

construction, the index nevertheless represents an extremely important first step toward the measurement of underemployment. In all countries, rich and poor alike, the study and reporting of underemployment as a measure of the *quality* of working life is bound to become increasingly important.

The ten-ghetto subemployment rates are shown in table 7. The highest rate is found in the two Mexican-American slum areas surveyed in San Antonio; nearly one out of every two ghetto residents is unemployed or underemployed. For the predominantly black slums of New Orleans, the rate is only slightly lower: 45.3 percent. The lowest subemployment rate in the sample is the 24.2 percent rate in Boston's Roxbury area. In that community (over a quarter of whose population was still white in 1966), the labor market failed one out of four actual or potential workers.

Wage rates, even for full-time workers, were extremely low in the ten urban ghettos. In Harlem, when they worked, male household heads earned a median wage of $84 during the survey week in November, 1966. The median for all Harlem workers was only $73 a week. In the North Philadelphia ghetto, employed workers earned on the average only $65 a week—and were employed for only twenty weeks a year. In the slums of New Orleans, the average rate of pay was $58 a week. We may place these findings in some perspective by comparing them with available metropolitan area benchmarks, shown in table 8.[14] Here we find the lowest average wage to be the $1.45 per hour rate earned by machine operatives in San Antonio's slums. In the San Antonio SMSA, the mean manufacturing wage rate was $1.98 per hour. The highest slum rate in table 8 is $2.18 per hour for craftsmen in the Mission-Fillmore ghetto of San Francisco; compare this with the San Francisco-Oakland mean of $3.42 per hour in 1966. Finally, the average wage rate for the pooled sample—$1.85 per hour—was only 35 cents above the hourly equivalent of the 1966 "poverty line." All in all, the ghetto means averaged only 40–60 percent of the corresponding SMSA manufacturing wage means. This is a crude comparison, to be sure, but it is nevertheless the most specific glance we have yet had at the magnitude of the underemployment of ghetto workers, the "submerged seven-eighths" of the employment problem "iceberg."

Given the extent of low-wage work in the slums, it is perhaps not too surprising that so many families receive some sort of public assistance—Unemployment Insurance, Aid to Families with Dependent Children, and other income transfers. Nor is it surprising that many ghetto men leave (or do not form) families so that mothers and children will be eligible for welfare—what amounts to a desperately needed second income. Broken homes in the ghetto may sometimes represent a rational response to the need for multiple incomes, at least as often as they represent a casual attitude toward sex and

14. These wage rates are not deflated to adjust for intercity variations in the cost of living. Thus, the more meaningful comparisons are those between each ghetto and its respective city.

Table 8

Hourly Ghetto Wage Rates by Occupation,[a]
with SMSA Benchmarks[b]

N = 13,380

Ghetto and SMSA	Mean hourly money wage by occupation ($)				
	Professional	Clerical	Craftsman	Operative	Laborer
Roxbury	2.07	1.92	2.16	1.96	1.85
—Boston benchmark		(2.76 — manufacturing)			
Central Harlem	2.14	1.94	2.12	1.90	1.77
East Harlem	2.12	1.85	2.13	2.00	1.72
Bedford-Stuyvesant	2.12	2.00	2.21	1.98	1.73
—New York benchmark		(2.71 — manufacturing)			
North Philadelphia	2.19	1.88	1.97	1.86	1.80
—Philadelphia benchmark		(2.87 — manufacturing)			
North Side	1.99	1.79	2.06	1.85	1.87
—St. Louis benchmark		(3.02 — manufacturing)			
Slums of San Antonio	1.86	1.54	1.85	1.45	1.35
—San Antonio benchmark		(1.98 — manufacturing)			
Mission-Fillmore	2.05	1.99	2.18	1.95	2.05
—San Francisco benchmark		(3.42 — manufacturing)			
Salt River Bed	2.01	1.66	2.01	1.86	1.80
—Phoenix benchmark		(2.82 — manufacturing)			
Slums of New Orleans	1.92	1.73	2.00	1.70	1.87
—New Orleans benchmark		(2.83 — manufacturing)			

[a]Ghetto rates for November, 1966, were calculated by the author from the unpublished UES data files.

[b]U.S. Department of Labor, Bureau of Labor Statistics, *Employment & Earnings Statistics for States and Areas, 1939–66* (Washington, D.C.: Govt. Prtg. Off., 1966), annual averages.

marriage. Yet, the median incomes of female-headed ghetto households (including welfare receipts), added to the median individual incomes of "unattached" adult males, still sum to less than $4,000. In 1966, ghetto families with both spouses present received only about $3,500 in gross income. This is about $2,500 below the benchmark established by the USDL as a minimum family budget just adequate to sustain an urban family of four in a cheap, rented apartment, with an 8-year-old automobile, and subsisting on a diet consisting largely of dried beans.

Most of the remaining data in table 7 provide demographic information. The age distributions were surprising. I had expected to find that those whites who remained in the ghetto would be—if not elderly—then certainly much older than the nonwhites. But this was the case in only one of the ghettos— Roxbury. Almost everywhere else, the oldest group was the Spanish-surname population: Puerto Ricans in the Northeast areas and Mexican-Americans in the South, Southwest and Western cities. These results hold up even when the complete distributions are examined.[15] Another surprise is found in the family size data. I had expected the Puerto Ricans and Mexican-born residents to have the largest families, and this is indeed the case. But I was completely surprised to find that, in seven of the ten ghettos, the "typical" black family was no larger—and was in many cases rather smaller—than the "typical" white family. Even if we make the absurdly extreme assumption that a male wage-earner is "missing" from every black family, the identity of black and white family sizes continues to hold for six areas.

Finally, we come to the data on education. Table 7 shows the median school completion of all persons aged twenty and over of each race in the UES sample. In six of the ten ghettos, blacks had completed at least as many years of school by 1966 as had the entire adult population of their respective cities in 1960 ("adult" is defined here as age twenty-five or over. SMSA or citywide education data are unavailable for people under the age of twenty-five). Moreover, within the slum areas, blacks' educational attainment exceeded that of whites in six cases. Spanish-speaking residents (principally Puerto Ricans and Chicanos) lagged behind both whites (or "Anglos") and blacks. In the San Francisco ghetto of Mission-Fillmore, which is about 45 percent black, the median educational attainment of Negroes was 12.1 years; i.e., better than a high school diploma.

The proportions of ghetto residents with at least a high school education, distributed by race and age, are given in table 9. Using the figures in table B-1 in Appendix B as benchmarks, we find that some of the ghetto dwellers have done remarkably well. With respect to the nation as a whole and to the set of all SMSAs, whites in the ghetto are relatively undereducated. But the ghetto blacks have completed substantially more schooling than either their national or their urban brothers. Moreover, the youngest ghetto residents—both white and black—display high school completion rates which exceed even the national white adult rate. Clearly, ghetto youth are staying in school.

Table B-2 in Appendix B permits a comparison of education attainment in each ghetto with attainment (albeit six years earlier) in the SMSA of which that ghetto is a part. In every case, the black population in the ghetto displays a higher frequency of high school completions than the total nonwhite population of the city. In five cases (Central Harlem, Bedford-Stuyvesant, North Side, Mission-Fillmore, and the UES area in San Antonio), the black community did at least as well as the entire SMSA population—whites and nonwhites together.

Because of disparities in the dates and ages being compared, we must be cautious in drawing inferences from these statistics. But one inference which is surely appropriate is the need for a revision of the conventional wisdom on the subject of the "educability" of and the "taste for education" by the black urban poor. This is confirmed by examination of the full education distribu-

15. This corroborates a similar finding for the twelve sets of SEO poverty areas; see figure 4 in Chapter Two.

Table 9

Proportion of Ghetto Residents Having Completed
at Least a High School Education by 1966

(in percent)

Ghetto and City	Aged 20–65			Aged 20–24 only		
	Black	White	Spanish-speaking	Black	White	Spanish-speaking
Roxbury (Boston)	45.4	42.8	19.8	57.1	61.2	13.6
Central Harlem (N.Y.C.)	45.2	46.0	26.6	69.2	76.5	44.9
East Harlem (N.Y.C.)	38.0	38.3	18.1	47.1	67.0	33.3
Bedford-Stuyvesant (N.Y.C.)	47.3	46.4	25.4	64.5	44.4	37.9
North Philadelphia	33.8	48.2	14.1	53.5	64.7	13.2
North Side (St. Louis)	29.7	27.0	44.4	52.9	57.1	50.0
Slums of San Antonio	43.4	47.8	17.7	80.6	53.3	39.0
Mission-Fillmore (San Francisco)	52.5	54.3	37.5	71.7	79.7	57.9
Salt River Bed (Phoenix)	23.6	28.4	15.9	49.1	53.7	24.5
Slums of New Orleans	23.1	35.2	34.5	49.2	63.6	–

Source: Appendix C, tables C-1–C-10. N = 37,330.

tions for the ten ghettos, contained in tables C-1 through C-10 in Appendix C. Finally, we note that the UES sample displays considerably greater educational attainment than the (less geographically compact) SEO sample studied in the previous chapter.

THE MARGINAL EFFECT OF EDUCATION ON EARNINGS

The general models to be examined in the following pages were discussed in the Introduction to this chapter. We begin with an investigation of the magnitude of the relationship between hourly earnings (w) and years of school completed (E). The sample to be studied consists of 13,380 individuals aged twenty or older who were employed and who reported earnings when interviewed in November, 1966.

First, we pool the data. As with the earlier twelve-city SEO sample, it is necessary to deflate the dependent variable in order to adjust for intercity variations in money wages. The possibility of additional variation attributable to intercity differences in economic and institutional conditions is introduced through the use of city dummies. Once again, both linear and nonlinear specifications of the policy variable (E) are examined, with and without interaction terms.

Then, each individual ghetto is studied. The ten resulting w–E structures are compared by examining two different estimated statistics: (1) the earnings effect of four years of high school for ghetto males of prime working age;

and (2) the maximum expected ("asymptotic") hourly wage for all adult workers in the ghetto.[16]

Throughout Chapter Three, race is specified as a single dichotomous variable:

$$R = \begin{cases} 1 \text{ if individual is white} \\ 0 \text{ if individual is black,} \\ \quad \text{Puerto Rican, Mexican-} \\ \quad \text{American or "other"} \end{cases}$$

despite the more detailed racial-ethnic-national distinctions recorded in the UES. In fact, a four-way racial specification was tried first, with the result that several of the nonwhite terms were always insignificant. This apparent collinearity is surmounted by using the more aggregative variable (R) to control for the effect of race on earnings.[17]

The Pooled Sample. As in Chapter Two, it is necessary to adjust the wage variable in order to eliminate as best we can the effect of intercity variations in the cost of living on the money wages paid in each city. Again, it is convenient to employ the schedule of costs of the "lower level market basket" for a family of four, constructed by the BLS in the Spring of 1967. Thus, the eight appropriate relative cost indices in table 2 are used as deflators to transform the 13,380 money wage observations into measures of "real wage."

The first experiments with the pooled sample embody linear and nonlinear specifications of (E) without allowing for interactions. The hourly wages variable is regressed on years of schooling, race, sex, age, and city of residence (see equations [22] and [23] in Appendix C).[18] The resulting education-wage relations are graphed in figure 8. Earnings increased on the average by nine cents an hour per additional year of school completed. The five-way nonlinear specification of education (0-7, 8, 9-11, 12, 13+ years) did not substantially improve the quality of the estimates; in going from model (22) to model (23), R^2 rose from 0.257 to only 0.261 and the standard error fell from 0.472 to 0.471. Of course, the step-function model yields more information, e.g., the presence of (modestly) increasing returns to education after the ninth grade.

16. Given by the term e^{a} in the model

$$w = e^{a - \beta/E} \text{ or } \log_e w = a - \frac{\beta}{E}$$

17. A Chow test showed that—unlike the SEO areas—the individual UES neighborhoods are not sufficiently heterogeneous (in terms of variable R) to warrant running separate regressions for "whites" and "nonwhites."

18. Again, complete regression results may be found in the dissertation.

The results of running interaction models containing linear and nonlinear specifications of (E) (equations [24] and [25] in Appendix C) strongly reconfirm the existence of many of the effects discussed in Chapter Two. In the absence of interaction, we are permitted to treat the other variables (A, S, R, C) as "shift parameters" of the w-E curve. Thus, in figure 8,

Figure 8

Additive Regression Models

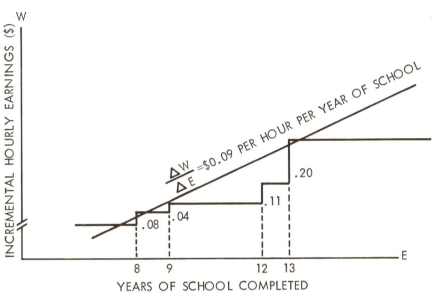

YEARS OF SCHOOL COMPLETED

changes in levels of these other variables affect the intercepts but not the slopes of the two curves. With interaction, however, such changes affect both intercepts and slopes; the shape of the curves are themselves sensitive to the values of other variables. It is this sensitivity that we now evaluate.

For model (24), the interactions between (E) and four of the city dummies (A_{20-24}), and (S) were all significant at the 95 percent level of confidence. Computing all possible combinations, we may identify the weakest and the strongest earnings effects of education. These extreme values are displayed in figure 9. Recalling the size of the sample (N = 13,380) and noting the extent of variability of the factors in question (e.g., $0.20/hr. < w < $5.00/hr; 3 < E < 18 years), the very small magnitude of the differences in the estimated effect of schooling on earnings for people with very different clusters of characteristics—a maximum of six cents an hour—is surprising.

Figure 9

Maximum and Minimum Effects in the Interaction Model
with Continuous-E

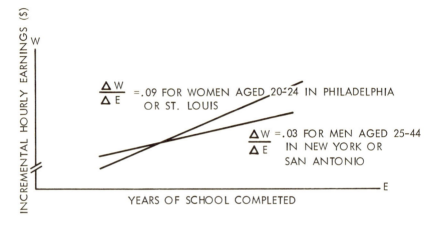

YEARS OF SCHOOL COMPLETED

This result is substantially modified when we examine model (25), where each education step is interacted with (C), (A), (S), and (R). All but five of the forty-eight estimated regression coefficients are significant at the 95 percent level. The maximum and minimum values corresponding to each step are shown in table 10. Notice the relatively modest interracial and inter-age differences. Differences by sex are somewhat greater. Differences by city are the greatest of all. Thus, for example, San Francisco high school graduates can expect an incremental return which is about $0.50 per hour (or $20 per week) greater than the return expected by a San Antonian of the same age, sex, and race. The policy implication which follows from this finding can be restated: *urban minority manpower development programs must be city-specific.* A federal program lacking the flexibility to accommodate intercity variations in the labor market processes which affect ghetto workers will have an unpredictable impact on minority underemployment.

To summarize: the interaction models, embodying first linear and then nonlinear specifications of (E), and with properties that conform to many of our a priori theoretical expectations, indicate that education has on the average been a statistically significant but numerically weak determinant of individual earnings in a pooled sample of over 13,000 ghetto workers, although the specific interaction estimates vary substantially from one city to another. For one reasonably "typical" example, the expected difference in the North Philadelphia ghetto between the hourly earnings of a 30-year-old, nonwhite, male, high school graduate and another nonwhite man of the same

Table 10

Maximum and Minimum Statistically Significant "Steps"
in the Discontinuous Education-Earnings Interaction Model[a]

Education Steps		City		Other Independent Variables						
				Age		Sex		Race		
E_8	Max. step	New York	= 0.30	A_{45-54} =	0.01	Male =	0.46	White =	0.08
	Min. step	San Antonio	= −0.34	A_{20-24} =	−0.12	Female =	0	Nonwhite =	0
E_{9-11}	Max. step	San Francisco	= 0.28	A_{55+} =	0	Male =	0.43	White =	0.06
	Min. step	San Antonio	= −0.27	A_{20-24} =	−0.23	Female =	0	Nonwhite =	0
E_{12}	Max. step	San Francisco	= 0.29	A_{55+} =	0	Male =	0.40	White =	0.08
	Min. step	San Antonio	= −0.20	A_{20-24} =	−0.12	Female =	0	Nonwhite =	0
E_{13}	Max. step	Philadelphia	= 0.43	A_{45-54} =	0.28	Male =	0.14	White =	0.09
	Min. step	Phoenix	= −0.01	A_{55+} =	0	Female =	0	Nonwhite =	0

[a]Coefficients represent incremental hourly earnings associated with the appropriate educational attainment and membership in the appropriate (city, age, sex, race) class. Only 95 percent−significant coefficients were evaluated in searching for the various maximum and minimum "steps."

age who dropped out of school after the eighth grade is roughly eighteen cents—less than $400 per year (and even less if the individual does not work a full year—which is probably the case). Over a fifty-year working lifetime, at a 6 percent discount rate, the present value of this expected lifetime return to a high school education is about $5,400. This is very close to the estimated return resulting from Chapter Two's studies of the SEO poverty areas (see page 57). This similarity increases our confidence in the reliability of the estimates.

Interghetto Comparisons. In the previous section, we learned that the city in which the individual's neighborhood is located often "counts" significantly, not only in affecting wage rates directly, but also in estimating the true marginal relationship between wages and education. For this reason, it will be instructive to look further at the intercity variation in the $w-E$ relation.

For this purpose, the nonlinear interaction model (25) (minus the terms in [C]) was re-estimated, this time for each of the ten ghetto subsamples in the 1966 UES. One convenient way of appreciating the complex results of this process (there are some 200 coefficients involved) is to select one specific subset of the labor force and focus our interarea comparisons on them. Column one of table 11 shows the differences between the expected hourly earnings of nonwhite male high school graduates of prime working age (25–44) and those of nonwhite men in the same age group who dropped out of school after the eighth grade. The weighted average of these ten estimates is $0.20 per hour, which is equivalent to a weekly rate of about $8.00—precisely our estimate for nonwhites in the twelve sets of poverty areas studied in Chapter Two. This similarity between the findings on two entirely distinct data sets is intriguing. For the $(C_2^{10} = \frac{10!}{2!8!} =)$ forty-five pairs of coefficients in column one of table 11, the differences between payoffs are statistically significant (at the 0.10 level or better) in thirty-one cases.

A second interesting approach is to estimate and compare the expected *upper limits* to hourly wage as a function of education (see note 16). The largest (or "highest") of these limits—$2.04 per hour in Bedford-Stuyvesant—is shown in figure 10. The ten estimates are given in column two of table 11. All are significantly different from zero, but—unlike the figures in column one—the differences between them are significant in only a few cases. For comparative purposes, I first multiplied these figures by forty to obtain the expected *weekly* earnings "ceilings" shown in column three of table 11, and then estimated the same upper asymptotes for the weekly wages recorded in the SEO and analyzed in Chapter Two. All six asymptotes were significantly different from zero at the 0.05 level, and ten of the fifteen pairs contained statistically different elements:

	Value of Asymptote (e^a)	
Sample Area	Whites	Nonwhites
Central city poverty areas	$ 85.93	$67.44
Rest of central city	132.08	90.50
Suburban ring	132.02	86.97

Notice the similarity between the ghetto estimates in column three of table 11 and these poverty area estimates.

Table 11

Interghetto Variation in the Marginal
Returns to Education

Ghetto and City	Marginal Contribution of High School Graduation to Hourly Earnings: Nonwhite Men Aged 25–44[a]	Maximum Expected Hourly Earnings for All Ghetto Workers[b]	
	$/hr.	$/hr.	$/hr. × 40
Central Harlem (N.Y.C.)	.24[c]	1.94	77.60
Mission-Fillmore (S.F.)	.21[c]	1.90	76.00
Roxbury (Boston)	.20[d]	1.93	77.20
North Philadelphia	.18[c]	1.88	75.20
North Side (St. Louis)	.17[c]	1.74	69.60
Slums of New Orleans	.14[d]	1.64	65.60
Salt River Bed (Phoenix)	.13	1.78	71.20
Slums of San Antonio	.06	1.56	62.40
Bedford-Stuyvesant (N.Y.C.)	.05[d]	2.04	81.60
East Harlem (N.Y.C.)	.02	1.96	78.40

[a] $\left[\dfrac{\Delta w}{\Delta E_{12} \text{ years}} \right] \Bigg|_{\substack{\text{nonwhite} \\ \text{male} \\ \text{age } 25-44}} - \left[\dfrac{\Delta w}{\Delta E_8 \text{ years}} \right] \Bigg|_{\substack{\text{nonwhite} \\ \text{male} \\ \text{age } 25-44}}$

[b] Given by e^a in the function $\log_e w = a - \beta E^{-1}$. All ten asymptotes are significantly different from zero at the .05 level.

[c] Significant at the .05 level (the standard error of the difference between two coefficients β_i and β_j within a regression is estimated by $\sqrt{\text{Var}_i + \text{Var}_j - 2 \text{Cov}_{ij}}$).

[d] Significant at the .10 level.

Summary. From a sample of over 13,000 employed adults living in ten urban ghettos in the fall of 1966, we have learned that education has a positive but small impact on their hourly earnings. Without attempting to account for nonlinearities, our experiments indicated marginal returns to education rang-

Figure 10

Maximum Expected Hourly Earnings
in the Bedford-Stuyvesant Ghetto

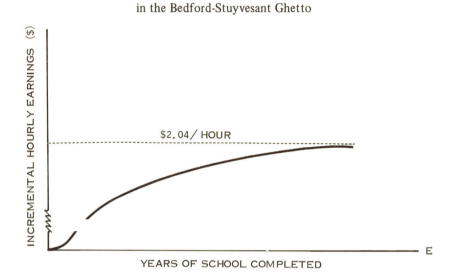

ing from three to nine cents per hour per year of school completed. Additive models nonlinear in education indicated a return to the high school diploma of roughly fifteen cents per hour above the return to completion of grammer school. In the latter, completion of at least some college added only about twenty cents per hour to the ghetto worker's expected wage rate. Individual ghetto interaction models with a nonlinear specification of education generated incremental returns to high school attendance and completion ranging from a mean of two cents per hour in East Harlem to a mean of twenty-four cents per hour in Central Harlem. Among all ten ghettos, the largest asymptotic maximum expected wage rate—in Bedford-Stuyvesant—was found to be only about $2 per hour, or $4,000 per year, regardless of how much education the worker had acquired (the smallest asymptote was $1.56 per hour in San Antonio). This is a particularly powerful result, because exactly half of the original observations showed a wage rate exceeding $2.00. Thus, the result cannot be attributed to the presence of a skewed wage distribution.

THE MARGINAL EFFECT OF EDUCATION ON UNEMPLOYMENT

We turn now from the study of earnings as a measure of payoff to a different indicator: whether or not the ghetto worker was unemployed during the survey week in 1966. Symbolizing this new dependent variable by (u), we expect that increased schooling should reduce the individual's chances of being out of work in any given week. In what follows, the sample consists of 15,363 adults (aged 20 or older) who were in the labor force—employed or unemployed but actively seeking work—when interviewed in November, 1966.

Regression analysis must be applied with certain methodological modifications when the dependent variable is dichotomous, as it is here (u = 0 or 1). The procedure, which is described in Appendix C, is particularly expensive in terms of computer time, especially with a sample of over 15,000 observations. Therefore, only two regression equations are estimated in this section. The first model is linear in the policy variable (E), and is fitted to the pooled data. The second model is nonlinear in (E), and is fitted to each of the ten ghetto subsamples. Given our earlier discovery of substantial interaction in the UES data, both of the unemployment models include interaction terms.

The Pooled Sample. The pooled model is the same as model (24) with the variable (u) substituted for (w). Although the overall regression was highly significant (F = 46.8), only about 7 percent of of the variation in (u) was explained by the model. This is substantially below the power of the same model to explain wage variation earlier, where $R^2 = 0.275$. Moreover, neither the age nor the sex terms were significant in the unemployment model.

The marginal effects of an additional year of school on the probability of being unemployed may be summarized briefly (as before, details may be found in the original dissertation). As expected, the u–E relation is numerically stronger for whites than for nonwhites, but the 0.002 difference is not statistically significant. In six of the UES cities, the ability of education to reduce the worker's chances of being unemployed is significant but, again, quite small (none of the interghetto differences are significant, however). In Philadelphia, for example, a black twelfth grade graduate now living in the North Philadelphia ghetto has only a 3 percent smaller chance of being unemployed than a black North Philadelphian who dropped out of school after the eighth grade. In St. Louis, the difference is only 5 percent.

In the interaction models of Chapter Two, we discovered instances where education actually *increased* the chances of joblessness. Here, in three of the UES cities (Boston, Phoenix, and San Francisco), the u–E relation again has the opposite sign; increased education increases the individual's chances of being unemployed (only two of the three values are statistically significant, however). For example, a high school graduate now living in the Roxbury ghetto of Boston has (depending on race) either a 6.4 percent or a 7.2 percent *higher* probability of finding himself or herself out of work in any given week than a dropout who never even began high school. This is something which a colleague and I began to suspect during the researching of a previous monograph. In our Harlem study, Professor Thomas Vietorisz and I stratified both unemployment and labor force participation rates by age, sex, and clusters of years of school completed (0-8, 9-12, 13+).[19] The resulting tables displayed a surprising absence of the expected inverse relationship between education and unemployment and the expected direct relationship between education and labor force participation. In fact, many of the cells showed precisely the opposite effects. From this, we hazarded a (most tentative) explanation, about which I now feel considerably more confident. Perhaps education increases the expectations and standards of ghetto workers which, when unmet by discriminating or exploitative employers, leads to frustration. This, in turn, may reduce the job attachment of the worker. If presently employed, he or she may display greater absenteeism, more frequent recalcitrance when given orders by foremen, less patience with the more experienced and sometimes racist coworkers, and so forth. If the ghetto worker is not presently employed, then, although he is indeed searching for work, the change in his standards or expectations means that he will no longer accept just any job offered to him. If the positions readily available to him are beneath his new standards, then he may reject the job and continue to search further, or turn to other income-generating activities such as public welfare or "the hustle" (see Chapter Five). Ms. Helen Wood, editor of the *Manpower Report of the President*, informs me on the basis of her studies that well-educated blacks frequently maintain a reservation (i.e., minimum acceptable asking) wage which is higher than the average for their particular labor market. Either of these processes, or some combination of the two, might well explain the apparently perverse results we have found in the ghettos of at least two large cities.[20]

There is now some independent evidence to support these speculations. Peter Doeringer has observed that, while Boston's antipoverty agency set up neighborhood employment centers in the slums to recruit ghetto workers for Boston industry, "many of these jobs pay only $2.00 an hour or less."[21] Thus, says Doeringer, "the main benefits of the system have come from prompt referrals to jobs similar to those already available to the ghetto community."[22] This lack of upward mobility in the placement system probably contributes to the poor work habits (such as tardiness and high quit rates) which then frighten off other and perhaps genuinely concerned businessmen. Doeringer hypothesizes that

19. Thomas Vietorisz and Bennett Harrison, *The Economic Development of Harlem* (New York: Praeger, 1970), pp. 24 ff.

20. Harold Sheppard's famous studies of "workers with the 'blues' " have shown that "the greater a person's education achievements, as measured by years of school, the greater are his life and job aspirations," and the greater his discontent if he fails to achieve those goals. Cf. Harold L. Sheppard, "Discontented Blue-Collar Workers," *Monthly Labor Review*, April 1971, p. 28.

21. Peter B. Doeringer, "Ghetto Labor Markets—Problems and Programs," Program on Regional and Urban Economics, Discussion Paper no. 35 (mimeographed, Harvard University, May 1968), p. 9.

22. *Ibid.*, p. 17.

... the availability of alternative low wage job opportunities and the unattractiveness of such low wage work interact to discourage the formation of strong ties to particular employers ... for wage rates higher than the "prevailing" ghetto wage, disadvantaged workers are more likely to be stable employees than other workers.[23]

Doeringer presents further evidence that education may not contribute to improved employment status for ghetto workers. Job tenure, of course, is inversely related to unemployment. Doeringer has found that the relationship between tenure and schooling displays all the ambiguities we discovered above in relating (u) to (E). He regressed number of weeks on the job (T) on several background variables for each of three Roxbury samples. In one regression, the coefficient on education was positive but insignificant. In the second regression, it was negative but insignificant. In the third (fitted to a sample of 186 workers aged 16–25), it was positive and significant, but extremely small. A high school graduate from Roxbury might be expected to "last" only a little over six weeks longer on the job than a worker who dropped out after the eighth grade.[24]

Interghetto Comparisons. We now fit nonlinear regressions similar to model (25) to each of the ten ghetto subsamples, substituting the new dependent variable (u) for (w).

Very few of the two hundred regression coefficients were significant, reinforcing the impression that the relationship between education and unemployment is tenuous indeed. In fact, in seven of the ghettos, there was no statistically significant relationship at all, with the (F)s all less than unity. Only Salt River Bed in Pheonix (an area which is 44 percent Mexican-American, 33 percent black, and 23 percent white or "Anglo") and the Roxbury area of Boston display what might be called a "normal" result. In Phoenix, a young male Anglo with a high school education has nearly a 13 percent lower probability of being out of work than a grammar school graduate of the same race and sex but with no further education. The effect is also seen to be about 5 percent "stronger" for Anglos than for the minority workers living in the Phoenix ghetto, as we would expect. In Roxbury, the return to high school completion is a 6 percent reduction in the conditional probability of unemployment.

At the other extreme, in the slums of San Antonio (which are 86 percent Mexican-American), a male chicano, even with some college training, has (at least up until 1966) faced almost certain unemployment (7 percent of the San Antonio sample had attended college). So low has been the apparent San Antonio demand for college-trained minority workers that the probability of

23. *Ibid.*, pp. 10–11.
24. Peter B. Doeringer, *Programs to Employ the Disadvantaged* (Englewood Cliffs, N.J.: Prentice-Hall, 1969), p. 252, table 2.

unemployment is 8 percent higher for the latter than for workers who never attended college at all.

Summary. From the more reliable pooled sample, we have found that increased education has a significant but very small effect on a ghetto worker's chances of being unemployed in any given week. In the Boston and San Francisco ghettos, a high school diploma or some college training may actually reduce his ability to find and/or hold a job, perhaps because his standards have risen faster than the effective local demand for his labor. In any case, we can report with confidence that there is no evidence of a substantial inverse relationship between education and unemployment, as one would expect from reading the literature on the subject and by consulting the conventional wisdom. The ten individual ghetto models confirm this conclusion.

CONCLUSIONS ON THE RETURNS TO EDUCATION IN THE TEN URBAN GHETTOS

With the limitations of the 1966 UES data (and the model specifications which it permits) clearly in mind, we may hazard some conclusions. In brief, education has only a limited (but statistically significant) impact upon hourly earnings, and an even weaker effect upon the conditional probability of unemployment in any given week.

Because of the relatively greater homogeneity of the population within each UES ghetto (in terms of socioeconomic status), the regression results were not very sensitive to race, so interracial comparisons of the kind made in Chapter Two are not relevant here.

A number of different earnings models yielded estimated returns of from three to nine cents per hour for each additional year of schooling, and—over the discrete interval of 9–12 years inclusive—anywhere from two to twenty-four cents per hour. Workers with at least some college received, on the average, less than twenty cents per hour above the rate for high school graduates. The asymptotic maximum expected hourly wage rate given education ranged from a low of $1.56 per hour in San Antonio's Mexican-American slums to a high of $2.04 per hour in the Bedford-Stuyvesant ghetto of New York City.

In none of the ghettos was the effect of education on unemployment even as great as a 2 percent reduction per year of schooling. In several cases, increased education actually increased the conditional probability of unemployment. This result is consistent with an earlier research finding of the author, published elsewhere, and appears to obtain for ghetto labor force participation rates as well: education increases workers' expectations and standards which, when frustrated by discrimination, lead to discouragement and non-participation.

All of these findings on the relative marginal inefficiency of education are fully consistent with those developed for the SEO poverty areas in Chapter Two. In the next chapter, we shall examine samples of white and nonwhite individuals who live *outside* the slum areas in the twelve largest cities. This should provide a valuable benchmark against which to judge the results of these studies in the structure of the ghetto economy.

Barring blacks from the new suburbs also bars them from the better jobs, because [these] are now in the suburbs.
— Robert C. Maynard,
in *The Washington Post*

PLAYBOY: But wouldn't many blacks have higher incomes and live better if they could be integrated into the suburbs?

CLEAVER: I emphasize again that until black people as a whole gain power, it's not a question of where you are geographically, if you're black; it's a question of where you are psychologically. No matter where you place black people under present conditions, they'll still be powerless, still subject to the whims and decisions of the white political and economic apparatus.
— Eldridge Cleaver

4.

NONPOVERTY AREAS IN THE TWELVE STANDARD METROPOLITAN STATISTICAL AREAS

INTRODUCTION

Two research objectives are pursued in this chapter. First, as indicated in Chapter One, it is at least plausible that a sample consisting exclusively of "ghetto" residents will be inherently biased since those for whom human capital investments have brought substantial returns may have moved out, leaving behind a population with an abnormally high proportion of "failures." In the present chapter, we therefore fit the three general models (8), (9), and (10) to data for whites and nonwhites living outside the twelve sets of central city poverty areas analyzed in Chapter Two. We expect that white economic opportunity will increase—underemployment will fall and the marginal efficiency of education will rise—as our focus shifts outward from the core poverty areas. Indeed, if the data do not show such a pattern, we should be most suspicious of the quality of the SEO files. Although many writers have assumed a similar pattern for nonwhites,[1] no one (to my knowledge) has ever before been in a position to subject the assumption to rigorous quantitative tests.[2] If the assumption is invalid—if nonwhite educational returns are insensitive to residential location within the metropolitan area—then our confidence in the results of Chapter Two will be substantially increased.

The SEO is an especially attractive data source for our purposes because it permits us to distinguish among three areas or "regions" within the SMSA: (1) central city poverty neighborhoods, (2) all other central city neighborhoods, and (3) suburban communities. Too many policy discussions about minority economic opportunity or urban poverty pose the completely artificial dichotomy of ghetto versus suburb as the *situs* for development investment. Between the two—both figuratively and geographically—lies the area where the greatest nonwhite urban population growth has occurred and will undoubtedly continue to do so: the nonghetto central city. Every important policy consideration—from transportation investment to the location of daycare centers for children of working mothers—is highly sensitive to the decision (or the prediction) about where the greatest nonwhite urban population growth is likely to occur. A second objective in this chapter is therefore to compare the economic opportunities of nonwhites living in nonpoverty central city neighborhoods with the opportunities of nonwhites who have "suburbanized." This comparison is drawn against the background of our previous findings on the ghetto and parallel findings on the sensitivity of white underemployment to residential location within the SMSA.

SPATIAL VARIATIONS IN INTRAMETROPOLITAN EMPLOYMENT OPPORTUNITIES

We begin with a brief descriptive analysis of the three indicators of relative well-being: weekly earnings, annual unemployment, and occupational status.

---

1. See the discussion of "ghetto dispersal" on p. 116 and in Chapter Six.
2. For the one limited exception, see the summary of George M. von Furstenberg's study of Detroit on p. 110 in this book.

Because so many women outside of the ghetto have traditionally acted as "secondary" workers, whose labor supply decisions have depended upon the status of males in the family, we shall simplify the analysis considerably by concentrating in this section on the males in the SEO sample.

Earnings. The weekly earnings distributions for the 6,797 males in our SEO twelve-SMSA sample are displayed in figures 11 and 12. For white males the conventional wisdom is valid. As we "move" out from the core city "ghetto" through the rest of the central city and into the suburban "ring," expected white earnings rise monotonically. The greatest change occurs at the mode; the suburban white mode is roughly $100 per week "to the right of" the central city white mode. In figure 12, the three curves are clearly distinct and widely spaced. White earnings (for males, at any rate) are indeed highly sensitive to the intrametropolitan residential location of the worker.

This is not, however, true for nonwhites. The three curves in figure 11 are clustered much more closely together than was the case for whites. Moreover, the largest frequency of relatively high earnings (i.e., above approximately $160 per week in figure 11) occurs, not in the suburbs, but in the rest of the central city, while both of these distributions have the same mode. The most dramatic property of these figures is, of course, the extent to which the nonwhite earnings distributions—even outside the ghetto—lie far to the left of the white distributions. This comparison of the full distributions is much more informative than the simple comparisons of white and nonwhite medians or means found in much of the poverty literature. In particular, it suggests that nonwhite economic opportunity would not necessarily be increased by "suburbanization." Moreover, there is much less dispersion among nonwhite than among white earnings, in every part of the metropolis. Intrametropolitan employment opportunities are highly variegated for whites. But the constraints on the opportunities for nonwhites are such that most find themselves in much the same situation vis-à-vis the urban labor market.

Unemployment. The conventional wisdom asserts that unemployment is less prevalent in the suburbs than in the central city, particularly as private manufacturing and retailing industries continue to "suburbanize." According to John F. Kain, for example,

> the most central parts of metropolitan areas are losing employment to outlying areas and . . . this process is, if anything, accelerating. Slow growth and not infrequent decline of central city areas have accumulated to the point where absolute declines in central city employment are now commonplace.[3]

3. John F. Kain, "The Distribution and Movement of Jobs and Industry," in *The Metropolitan Enigma*, ed. James Q. Wilson (Cambridge, Mass.: Harvard University Press, 1968), p. 27. The "suburbanization" phenomenon is examined more closely in Chapter Six.

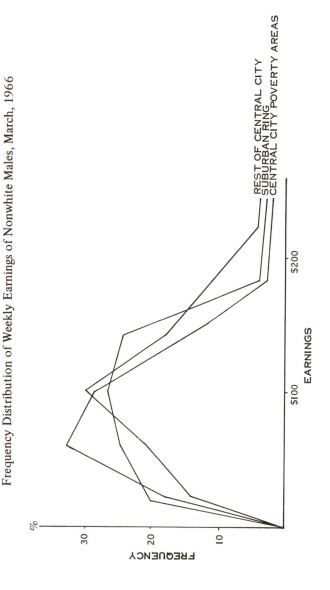

Figure 11

Frequency Distribution of Weekly Earnings of Nonwhite Males, March, 1966

Figure 12

Frequency Distributions of Weekly Earnings of White Males, March, 1966

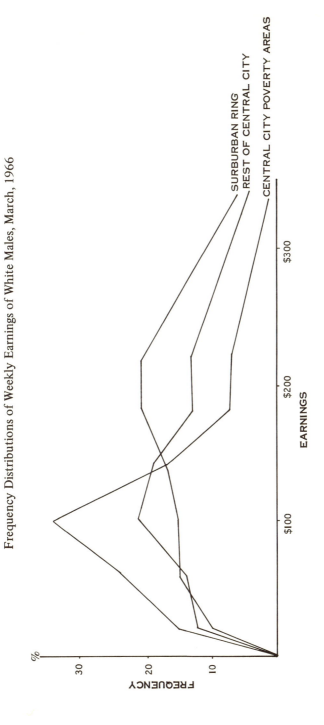

The whites in our twelve-city sample display behavior consistent with this aggregate benchmark. The median unemployment rates associated with the three frequency distributions in figure 13 fall as we "move" from the central city poverty areas "out" to the suburban ring. Again, the three curves are fairly distinct; white unemployment is sensitive to residential location within the SMSA.

The nonwhite curves in figure 14 do not share these attributes. Median nonwhite unemployment in the suburbs exceeds the rate for the (non-poverty) central city; it is especially difficult to distinguish between the non-white ghetto and the nonghetto central city distributions.

Occupational Status. When the 308 occupational titles are mapped into the 100 Duncan-NORC prestige scores and distributed over all males in the sample (by residential location), the results are as shown in figures 15 and 16. Again, the pattern for whites is precisely what we would expect: the occupational status distribution for suburban whites lies to the right of the distribution for central city whites, which, in turn, lies to the right of the distribution for whites in the ghetto. While the latter is clearly skewed left, the suburban white distribution is much more nearly "rectangular," indicating that suburban whites are distributed more or less uniformly throughout the range of occupations, from very low status to very high status positions. White occupational status is, in other words, sensitive to location.

For nonwhites, on the other hand, all three distributions are sharply skewed left and are, in fact, almost indistinguishable. Well over half of the nonwhite males in the sample—even those living in the suburbs—are (to employ Barbara Bergmann's phrase) "crowded" into the lowest fifth of the occupations, in terms of status. Figure 16 makes it clear that a nonwhite worker's chances of attaining a *high* status occupation are—regardless of his educational achievements—very small.

Comparisons of the full distributions have shown rather clearly that white employment opportunities are indeed sensitive to variations in residential location. For nonwhites, on the other hand, the full distributions of earnings, unemployment, and occupational status are much more similar to one another. It is, in other words, difficult to distinguish ghetto from nonghetto nonwhite workers.

It is particularly noteworthy that these descriptive materials do not provide support for the widespread belief that nonwhite economic opportunity would be enhanced by an open housing policy to facilitate the "suburbanization" of the nonwhite ghetto population[4] (neither, of course, do they provide definitive evidence against such an outcome). The central tendencies which permit such an inference are summarized in figures 17–19. It is easily

---

4. Anthony Downs, for example, writes that, "if [ghetto] residents were to move to suburban areas, they would. . . have a far better chance of getting decent employment." See "Alternative Futures for the American Ghetto," *Daedalus*, Fall 1968, p. 1364.

Figure 13

Frequency Distributions of Annual Unemployment
of White Males, 1965

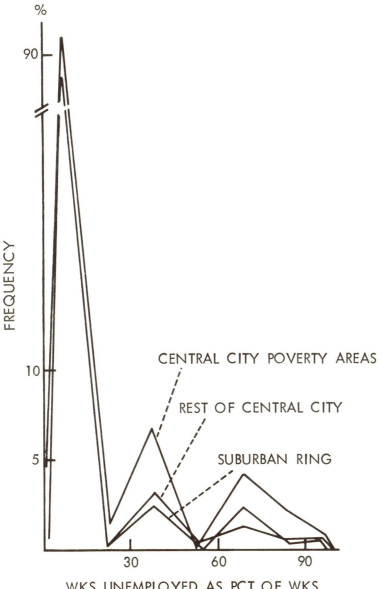

Figure 14

Frequency Distributions of Annual Unemployment
of Nonwhite Males, 1965

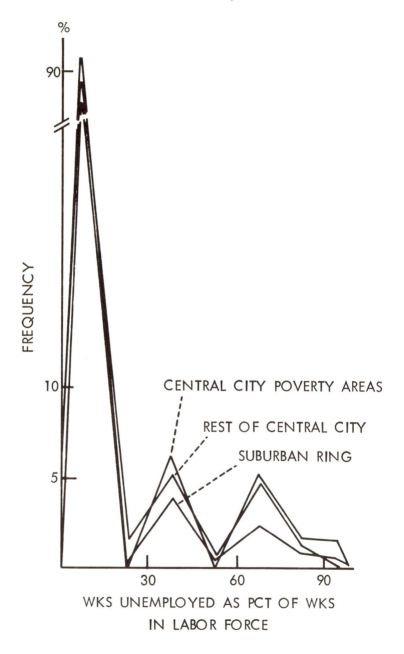

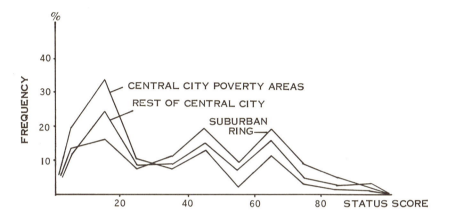

Figure 15

Frequency Distributions of Occupational Status
of White Males, March, 1966

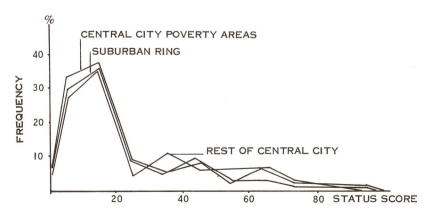

Figure 16

Frequency Distributions of Occupational Status
of Nonwhite Males, March, 1966

Figure 17

Median Male Earnings by Intrametropolitan Residential Location,
March, 1966

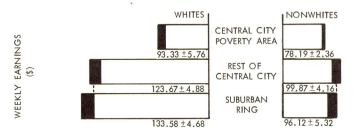

Figure 18

Median Male Unemployment Rates
by Intrametropolitan Residential Location, 1965

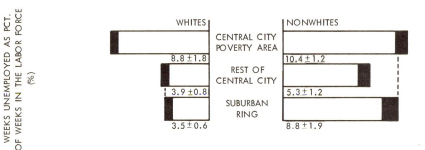

Figure 19

Median Male Occupational Status
by Intrametropolitan Residential Location, March, 1966

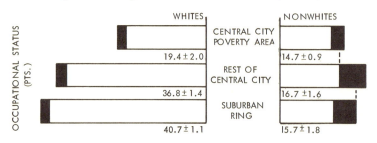

seen that—for all three measures—average white employment opportunity improves monotonically with "distance" from the core, while nonwhite opportunity increases somewhat with the "move" from the ghetto to the nonpoverty central city, but falls again with the further "move" out to the suburban ring (the quotation marks are designed to remind the reader that this is a cross-section analysis, so that it is our perspective which is "moving," and not the households themselves). When 95 percent confidence intervals are constructed around these means or medians (shaded bands in figures 17–19), the contrast is even more dramatic. For whites, employment opportunity definitely rises (or at least does not fall) with distance from the ghetto. For nonwhites, however, the three descriptors of employment opportunity show relatively little sensitivity to intrametropolitan residential location. Nonwhite earnings are significantly higher outside the ghetto than inside, but—once outside—there is no significant difference between the average levels associated with central city and suburban residence. Nonwhite unemployment rates in the ghetto and in the suburbs are not statistically different from one another, and are only slightly lower in the nonpoverty central city. Finally, the indicator of occupational status for nonwhite men is completely insensitive to residential location.

The Role of the Male Family Head. Another aspect of underemployment with especially important implications for the stability of family structure is the contribution of the male family head to the total income of the family. Underemployment of the male head—sporadic work at substandard wages in low-status occupations or jobs to which the worker has only a loose attachment—forces the family to resort to other means of acquiring income. Other family members—including children—may have to go to work. The family may enroll for public assistance, although in many cities (at the time of the survey) this required the father to leave (or to pretend to leave) the home. As a composite measure of economic opportunity, the share of gross family income contributed by the male head is an important summary indicator.

Table 12 shows the relevant estimates for the six SEO subsamples. The income and earnings figures display the same pattern as the one we have just seen: mean white income and earnings increase monotonically with distance from the core, but mean nonwhite income and earnings are lower in the suburbs than in the nonghetto neighborhoods of the central city.

Table 12 also contains several indicators which reflect the impact of underemployment of the male head on the urban family. On the average, the head of the white family contributes 46 percent of the family's gross income in the ghetto. At the margin, a 1 percent increase in the family's income is associated with a 0.65 percent increase in the head's earnings. Within any given part of the metropolis, the head is relatively less important as a breadwinner to the nonwhite family than to the white family, by all three indicators in the table. Across areas of the metropolis, the relative importance of the white

Table 12

Contribution of the Male Family Head to 1965 Family Income,
by Intrametropolitan Residential
Location and Race

Residential Location	1965 Means		Average Importance of the Head $(\overline{W}/\overline{Y})$	Marginal Importance of the Head $(\Delta W/\Delta Y)$	Relative Importance of the Head $\left[\dfrac{\% \,\Delta\, W}{\% \,\Delta\, Y}\right]$ [a]
	Gross family income $(\overline{Y})$	Earnings of the head $(\overline{W})$			
Central city poverty areas					
White families	$ 8,120	$ 3,815	0.46	0.30	0.65
Nonwhite families	5,995	3,102	0.52	0.29	0.56
Rest of the central city					
White families	10,468	5,234	0.50	0.33	0.66
Nonwhite families	8,458	4,080	0.48	0.26	0.54
Suburban ring					
White families	10,839	5,710	0.53	0.36	0.68
Nonwhite families	7,285	3,520	0.48	0.25	0.52

[a]Elasticity $= \hat{B}\left[\dfrac{\overline{Y}}{\overline{W}}\right]$ where $\hat{B}$ is an estimate of the slope in the regression $W = B_0 + B_1\,Y$.

head increases monotonically with "distance" from the ghetto, but the relative importance of the nonwhite head decreases, and this decrease is also monotonic. Thus, while 52 percent of the average nonwhite family income in the ghetto is contributed by the earnings of the male head, only 48 percent of the suburban nonwhite family's income derives from the labor of the family head.

This evidence on the implications of nonwhite underemployment outside the ghetto directly challenges two strands in the conventional wisdom frequently associated with the names of Daniel P. Moynihan and John F. Kain. If the absence of a strong nuclear and patriarchal family structure among ghetto blacks is a major cause of the pervasiveness of urban poverty—as Moynihan argues[5]—and if economic opportunity for urban blacks is greatest in the suburbs—a position taken (on very little evidence) by Kain[6]—then we should certainly expect that the economic importance of the nonwhite family head would be greater in the suburbs than in the ghetto. Instead, we find just the opposite to be the case. Table 12 records central tendencies, but an analysis of the complete distributions tells the same story. The earnings distributions of nonwhite male family heads living in the three "regions" overlap almost completely, while the nonwhite gross family income distributions shift somewhat to the right as we "move" out from the ghetto. These findings imply that suburban nonwhite families finance their living expense through some combination of greater labor force participation within the family, multiple job-holding by the spouse, or access to public assistance.[7] According

5. Cf. Moynihan's "Employment, Income, and the Ordeal of the Negro Family," *Daedalus*, Fall 1965; and U.S. Department of Labor, *The Negro Family: The Case for National Action* (Washington, D.C.: Govt. Prtg. Off., 1965).

6. Cf. "Housing Segregation, Negro Employment, and Metropolitan Decentralization," *Quarterly Journal of Economics*, May 1968; John F. Kain and Joseph J. Persky, "Alternatives to the Gilded Ghetto," *Public Interest*, Winter 1969.

7. Specifically, I am suggesting that suburban black families may work *more* total man-hours per year than white families, but in jobs which pay lower wages. Some fascinating indirect evidence consistent with this hypothesis has been unearthed by Duran Bell, who has generously shown me his unpublished worksheets. In 1966, according to Bell, the national black-white family earnings ratio was 0.53 for families without working wives, but 0.80 for families in which wives worked at least part time. The explanation was *not* that the economy had opened lots of jobs to black women. Rather, it appears that white men work *less* when their wives work, while black men work as hard or harder when *their* wives work:

	1966 Average Male Earnings	
	Black	White
Wives work	$5,044	$6,464
Wives don't work	$4,673	$8,678

Source: *1967 Survey of Economic Opportunity.*

(White wives averaged $2,769, compared to the average black wife's income of $2,416. Taken together, these figures yield the black-white ratios of 0.53 and 0.80.) Bell's

to the SEO files, there is reason to suppose that transfer payments including public welfare do indeed play an important role in aiding suburban nonwhites to defray expenses in the face of underemployment of the male head. Mean public assistance per family (not per case) in 1965 in the twelve SMSAs was as follows:

Whites in central city poverty areas	$ 42.73
Whites in the rest of the central city	15.86
Whites in the suburban ring	11.34
Nonwhites in the central city poverty areas	$ 87.12
Nonwhites in the rest of the central city	55.62
Nonwhites in the suburban ring	117.56

And, according to the executive director of the Connecticut Housing Investment Fund (CHIF), an organization which helps to place minority families in integrated suburban housing, 75 percent of the wives in CHIF's suburban client families work, with "many husbands holding down second jobs" as well.[8]

One recent study of subsidized housing project residents in the Detroit metropolitan area found that the gross family incomes of suburban blacks grew more rapidly during the late 1960s than the incomes of central city blacks with similar demographic characteristics. One of the "control" variables—the proportion of family members who were full- or part-time workers—had an even larger positive effect on family income growth than either race or residential location.[9] These results are fully consistent with my own. Unfortunately, the author of the study attempts to draw inferences from these results about the differential (central city-suburban) *earnings* opportunities for black household heads. Such inferences are not possible from his data, which do not distinguish between income and earnings. Yet this is—so far as I can tell—the only empirical study of intrametropolitan spatial income variations ever published.

These analyses certainly lead to the conclusion that nonwhite underemployment, in all of its many manifestations, is pervasive throughout the metropolitan area. On the average, central city residents living in nonpoverty neighborhoods, i.e., outside the "ghetto" but inside the city, appear to enjoy a slight advantage. They receive somewhat higher earnings, display lower unemployment rates, find their way into slightly higher status occupations, enjoy the highest family incomes, and receive smaller welfare supplements

---

purpose in making these calculations is to temper the enthusiasm of those social scientists and policy-makers who see a declining black-white income gap as evidence of increased economic opportunity for blacks.

8. "A New Way to Integrate the Suburbs," *Business Week*, March 28, 1970, p. 168.

9. George M. von Furstenberg, "Place of Residence and Employment Opportunities within a Metropolitan Area," *Journal of Economic Issues*, June 1971.

than either ghetto or suburban nonwhites. In every aspect of working life, nonwhites who live in the suburbs tend to be more seriously underemployed than nonwhites living in the (nonpoverty) central city.

However, when the statistical variation about these mean and median indicators of employment opportunity is taken into account, we find that nonwhite underemployment is rather insensitive to intrametropolitan residential location, the conventional wisdom notwithstanding. It remains to be seen whether the same is true of the nonwhite returns to education.

THE RETURNS TO EDUCATION AND TRAINING OUTSIDE THE GHETTO

In Chapter Two, models both linear and nonlinear in education (E) were fitted to data on the central city poverty areas of the twelve largest SMSAs in the United States. Both to examine the sensitivity of the education and training "payoffs" to variations in intrametropolitan residential location, and to determine whether or not the "ghetto" findings were biased, we now fit these same models to two other data files: All persons aged fourteen or more, in the labor force for at least fourteen weeks in 1965, no longer in school in March, 1966, and residing (1) in nonpoverty neighborhoods of the twelve central cities, and (2) in the suburban rings of the twelve SMSAs. The reader is reminded that our information concerns the *current* residence of each individual in the sample, *not* his or her residence while attending school. The results, therefore, reflect on the sensitivity of nonghetto employment opportunities to a worker's education, but *not* on the efficacy of nonghetto schools.

The regression coefficients for the policy variables are listed in table D-1 in Appendix D.[10] For convenience, the ghetto results reported in Chapter Two are reproduced in this table. Since the training variables continue to be largely insignificant—which may or may not be a meaningful finding, given the very small number of trainees (and former trainees) in the SEO—the following discussion is addressed exclusively to the payoffs to education outside the ghetto.

Figures 20 and 21 display the education-earnings step-functions for both racial groups, in the rest of the central city and in the suburban ring, respectively. As in Chapter Two, only those steps which are significantly different from the previous step are shown. Whites clearly benefit from education. Attendance at school brings substantial monetary returns, even when credentials have not been earned. For example, white city dwellers with some college experience but without a college diploma earn about $13 per week more than white workers who do not go beyond high school. For suburban whites, the differential is even greater: nearly $20 per week. The credentials do, however,

10. Again, readers interested in the detailed results are referred to the thesis.

Figure 20

Additive Earnings Model—Rest of Central City

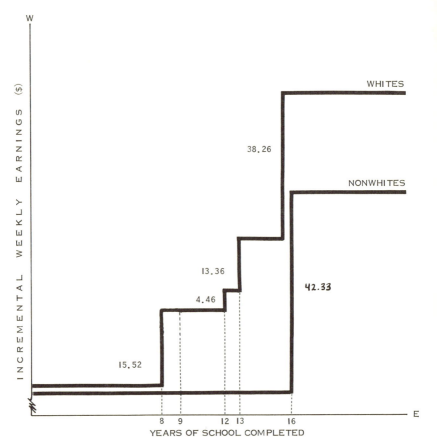

make quite a difference. Relative to the person who does not go beyond the eighth grade, a high school diploma adds $4.46 to the expected weekly earnings of white central city dwellers. In the suburbs, the comparable estimate is $10.54. The payoff to educational credentials is even more pronounced at the college level. Central city white college graduates can expect nearly $52 per week more than people who go directly to work after high school, as compared with the $13 per week differential accruing to collegians lacking the degree. For suburban whites, the respective expected returns are $65 and $20. In summary, with weekly earnings as the measure of "payoff," there are everywhere positive returns to education for whites, and the entire schedule of returns shifts up with "distance" from the core city ghetto. The pattern is

Figure 21

Additive Earnings Model—Suburban Ring

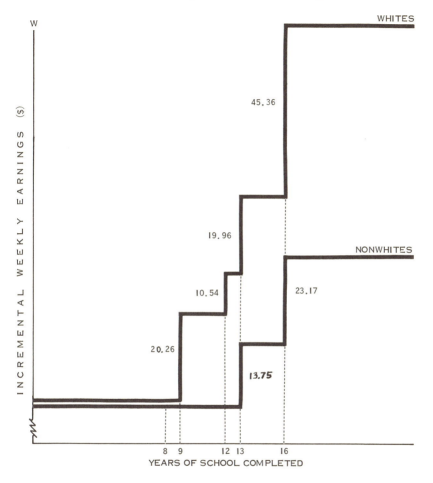

precisely what the conventional wisdom on the marginal efficiency of education would lead us to expect.

For nonwhites, the results are strikingly different. There is apparently no
earnings payoff at all for nonghetto nonwhites who did not at least begin a
college program. In the nonpoverty central city, nothing short of a college
degree brings statistically significant returns to nonwhites. For "suburbanized" nonwhites, college attendance short of graduation is efficient in
terms of earnings (although graduation from college is numerically much
more important), but a high school diploma has zero value in terms of its

contribution to earnings. One of the most remarkable findings is that the cumulative impact of education on nonwhite earnings is no greater in the suburbs than in the ghetto. In fact, the pattern is similar to the one found earlier in this chapter: cumulative nonwhite marginal earnings are slightly higher in the nonpoverty central city than in the ghetto, but fall as we "move" to the suburbs. In the present case, however, the suburban return is even lower than the ghetto return. This is certainly not consistent with the conventional wisdom.

Table D-1 also displays estimates of the returns to education with unemployment as the measure of payoff. The unemployment results for whites are symmetrical to the earnings results reviewed a moment ago. For metropolitan whites living outside the ghetto, expected unemployment falls as education increases. Moreover, the suburban schedule is lower ("better") than the nonpoverty central city schedule. This is displayed graphically in figures 22 and 23. Since the same result held for ghetto whites as well, we are again led to conclude that the prevailing assumptions about the marginal efficiency of

Figure 22

Additive Unemployment Model—Rest of Central City

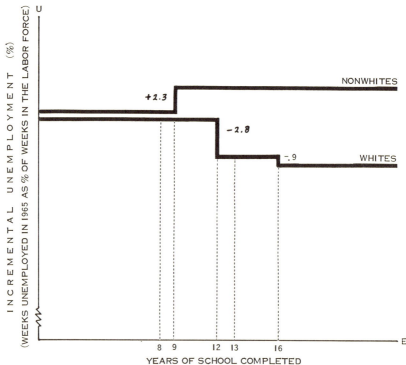

YEARS OF SCHOOL COMPLETED

Figure 23

Additive Unemployment Model—Suburban Ring

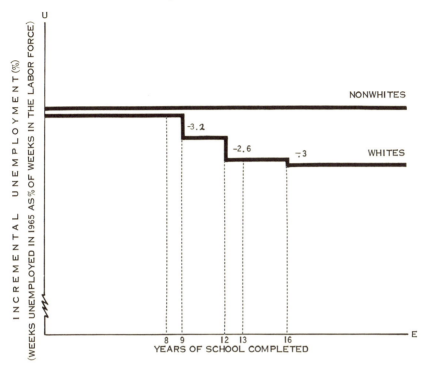

education adequately describe the status of urban white workers—even if they live in the ghetto.

But—once again—it is equally clear that the conventional wisdom does not apply to urban nonwhites. Even in the suburbs, no amount of education up to and including completion of college has any significant effect on the risk of unemployment for nonwhites. Indeed, central city (but nonghetto) non-white workers who are high school dropouts are likely to be unemployed for a *longer* period of time than workers who make no attempt to go beyond the eighth grade. The very normality of the white education-unemployment functions increases our confidence in these nonwhite results—and provides a stark contrast.

The results for occupational status as a measure of payoff are similar to what we found in our earlier study of the ghetto in Chapter Two. For both racial groups, education is associated with increased mobility into what are nationally considered to be higher-status occupations. For whites, this promise is realized; as their education increases, whites move into new occupations where they receive higher earnings and face lower expectations of unemployment. For nonwhites, the promise is not realized; as their education increases, nonwhites move into new occupations, but their earnings are hardly affected at all by anything short of a college degree, and there is no effect whatever on their chances of finding themselves unemployed over the course of a year.

For both races, table D-1 shows that the impact of higher education on occupational status is not very sensitive to residential location.

CONCLUSION

The previous findings yield no evidence to support the popular contention that education would facilitate the "suburbanization" of unskilled or semi-skilled nonwhite workers presently living in the ghetto. The returns to non-white schooling are no higher "outside" than "inside" the core city. There is, therefore, reason to doubt that the economic opportunities of minorities would be enhanced by suburbanization, as has been argued by John F. Kain. Government programs, says Kain, "should emphasize the strengthening of the Negro's ability to break out of the ghetto [by] education and job training and the expansion of suburban housing opportunities."[11]

These findings are, of course, by no means conclusive. Further research with explicitly longitudinal data is needed, so that we can "track" families actually undergoing "suburbanization." Nevertheless, from the resources at hand, it appears that urban nonwhites are severely constrained in their economic opportunities, regardless of where in the metropolis they reside. The implication is that there may be little to be gained from policies designed to rearrange the intrametropolitan spatial configuration of minority residences. In no part of the American city does the labor market "work" for nonwhites. In particular, there is no evidence to support the assertion that nonwhite economic opportunity in the suburbs is unambiguously greater than in the ghettos. Taken together with the widespread resistance of white suburbanites to residential integration through the construction of subsidized low-income housing, and educational integration through "busing"—a resistance which suggests that the social costs of enforced integration would be extremely high—one cannot react to these materials with anything other than the deepest pessimism about the potential effectiveness of policies for "suburban-izing" nonwhites in the urban ghetto. The known costs of such policies would be very great, and the expected benefits very small, at least in terms of employment opportunity.

11. John F. Kain, "The Big Cities' Big Problem," *Challenge*, September/October, 1966; reprinted in *Negroes and Jobs*, ed. Louis A. Ferman *et al.* (Ann Arbor, Mich.: University of Michigan Press, 1968), p. 243.

... our potential for solving underemployment among ghetto workers depends fundamentally on the capacity of programs for opening large numbers of "primary" jobs and guaranteeing opportunities in those jobs for disadvantaged workers [but] this is becoming increasingly impossible in the American economy. For a variety of critical historical reasons, the labor market is becoming increasingly segmented, avenues for internal job mobility are being restricted, and discrimination against demographically defined classes of workers has grown functionally more important.

— David M. Gordon

In large measure the American welfare state is a myth. The people at the bottom tend to survive because America is prosperous, not because it is just.

— Tom Hayden

5.

EDUCATION, POVERTY, AND THE THEORY OF THE DUAL LABOR MARKET

INTRODUCTION

Up to this point, we have been concerned with measuring the quantitative magnitudes of underemployment in the ghetto. It is time to place the findings of the previous chapters into some theoretical context. There are several competing contexts from which to choose.

Neoclassical explanations of unemployment and underemployment have, until very recently, been oriented almost entirely toward analysis of labor supply. During the 1950s, discussions of "structural unemployment" turned on the premise that certain kinds of labor (distinguished by ethnic origin, education, or location) were unable to respond "normally" when effective demand for goods and services was translated into derived demand for labor. Then,

> . . . as aggregate demand lowered unemployment and the structural hypothesis became less tenable as an explanation of high unemployment, the manpower training programs gradually shifted character and became anti-poverty programs. . . . They readily harmonized with the early puritan ethic of the war on poverty. Poverty was to be eliminated by raising everyone's marginal product to the level where [they] would be able to earn an acceptable income. Education and training programs were to be the principal means for raising marginal products . . . [i]ncreasing workers' human capital could eliminate poverty. . . . [1]

The author of the previous statement, Lester Thurow, is one of the most prominent members of the "human capital" school. His assessment is shared by Thomas Ribich, whose analysis of the relationship between education and poverty begins with the proposition that "a major presumption of the war on poverty is that education and training are especially effective ways to bring people out of poverty."[2]

But investments in the human capital of ghetto workers have not eliminated poverty. The results of the previous chapters of this monograph demonstrate a fundamental flaw in the conventional wisdom, and call for a revision of the current orthodoxy which asserts that poverty is a function of inadequate human capital.

POVERTY AND DISCRIMINATION

A few neoclassical economists have attempted a modest revision, according to which minority underemployment is explained by the "market imperfection"

1. Lester Thurow, "Raising Incomes through Manpower Training Programs," in *Contributions to the Analysis of Urban Problems*, ed. Anthony H. Pascal (Santa Monica, Cal.: RAND Corporation, August, 1968), document no. P-3868, pp. 91-92.

2. Thomas I. Ribich, *Education and Poverty* (Washington, D.C.: Brookings Institution, 1968), p. 1.

of racial discrimination.[3] These theorists have been criticized for attributing unrealistically calculated, marginalist decision-making behavior to discriminating employers, and for their inability or unwillingness to recognize that discrimination by employers takes place within the larger context of institutional racism throughout the economy.[4] Limited though they may be, however, the neoclassical studies are at least addressed to the "demand side" of the problem.

Gary Becker's analysis of discrimination is founded on the notion that every employer has his price for hiring blacks. "For each employer, for each job, there is a crucial wage differential which would make the hiring of a white and an equally qualified Negro a matter of indifference to him. This crucial wage differential, expressed as a ratio of the white wage, Becker calls the 'discrimination coefficient.' "[5] The market acts so as to cause the available supply of Negroes to be hired by employers with relatively low discrimination coefficients. The observed differential between Negro and white pay is the discrimination coefficient of the employer on the margin, the employer of Negroes who is most prejudiced against them. For Becker, in other words, discrimination takes place at the point of job entry. Thurow's approach is similar in placing the focus of discrimination within the firm which pays Negroes a wage discounted to take into account the employer's "psychic cost" of integrating his workforce.

For Barbara Bergmann, on the other hand, the focus is on those employers who will not hire blacks at any wage. This is the crowding hypothesis:

> The most important feature of an economy in which discrimination is practiced is the simple fact that some jobs are open to Negroes and some are not. The jobs open to Negroes are not a random selection, even allowing for Negroes' relatively lower education. They tend to be predominantly low in status, and to be concentrated very heavily in a few occupations. Following Donald Dewey, we might call this a "racial division of labor. . . . " Another major difference with the view of this paper is the identification of the villain of the piece. For Thurow, he is the man who

3. Cf. Kenneth J. Arrow, *Some Models of the Racial Discrimination in the Labor Market* (Santa Monica, Cal.: RAND Corporation, February, 1971), document no. RM–6253–RC; Gary S. Becker, *The Economics of Discrimination* (Chicago: University of Chicago Press, 1957); Barbara R. Bergmann, "The Effect on White Incomes of Discrimination in Employment," *Journal of Political Economy*, March/April 1971; Anne O. Krueger, "The Economies of Discrimination," *Journal of Political Economy*, October 1963; and Lester Thurow, *Poverty and Discrimination* (Washington, D.C.: Brookings Institution, 1969).
4. Cf. Raymond Franklin and Michael Tanzer, "Traditional Microeconomic Analysis of Racial Discrimination: A Critical View and Alternative Approach," in *Economics: Mainstream Readings and Radical Critiques*, ed. David Mermelstein (New York: Random House, 1970); Michael Reich, "Economic Theories of Racism," in *Problems in Political Economy: An Urban Perspective*, ed. David M. Gordon (Lexington, Mass.: D. C. Heath, 1971).
5. Bergmann, "Effect on White Incomes," p. 308.

hires Negroes and pays them low wages. Under the crowdedness hypothesis . . . the villain is the entrepreneur who will not hire Negroes, perhaps on behalf of or under pressure from his white workers. The entrepreneur who does hire Negroes acts towards them the way he is presumed to act towards any other factor of production: he pays them the price for which he can get them. The fact that the price for Negro labor is a lower price than he need pay white workers is attributable not to the entrepreneur who hires Negroes, but to the entrepreneur who refuses to do so, and so crowds them into the janitorships at low pay.[6]

Kenneth Arrow's analysis is similar to Bergmann's in emphasizing the significance of "corner" (i.e., either-or) solutions to the intrafirm (or intrashop) labor allocation decision.

The emphasis in this monograph has also been on minority workers, especially blacks, and we, too, have often spoken of racial discrimination. But this study has also shown that lower-class whites—those who still live in the central city poverty areas and "ghettos"—receive returns to their human capital which are substantially lower than the returns received by whites who have "escaped" the ghetto. Our analysis, in other words, leads us to hypothesize the existence of *class* as well as *race* discrimination.

Bradley Schiller has succeeded in making a quantitative distinction between the effects of class discrimination (with "class" defined by income stratum) and racial discrimination, as these are manifested through restricted access to educational and occupational opportunities.[7] Schiller estimates that, if working sons in black families enrolled in the Aid to Families with Dependent Children (AFDC) program could convert their inherited status[8] and their own years of schooling into occupational status at the same "rate" that poor (i.e., AFDC-enrolled) *white* sons do, they would gain 3.32 occupational status points (on the same ordinal scale of 0-100 used in the earlier chapters of this monograph). This is, therefore, a kind of measure of the extent of racial discrimination, holding "class" constant.

If poor white sons could convert *their* inherited status and their own education into occupational status at the same "rate" that *non-poor* white sons do, they would gain 2.74 status points. This is Schiller's measure of class discrimination, holding race constant.

Finally, if poor black sons could convert their inherited status and their own schooling into occupational status at the same "rate" that nonpoor white sons do, they would gain 5.66 status points. This is a measure of the *joint* effects of racial and class discrimination.

These findings require us to ask whether common structural characteristics of the economic system underlie both white and black poverty. If such is the

6. *Ibid.*, pp. 295, 310.
7. Bradley R. Schiller, "Class Discrimination vs. Racial Discrimination," *Review of Economics and Statistics*, August 1971.
8. Defined by parental occupation and education.

case, then neither appeals to racial justice nor coercive antidiscrimination policies will be sufficient to eliminate poverty. As Barry Bluestone observes,

[W]hile particular individuals now denied high-wage jobs may benefit from a removal of market barriers, low-wage jobs will still exist. At best, increased mobility will distribute workers more "fairly" over the existing set of jobs. . . . Some black workers will exchange places with some white workers in the occupational hierarchy and some women will replace men, but increased mobility will *not*, in general, increase the number of high-wage jobs or reduce the number of jobs at poverty wages.[9]

This important proposition has received some support from Ms. Bergmann's study of the income effects of occupational "crowding." Under varying assumptions about the rate of growth of national income, the elimination of occupational discrimination by race would (according to the Bergmann equations) cause a 6-9 percent reduction in the incomes of white men lacking an eighth grade diploma—a group which constitutes 14 percent of all adult white men in the United States. The displacement of white women would be even greater. Even high school graduates would be affected to some extent. For both sexes, the conflict becomes greater the less substitutable we assume capital, white workers, and nonwhite workers to be in production.[10] These calculations imply that the oft-times vocal opposition of lower-class white ethnic groups to government programs designed to expand job opportunities for blacks is—in an economy such as ours—not without some rationale.

Confronting the facts of class conflict and continued poverty in the United States, even after a decade in which "the federal government directed between $140 and $170 billion in aid to the poor,"[11] a small (but growing) number of young economists have begun to develop an alternative theory—what David Gordon (after Thomas Kuhn) calls a new "paradigm"[12]—to explain these phenomena.

Some of this new research to which I have alluded has grown out of what began as fairly pedestrian evaluations of various training and education programs connected with the federal "war on poverty." These studies frequently showed that training programs had little positive effect on the work situation of the poor. Enrollees in such programs typically earned no higher wages after

9. Barry Bluestone, "The Tripartite Economy: Labor Markets and the Working Poor," *Poverty and Human Resources*, July/August 1970, pp. 23-24.
10. "Although the groups of whites which can be designated as suffering nontrivial damage do not change when we change the assumption about the elasticity of substitution of factors in production, the degree of damage to whites does vary. At low elasticities of substitution, the damage to whites is greater." Bergmann, "Effect on White Incomes," p. 304.
11. Bluestone, "Tripartite Economy," p. 15.
12. David M. Gordon, *Theories of Poverty and Underemployment* (Lexington, Mass.: Heath-Lexington Books, 1972). Gordon builds upon an excellent history of science by Thomas S. Kuhn, *The Structure of Scientific Revolutions* (Chicago: University of Chicago Press, 1962).

graduation than before undertaking training. Many refused to take the programs seriously at all, remaining in them for short periods of time, earning small training stipends, and then dropping out. In fact, many enrollees told evaluators frankly that they thought of the manpower training system in the same way they thought of any other form of low wage, marginal activity: as a temporary source of income, a place to go for short periods of time to supplement family income. They entertained little hope or expectation of actually acquiring decent permanent employment as a result of their participation in the program.

At about the same time, other researchers discovered an important flaw in the conventional wisdom about welfare recipients. It was popularly held that there exists in the economy a large, permanent "welfare class," consisting of individuals and families who themselves remain on the relief rolls for long periods of time and who not infrequently raise their children to become similarly dependent on public assistance. The researchers found, instead, that people tended to move on and off the welfare rolls, over and over again, in a fashion reminiscent of the behavior of the manpower trainees. The analogy was reinforced by the publication in 1967 of the BLS Lower Level Urban Family Budgets, which showed clearly that families in even the richest states whose incomes derived entirely from welfare would be "enjoying" a seriously deficient standard of living. High turnover and low rates of income seemed to characterize both of our major antipoverty programs.

Anecdotal accounts of the extent to which the urban poor are forced to depend for part of their livelihood on illegal or other "irregular" activities have been available at least since the publication of the autobiographies of Claude Brown, Eldridge Cleaver, and Malcolm X.[13] Gradually, economists and sociologists began to realize that these activities were themselves organized into "markets," and that—given the unalterable constraint of the 24-hour day—ghetto workers might logically be assumed to allocate part of their labor time to "work" in the irregular market at the expense of time spent in other forms of income-bearing activity. When the structure of this "market" was explored, it was quickly found to be characterized by high turnover, unstable participation, and (after accounting for the high risks involved) relatively low average "wages." The similarity to the training and welfare "markets" was unmistakable—and quite dramatic.

Even before these discoveries were made, a few scholars had documented the existence and magnitude of "working poverty." In 1966, more than 7.3 million men and women in America were labor force participants and yet were poor.[14] In 1968, 1.3 million family heads worked thirty-five hours per

13. Claude Brown, *Manchild in the Promised Land* (New York: Signet, 1965); Eldridge Cleaver, *Post-Prison Writings and Speeches* (New York: Random House, A Ramparts Book, 1969); Malcolm X, *The Autobiography of Malcolm X* (New York: Grove Press, 1966).

14. Harold L. Sheppard, *The Nature of the Job Problem and The Role of New Public Service Employment* (Kalamazoo, Mich.: The W. E. Upjohn Institute, January, 1969), p. 4.

week, fifty weeks a year, but still earned less than $3,500, (then) the official poverty line; 1.6 million part-time working family heads were also poor.[15] In terms of the much higher (but hardly luxurious) BLS Lower Level Urban Family Budget, the incidence of working poverty was considerably greater: perhaps a third of all American families and 40 percent of the labor force had incomes in 1967 which fell below the BLS "minimum" budget standard.[16] These workers occupied a class of jobs which bore precisely the characteristics found to be associated with the abovementioned nonlabor market activities: low pay and high turnover. Moreover, evaluations of government institutions designed to place low-income workers into "good" jobs concluded that these placement programs were succeeding only in recirculating the poor among the very low-paying, unstable jobs which they already held.

Thus, a substantial number of seemingly disparate work activities and public programs were found to share certain important commonalities. Could these interrelationships be systematic? And if so, how did these various poverty income level activities relate to the conventional American mode of family support: nonpoverty wage labor? These are some of the questions that have led to the development of the germ of a new labor market theory, often referred to as the "theory of the dual economy" or the "theory of labor marked segmentation."[17]

THE "CORE" OF THE ECONOMY

Dual market analysts believe the economy to be segmented into what Barry Bluestone calls a "core" and a "periphery" (see figure 24). The division is functional and not simply semantic; workers, employers, and even the underlying technologies in the two segments behave very differently in important qualitative ways. The central institution of the "core" has been called the "primary labor market," and this is the part of the core which we shall study here.[18] In the primary labor market, the attributes of jobs and the behavioral

15. U.S. Department of Labor, *1970 Manpower Report of the President* (Washington, D.C.: Govt. Prtg. Off., 1970), pp. 121–22. Barry Bluestone notes that the Census Bureau's sexist designation of families with working wives and unemployed husbands as "families with an unemployed head of household" tends to understate the number of working poor household heads.

16. In 1967, one-third of all families earned less than the $6,000 BLS family standard. The median number of full-time earners per family was 1.2. The equivalent BLS standard for individuals is therefore $5,000. In 1967, two-fifths of all persons earned less than $5,000. By 1970, the BLS standard had risen to about $7,000, and the full-time-equivalent family LFPR per families below this level was only 0.88. With these parameters, it was the case in 1970 that 48.7 percent of those who worked at all during that year had substandard earnings—27.2 million workers. If we count only those who worked 35 hours a week or more for 50–52 weeks, the proportion earning beneath the standard of minimum decency was 30.1 percent: 10.9 million people.

17. For a good working bibliography on economic dualism in the American context, see the references cited in Gordon, *Theories of Poverty*; and in Bennett Harrison, "Human Capital, Black Poverty, and 'Radical' Economics," *Industrial Relations*, October 1971.

18. Some of the other interlocking institutions in the core include the schools that prepare people to work in the primary labor market, the financial intermediaries which

Figure 24

The Dual Economy

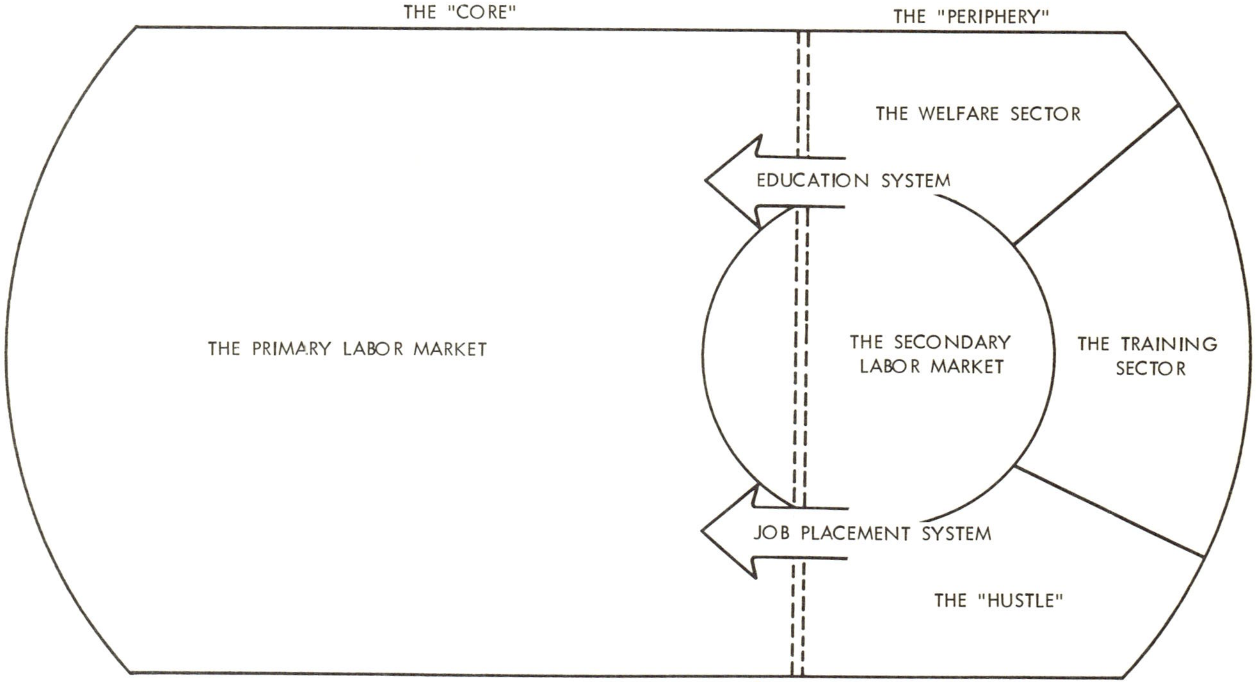

THE "CORE"

THE "PERIPHERY"

THE WELFARE SECTOR

THE TRAINING SECTOR

EDUCATION SYSTEM

THE SECONDARY LABOR MARKET

THE PRIMARY LABOR MARKET

JOB PLACEMENT SYSTEM

THE "HUSTLE"

traits of workers interact (e.g., by mutual reinforcement) to produce a structure characterized by high productivity, nonpoverty wages, and employment
stability.

The high productivity of primary labor is a function not only of the
knowledge and skills (i.e., the "human capital") of the workers, but also (and
perhaps more fundamentally) of the capital equipment with which they
generally work. The market power of the typical primary firm, and the
relatively high degree of profitability which is the usual corollary of such
power, enable the employer to invest in modern capital equipment (frequently embodying "leading edge" technologies), to maintain that equipment, and to replace it when necessary. The same factors make it possible for
such firms to invest in the "human capital" of their employees, so that the
equipment will be used efficiently. While this is, of course, an ideal construct,
it does seem to be broadly descriptive of the technical conditions of production in the leading, highly concentrated industries in the American economy,
and provides a plausible (albeit partial) explanation of the relatively high
average productivity of the core of the American labor force.[19]

Primary employers typically pay nonpoverty wages. This may be partly
explained by the aforementioned high average and marginal productivity of
core labor, but most dual market theorists prefer a more institutional explanation. The very economic power which underlies the profits which enable
primary employers to make productivity-enhancing investments also permits
them to pass along a share of wage (and other cost) increases to their cus-
tomers. In other words, their oligopoly position *permits* them to maintain
nonpoverty wage levels without seriously eroding their profit margins. At the
same time, the economic power of concentrated primary industries has
induced the organization of what John Kenneth Galbraith calls "countervail-
ing power" by labor unions. The evidence on how unions have affected the
American wage structure is surprisingly ambiguous; there is, however, no
question about the ability of unions to prevent employers from paying
poverty-level wages.

---

fund the activities of primary employers, and the federal government which serves as a
Keynesian "regulator," of aggregate demand and—more recently—as guarantor of demand
through direct contracts. See Robert Averitt, *The Dual Economy* (New York: W. W.
Norton, 1968); John Kenneth Galbraith, *The New Industrial State* (New York: Houghton Mifflin, 1967); and Herbert Gintis, "Repressive Schooling as Productive Schooling,"
in Gordon, *Problems in Political Economy.* We shall have more to say about the role of
the education system at the end of this section.

19. According to Michael Tanzer, "the degree of discrimination against Negroes of
either sex is highly correlated with the job structure of the industry. Specifically, the
greater the proportion of total jobs in an industry which are laborer jobs, the greater the
proportion of Negroes found in the industry as a whole and in each occupational job
category separately." Franklin and Tanzer, "Traditional Microeconomic Analysis,"
p. 120*n.* In other words, labor-intensive industries tend to employ nonwhites—both ag-
gregatively and in many different positions—while capital-intensive industries are less
likely to do either.

There is an important feedback mechanism at work here. In conventional ("neoclassical") price theory, profit-maximizing employers are assumed to hire workers up to the point where the wage rate is equal to the value of the marginal product of labor: the contribution of the last worker hired to the firm's revenue. Some economists believe that the relationship between wages and productivity is more complex, that (in particular) work effort (and therefore measured productivity) may well be an increasing function of wages.[20] If this view is correct, then the relatively high wages which primary employers are able to pay (and which primary unions "encourage" them to pay) in turn induce the productivity increases by labor which (coming full circle) generate the revenues out of which those nonpoverty wages are paid.

Workers in the primary labor market tend to be relatively stable.[21] There are at least three plausible explanations of why primary employers value workforce stability. First, their investments in the "specific training" of their workers—training highly specific to the particular conditions of this particular firm (or plant) and not easily transferred to other work environments—represents a "sunk cost" which they naturally wish to recoup. Workers who quit before repaying this investment in the form of contributions to output must be replaced, and the replacements must then be trained. In the primary labor market, turnover is *obviously* expensive and therefore undesirable from the point of view of the employer.

A second and somewhat more controversial explanation has to do with the development within large firms of what Doeringer and Piore call the "internal labor market."[22] During the 1950s, economists discovered that large corporations had developed internal capital "markets" in the form of large pools of retained earnings, the existence of which helped to insulate them from the periodic increases in the external cost of capital[23] (and, as it turns out, from

20. Cf. Harvey Leibenstein, *Economic Backwardness and Economic Growth* (New York: Wiley-Science Editions, 1963), pp. 62–69. This is one of the earliest discussions of "the interesting possibility that the energy level of a tenant or worker rises as his income rises." At a more aggregative level, a recent United Nations study developed "social profiles" for developing countries, composed of indicators of nutrition, education, health, housing, and leisure. The researchers found that "those developing countries which had a favorable social profile in the early 1950's also tended to show more rapid economic growth in the following ten years." Salvatore Schiavo-Campo and Hans W. Singer, *Perspectives of Economic Development* (New York: Houghton Mifflin, 1970), pp. 76–78. It is not at all uncharacteristic of the dual labor market theory that some of its roots are to be found in studies of the Third World.

21. "The most important characteristic distinguishing jobs in the primary sector from those in the secondary sector appears to be the behavioral requirements which they impose upon the work force, particularly that of employment stability." Michael J. Piore, "The Dual Labor Market: Theory and Implications," in Gordon, *Problems in Political Economy*, p. 91.

22. Peter B. Doeringer and Michael J. Piore, *Internal Labor Markets and Manpower Analysis* (Lexington, Mass.: D. C. Heath, 1971).

23. John R. Meyer and Edwin Kuh, *The Investment Decision* (Cambridge, Mass.: Harvard University Press, 1957). See also Galbraith, *New Industrial State*; and Robin Marris, *The Economic Theory of Managerial Capitalism* (Glencoe, Ill.: Free Press, 1964).

government anti-inflationary monetary policy as well). With large stocks of internal capital, firms could engage in long-run capacity expansion plans without having to concern themselves with changes in interest rates. During normal times, investment capital could be borrowed as usual. When interest rates rose (perhaps through government policy designed to slow down corporate investment in new plant and equipment), the firm could turn to its internal capital "market," thereby enabling the "plan" to continue. Doeringer and Piore believe that a similar process has now developed within large corporations with respect to labor as well as capital. Firms can go into the external labor market at times when conditions (such as excess supply) favor the firm in the wage-bargaining process (an obvious example is the extent to which corporations flood college campuses at graduation time each year). Since the employer-employee relation in the core of the economy is often characterized by the use of fairly long-term contracts, firms can then retain (or "hoard") this relatively cheaply bought labor against those times when external labor is more expensive. Such internal labor markets are, therefore, institutional manifestations of the employers' desire for workforce stability.

A third explanation of firms' demand for stability is derived from the work of Kenneth Arrow, who observed that most of what workers learn about the equipment and systems with which they work is probably really learned "on-the-job"; it is "learning by doing."[24] The more complex the job, i.e., the more intricate or subtle the technology and the equipment, the longer it takes the average worker to "learn" the job and to reach the point where—for all practical purposes—he has obtained his peak of efficiency. The concept is illustrated by figure 25, where the typical "learning curve" is represented by a logistic. However "productivity" is measured, the important question is: for any given job, how long does it take the average worker to reach his or her maximum efficiency? Is the concept of an asymptotic maximum (a limit to individual) efficiency meaningful for that job? If so, is the average learning period three weeks, three months, or three years? Consider the contrast between keypunch operators and computer operators. Both are very nearly unskilled (or at best semi-skilled) jobs (student computer operators are often trained by their colleges in a week). Any upper limit to the potential productivity of a computer operator is undoubtedly quite "high," so varied are the technical possibilities for performing the highly discretionary tasks associated with this job, e.g., filing, classifying and retrieving tapes, learning to take advantage of the capabilities of a system with respect to the batching of "jobs," discovering and accommodating oneself to the idiosyncracies of one's fellow operators. Contrast this with keypunch operators who—like clerk-typists—tend increasingly to be organized into large workpools and whose maximum efficiency is essentially determined by their

24. Kenneth Arrow, "The Economic Implications of Learning-by-Doing," *Review of Economic Studies*, June 1962.

Figure 25

Hypothetical Learning Curves in the Primary Labor Market

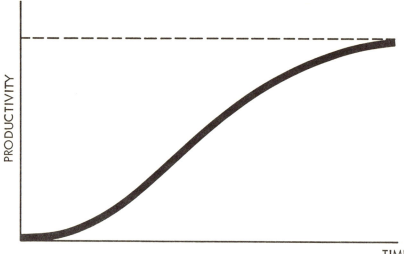

physical dexterity and the capacity of their machines. Once such workers reach their maximum punching (or typing) speed, continued tenure is unlikely to lead to significant improvements (and may very well lead to the opposite, as the job becomes "routine"). An even more dramatic contrast exists between the clerk-typist and the executive secretary. The latter may literally never "peak out"; he or she has to learn not only the mechanics of the job, but also be continually in the process of acquiring such subtle skills as the ability to locate the boss's business (and perhaps even extra-business) associates at any hour of the day at any of their favorite haunts. Clearly, it is to the employer's advantage to retain an employee whose capacity for improvement has not been exhausted.

At the same time, workers in most primary jobs seem to *want* to remain in those jobs (at least for a noticeably longer period than is the case for what we will later call "secondary workers." This is admittedly somewhat vague; while the threshold between "primary" and "secondary" wages seems to have been quantitatively identified—at from $1.75 to $3.50 per hour—very little quantitative work has yet to be performed on the tenure variable). The jobs pay relatively well, and employers (as we have seen) encourage the workers to stay. This stability of the workforce feeds back into the wage-bargaining process. Stable workers are more easily organized, and unions generally prefer to organize stable rather than unstable workers (perhaps because of the obvious consequences for strike funds, etc.). To the extent that this unionization is successful, it reinforces the maintenance of nonpoverty wages (as described earlier), which, in turn, induces the continued stability which, in turn, supports unionization, ad infinitum.

Efficient operation of the primary labor market requires the development of certain behavioral attitudes on the part of workers and employers, attitudes which it is the purpose of such social institutions as the educational system to inculcate. Herbert Gintis, referring to the literature which we surveyed in Chapter One, writes:

> Economists have long noted the relationship between the level of schooling in workers and their earnings.... Almost no attempt has been made, however, to determine the mechanism by which education affects earnings or productivity. In the absence of any direct evidence, it is commonly assumed that the main effect of schooling is to raise the level of cognitive development of students and that it is this increase which explains the relationship between schooling and earnings. This view of the schooling-earnings linkage has provided the conceptual framework for studies which seek to "control" for the quality of schooling through the use of variables such as scores on achievement tests and I.Q.
>
> The objective of this paper is to demonstrate that this interpretation is fundamentally incorrect.[25]

Instead, Gintis believes that "schools affect earnings" by creating an internal "social structure" whose "authority, motivational, and interpersonal relations" are designed to replicate "those of the factory and office." One of the most important instruments of this social development process is the grading system which, quite apart from (and beyond) its ostensible function of measuring cognitive ability, affords "independent reward to the development of traits necessary to adequate job performance."[26] Samuel Bowles has uncovered evidence that eighteenth and nineteenth century manufacturers consciously supported public education as a means of teaching young people (at public expense) discipline, punctuality, acceptance of outside authority, and individual accountability—behavioral traits crucial for the efficient operation of the factory system.[27]

Taken alone, there is nothing either novel or obviously pathological about these observations. Schools prepare students—behaviorally as well as technically—for the "world of work"; every manpower training agent and antipoverty warrior takes this for granted. The problem, according to Gintis, is that society and its individual members pay a very high price for the "prevo-

25. Herbert Gintis, "Education, Technology, and the Characteristics of Worker Productivity," *American Economic Review: Proceedings*, May 1971, p. 266.

26. *Ibid.*, p. 267.

27. Samuel Bowles, "Unequal Education and the Reproduction of the Social Division of Labor," *Review of Radical Political Economics*, Fall 1971; reprinted in *Schooling in a Corporate Society: The Political Economy of Education and the Alternatives before Us*, ed. Martin Carnoy (New York: David McKay, 1972).

cational training" which schools provide for primary employers. "The economic productivity of schooling is due primarily to the inculcation of personality characteristics which may be generally agreed to be inhibiting of personal development." Gintis analyzes a rich body of data on "649 upper-ability senior high school males (National Merit Scholarship Finalists)" who were scored on five achievement variables (e.g., scientific performance, humanities comprehension) and sixty-five personality variables, and a second group of 114 high school seniors "of varying ability." The measures of achievement were then correlated with the measures of personality. Gintis found that "schooling is conducive to the development of [those] traits . . . requisite for adequate job functioning in production characterized by bureaucratic order and hierarchical control." Personality traits such as perseverance, self-control, suppression of aggression, and deferred gratification were positively correlated with achievement scores. But the data also showed that "students are uniformly penalized for creativity, autonomy, initiative, tolerance for ambiguity, and independence, even after correcting for achievement."[28] From these results, and from the inference that "successful" students and workers even in the core of the economy must have learned to suppress their most creative and deeply human personality traits in order to *be* successful, Gintis concludes that "the 'economic productivity' of schooling must be measured against an 'opportunity cost' reflected in the development of an alienated and repressed labor force."[29]

THE "PERIPHERY" OF THE ECONOMY

The so-called periphery of the American economy is assumed to consist of at least four "segments," the manpower characteristics of which are remarkably similar to one another (figure 24). Mobility among these segments seems to take place regularly, while (by contrast) workers in the peripheral stratum are able to move into the core of the economy only very infrequently.

The "Secondary Labor Market." Research—much of it concerned with the study of ghetto labor markets[30]—has indicated the existence of a class of jobs

28. Gintis, "Worker Productivity," pp. 273–74.
29. *Ibid.*, p. 267. Bowles has posited a theory which integrates Gintis's conception of the function of schooling with the model of labor market segmentation and the findings on class discrimination. According to this theory, schools "reproduce" (i.e., preserve) class cultures from generation to generation. Labor markets then "translate" these differences in class culture into income inequalities and occupational hierarchies which in turn determine which schools the children of workers will be able to attend. See Bowles, "Unequal Education." We shall make use of this theory later, in the discussion of the role of public education as an instrument of mobility between the core and the periphery of the economy.
30. Cf. Peter B. Doeringer, with Penny Feldman, David M. Gordon, Michael J. Piore, and Michael Reich, "Low-Income Labor Markets and Urban Manpower Programs: A Critical Assessment," mimeographed (Washington, D.C.: U.S. Department of Labor,

which contrast sharply with the primary labor market along each of the three dimensions we have discussed.

Secondary workers tend to display relatively low average and marginal productivity. Until recently, one explanation for this was the dearth of "human capital" (particularly formal education of at least average quality) possessed by these workers. While this continues to provide a partial explanation, it is becoming increasingly less convincing as even ghetto blacks gradually close the education gap between themselves and the average American. By 1970, the gap between the median schooling of young whites and blacks had fallen to less than half a year, as the following figures show:

	Median Years of School Completed	
Age	Blacks	Whites
20–21 years	12.4	12.8
22–24	12.3	12.7
25–29	12.2	12.6
30–34	12.0	12.5

Source: U.S. Department of Commerce, Bureau of the Census, *Current Population Reports*, Series P–23, no. 38 (BLS Report No. 394), "The Social and Economic Status of Negroes in the United States, 1970" (Washington, D.C.: Govt. Prtg. Off., 1971), Table 65.

In any case, the importance of formal education in determining worker productivity is itself now in some doubt, as we have seen. Probably more important is the absence of economic power in this segment of the periphery of the economy. With little or no oligopolistic market control, and with small profit margins, secondary firms tend to use more antiquated capital which, of course, tends to diminish productivity. Finally, the jobs themselves often do not *require* skills of any great consequence, involving instead the kind of routine unskilled tasks which attract (and at the same time reinforce the lifestyles of) casual laborers.

Workers in the secondary labor market receive, and firms in this stratum of the economy pay, very low wages. During the period July, 1968, to June, 1969, 37 percent of the black and 51 percent of the Puerto Rican male household heads living in Harlem and working at least thirty-five hours a week, fifty weeks a year averaged less than $100 per week in earnings. Nationally, in 1966, 36.3 percent of all employees working in nursing homes and related facilities earned less than $1.60 per hour, the legal minimum wage. For employees of laundry and cleaning services, fertilizer manufac-

Manpower Administration, January 1969); Thomas Vietorisz and Bennett Harrison, *The Economic Development of Harlem* (New York: Praeger, 1970); and other references cited in Gordon and Harrison (cited in n. 17 in this chapter).

turers, eating and drinking places, gasoline service stations, and retail food stores, the 1966 percentages were 75.4 percent, 41.7 percent, 79.4 percent, 66.7 percent, and 47.6 percent, respectively.[31] Annual wage income is the product of an average wage *rate* and the number of hours, days or weeks during the year in which a person works. The instability of secondary labor (discussed shortly) drives down the duration of work, while the economic structure of the peripheral firm causes it to pay a low wage rate. Taken together, these factors guarantee that workers will be forced to subsist on a poverty-level income—to the extent that they rely for income entirely on what they can earn in the secondary labor market. Low productivity contributes to the explanation of these low wages, but so does the lack of market power among peripheral employers. Moreover (as indicated earlier), dual labor market theorists believe that these factors are interdependent; the marginal firm, by paying low wages and by not providing its workers with adequate complementary capital, discourages its labor force from taking those actions or developing those attitudes which would lead to increased productivity which, if capitalized, could increase the firm's capacity to pay higher wages. The lack of economic power which characterizes peripheral firms (as reflected, for example, in the relatively high elasticity of their output demand curves) also makes it impossible for them to raise wages and other input costs without eroding profit margins, often to the shutdown point. Finally, the low wages found in the secondary labor market are partly the result of the relative simplicity of the technologies in secondary industries: since skill requirements are minimal, the opportunity cost of secondary labor is low, given the large pool of readily available substitutable workers out "on the street."

While the primary labor market is characterized by a mutual employer-employee "taste" for stability, both firms and workers in the secondary labor market seem to benefit from unstable workforce behavior. That secondary labor is significantly more unstable than primary labor is incontestable. Robert Hall, for example, writes:

> Some groups exhibit what seems to be pathological instability in holding jobs. Changing from one low-paying, unpleasant job to another, often several times a year, is the typical pattern of some workers. The resulting unemployment can hardly be said to be the outcome of a normal process of career advancement. The true problem of hard-core unemployment is that a certain fraction of the labor force accounts for a disproportionate share of unemployment because they drift from one unsatisfactory job to another, spending the time between jobs either unemployed or out of the labor force. [Where they go when they drop out of the labor force will be discussed later.] The most compact evidence in favor of the hypothesis that such a group exists is provided by the data on the number of spells of unemployment experienced by the labor force. Among those who were unemployed at some time in 1968, sixty-nine percent had only one spell

31. Bluestone, "Tripartite Economy," p. 25.

of unemployment, fifteen percent had two spells and sixteen percent had three or more. Now the overall unemployment rate in 1968 was 3.6 percent. Suppose that the average person changing jobs required one month to find a satisfactory new job. Then the average duration between spells of unemployment would be about twenty-seven months. In order to have two, much less three, spells of unemployment in the same twelve months, an individual could hardly be making normal changes in jobs, even if it is true that the normal person changes jobs every twenty-eight months. Yet almost a third of those unemployed at all in 1968, more than three million individuals, had two or more spells. The existence of this group is surely a matter of social concern.[32]

In their studies of the hard-core unemployed in St. Louis, Edward Kalachek and his colleagues concluded that "the relatively high rates of unemployment experienced by St. Louis Negroes appear to be more the result of frequent job changes than of the inability to find employment. . . . Job stability develops and unemployment experiences diminish among older workers with dependents. . . . For our sample, however, the stabilizing influence of age was not discernible until respondents were in their early 30's."[33] The researchers tested for differential work attitudes and values between the young blacks who were their principal object of study and control groups of other workers.

A number of respondents, particularly young men in the fifteen to eighteen years of age category, admitted to engaging in nonlegitimate "hustles." . . . Still, like other younger members of the study population [such individuals] clearly see the value of jobs and education. . . . The high quit rates of young Negroes appear due not to a deviant value system, but to the frustration of low-wage-paying jobs. . . . Younger workers appear less willing or able to accept poverty level wages when they perceive the value system of the "American Dream" to be promising more.[34]

Secondary employers have several reasons for placing a low value on turnover, in sharp contrast to their fellows in the primary labor market. They can, as a rule, neither afford, nor do their technologies require them, to invest heavily in "specific training." Instead, they tend to rely on the "general training" (e.g., literacy, basic arithmetic) provided socially. With minimal investment in their current labor force, and given the ready availability of substitute labor outside the firm, such employers are at the very least indifferent to the rate of turnover. Moreover, these firms lack the size and wealth necessary for the development of internal labor markets. Nor have they any

---

32. Robert E. Hall, "Why is Unemployment So High at Full Employment?" *Brookings Papers on Economic Activity* (Washington, D.C.: Brookings Institution, 1970), no. 3, pp. 389–90.
33. Edward D. Kalachek and John M. Goering, eds., "Transportation and Central City Unemployment," Institute for Urban and Regional Studies, Washington University, Working Paper INS 5, March 1970, p. 8.
34. *Ibid.*, pp. 8–9.

reason to want to develop such institutions; since their skill requirements are minimal, they are unlikely to encounter periods where the labor they need is scarce and therefore expensive to recruit through conventional ("external") labor markets. Finally, everything we have hypothesized about the technology of secondary industries implies that the typical job is easily and quickly learned, so that learning curves probably look more like that depicted in figure 26 than that shown in figure 25. We have already discussed some of the implications of the shape of this function. It may be added at this point that to keep a worker employed for an extended period usually requires the granting of raises in pay and various employee benefits. Moreover, there is a definite correlation between labor force stability and the probability of that force being organized. It follows that employers who already have little to lose (in terms of foregone output) by discouraging long tenure of specific workers will have still other rational reasons for discounting stability.

Workers, for their part, seem similarly to have a rational preference for instability in the secondary labor market. The jobs are boring, and do not pay well. Employers seem not to mind—and perhaps even to encourage—casual attitudes toward work. The penalties for poor industrial discipline are generally not severe. Doeringer's studies of antipoverty programs in Boston led him to conclude that the job placement system for ghetto workers was seldom able to refer its clients to jobs paying more than they were earning before—"only $2.00 an hour or less." This lack of upward mobility in the placement system contributes to the poor work habits and weak job attachment of the "hard-to-employ":

> The availability of alternative low-wage job opportunities and the unattractiveness of such low-wage work interact to discourage the formation of strong ties to particular employers.[35]

That low wages are the principal motivating factor seems to be confirmed by the finding that, "for wage rates higher than the 'prevailing' ghetto wage, disadvantaged workers are more likely to be stable employees than other workers." These relationships between tenure and wage rates were found, at best, to be only weakly related to the educational attainment of the workers. And, of course, this entirely rational instability frustrates union organization so that there is no pressure for change, e.g., improvement in wages and working conditions—pressure which has been institutionalized in the core of the economy.

Thus, where primary employers and employees interact in an institutional setting characterized by high productivity, nonpoverty level wages and high workforce stability, the firms and workforces in the secondary labor market

---

35. Peter B. Doeringer, "Ghetto Labor Markets—Problems and Programs," Program on Regional and Urban Economics, Discussion Paper no. 35 (mimeographed, Harvard University, May 1968), pp. 10–11.

Figure 26

Hypothetical Learning Curves in the Secondary Labor Market

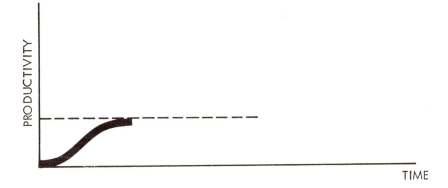

TIME

tend to organize themselves into production systems displaying low productivity, poverty level wages and low stability (high turnover). It is interesting to observe that what appeared to be "subemployment" or "underemployment" from the conventional perspective of an essentially unified economy (cf. Chapter Three) is now seen to be the normal mode of employment in a segment of that economy, a sector cut off from the mainstream.

How large *is* the secondary labor market? Definitive numbers await the development of more precise, quantitatively verified definitions of the boundaries between the "primary" and "secondary" sectors of the economy. By the criterion of wages alone—and using the BLS's standard of "adequacy"—40 percent or more of the jobs in urban America are substandard (see page 123). In an ingenious (if still tentative) quantitative analysis, David Gordon has developed a dichotomization of lists of "jobs" (specific industry-occupation combinations) in which hourly wages, annual incomes, and occupational status are held constant, and workers are stratified along a vector of other dual labor market characteristics, including stability (weeks worked per year, hours worked per week), commitment toward present job, job search techniques, and sex. This technique allows Gordon to identify two sets of "jobs" with the property that lifetime mobility is *far* greater within sets than across them. In non-ghetto Detroit, for example, there were 418 "jobs" (representing 3,516 workers) common to both the "present-job" and "first-job-out-of-school" data sets (workers interviewed by the Census Bureau had been asked to identify both their current and their first job). Among the present jobs, 52.2 percent were "primary," while 47.8 percent were "secondary." Among the first jobs, the estimates were 49.1 percent and 50.9 percent, respectively. Three hundred forty-three jobs (82.1 percent of the total) were labelled the same way both times. These 343 jobs covered 85.5 percent of the workers in the Detroit data set.[36] A small sample of the segmentation scheme developed by Gordon for Detroit is shown below:

Industry	Primary Labor Market	Secondary Labor Market
Manufactured durables	Cranemen, derrickmen Mechanics Filers, graders Polishers, welders Flame-cutters Laborers	Radio & TV mechanics Warehousemen
Manufactured nondurables	Craftsmen	
Construction	Painters Cement and concrete finishers	
Transportation	Officials Administrators	Packers and Wrappers
Wholesale trade	Truck drivers	Laborers
Retail trade	Managers, officials Proprietors Electricians Inspectors	Secretaries Housekeepers Bookkeepers
Business and repair services	Auto mechanics	Office machine operators Clerical workers Photo process workers
Entertainment		Waiters, waitresses Ushers
Real estate	Managers Building supervisors	

36. David M. Gordon, "Class, Productivity, and the Ghetto" (Ph.D. dissertation, Harvard University, 1971), chap. 4. Formally, Gordon examined a large set of variables for each of four samples of workers (nonghetto Detroit—present job of sample workers; nonghetto Detroit—first job; ghetto New York—present job; ghetto New York—first job. The data come from the 1969 UES). The workers were allocated among a large number of specific industry-occupation combinations, or "jobs." For each variable, an average was computed for each of these industry-occupation cells. First-order correlation coefficients were then calculated; for example,

$$r_{\text{hourly wage } (\bar{w}),\ \text{annual income } (\bar{y})}$$

$\bar{y}_{\text{job 1}}$	$\bar{w}_{\text{job 1}}$
$\bar{y}_{\text{job 2}}$	$\bar{w}_{\text{job 2}}$
$\vdots$	$\vdots$
$\bar{y}_{\text{job n}}$	$\bar{w}_{\text{job n}}$

The "Welfare Economy." The principle conclusion to be drawn from the previous description of the secondary labor market is that it is virtually impossible for an individual confined to that segment of the periphery to earn a living. This simple fact motivates the supply of part of the peripheral worker's time and effort to other income-bearing activities. The most obvious (or at least the most widely publicized) of these alternative "activities" is to "go on welfare." According to the Manpower Administration of the USDL,

> Another possible alternative to low-wage, irregular jobs for some slum residents, especially women with children but no husbands to help in family support, is public assistance. The division of the poor between those with jobs and those depending on welfare is by no means stable or clear cut. Women may receive assistance in some months of the year and work in other months, or they may be on welfare and at the same time work openly or covertly.[37]

> Recipients [of Aid to Families with Dependent Children] have been widely regarded as caught in a chronic, static condition of dependency, handed down from one generation to the next. Welfare has been viewed as an alternative to work, increasingly unrelated to such economic factors as the general level of unemployment or the participation of women in the labor force. . . . But there are also many families whose members are on welfare rolls for very short periods of time and never sever their connection with the labor force, even when they are on welfare.[38]

There is substantial evidence that many people on welfare display much the same kind of turnover found in the secondary labor market. In 1960 and 1961, for example, "about 35 percent of the then current recipients had previously received public assistance" at least once before. By 1967, "the

---

A factor analysis was performed on the correlation matrices for each of the four samples. The first (maximum variance-reducing) factor loaded on (consisted of a linear combination of) monetary and job status variables. A second factor loaded significantly on a set of stability and job commitment variables. When the original data observations were "plugged" back into the factors in order to calculate factor "scores" (values of the linear combinations), the first factor yielded continuous and right-skewed distributions for all four samples, precisely what we would expect from income distribution theory. The second factor, however, yielded *bi-modally* distributed scores in all four samples, a powerful discovery fully consistent with dual labor market theory but difficult to reconcile with the neoclassical paradigm. Gordon divided the distributions into two segments according to where they crossed (see especially p. 366); jobs in the left (lower-scoring) segment were termed "secondary," while jobs in the right (higher-scoring) segment were considered to be "primary" jobs. As Gordon himself indicates, the analysis is far from completely satisfactory. Nevertheless, Gordon's model represents the first—and may remain the best—attempt to quantify rigorously the boundaries of the segments into which urban jobs are thought to be divided.

37. U.S. Department of Labor, *1971 Manpower Report of the President* (Washington, D.C.: Govt. Prtg. Off., 1971), p. 97.

38. U.S. Department of Labor, *1968 Manpower Report of the President* (Washington, D.C.: Govt. Prtg. Off., 1968), p. 96.

proportion may have been as high as 40 percent."[39] In 1966, about 12 percent of the AFDC cases closed in that year were closed because of the employment (or re-employment) of the individual. In the same year, one million AFDC cases were carried over from the previous year, but 584,000 new cases were authorized and 508,000 cases were closed. "Averaged over the year, about 45,000 new families were added to the rolls each month, while 41,000 left." Moreover, "of the cases added in 1966 about thirty-four percent had received assistance previously"; i.e., had been on welfare, dropped off, and were now enrolling again.

In the same edition of the *Manpower Report of the President* from which I have been quoting, the USDL recognized that, according to the conventional wisdom, "welfare and employment are widely regarded as alternative rather than complementary or overlapping sources of income. The AFDC caseload is generally seen as made up of nonworking mothers."[40] In fact, however, large numbers of "welfare mothers" work—in the secondary labor market. Indeed, "public assistance often serves as a form of wage supplementation for the low-paid partially employed worker."[41] In 1961, some 26 percent of the white and 41 percent of the black children on the AFDC rolls had mothers who worked at least part-time, half of them regularly. A study of the Philadelphia AFDC caseload in 1962 showed that only 13 percent of the mothers had no history of work. Most remarkable of all, of those who did have a work history, "forty percent had been employed in skilled or semi-skilled jobs."[42] In a study of the Harlem economy, Thomas Vietorisz and I found that nearly 38 percent of the workers unemployed in November, 1966, lived in families which received some form of welfare during that year. Of the full-time employed, 6.7 percent, and of the part-time employed, 11.8 percent, of the

39. Bradley R. Schiller, "Turnover Rates in Public Assistance Programs," *Welfare in Review*, Sept.-Oct. 1970, p. 28.

40. U.S. Department of Labor, *1968 Manpower Report*, p. 97.

41. *Ibid.*, p. 98. Some analysts believe that "welfare" has also served as an instrument of social control. In the South, it has traditionally been used to keep "field hands alive at federal expense during the winter, then forcing them into the fields at low wages in the spring and summer. When civil rights activism disturbed the calm of Southern rural life, the welfare system was available for, and easily adapted to, discouraging 'troublemakers.' County officials systematically suspended commodity distributions and warned that benefits would be restored only when local blacks surrendered their 'uppity' ideas about changing the local balance of power." Lester M. Salamon, "Family Assistance: The Stakes in the Rural South," *New Republic*, February 20, 1971, p. 18. Piven and Cloward have just published a major work which argues that these two functions go hand in hand. Welfare has two functions: to buy off the poor so that they will not rebel, and to provide workers who will take the worst jobs at the lowest possible pay. The former is the primary purpose; welfare aids the rest of society by keeping the poor in what the affluent have determined is their proper place. Relief actually means social control, not social welfare. Frances Fox Piven and Richard Cloward, *Regulating the Poor* (New York: Pantheon, 1971). See also Herbert Gans, "Income Grants and Dirty Work," in Mermelstein, *Mainstream Readings*.

42. U.S. Department of Labor, *1968 Manpower Report*, p. 98.

workers had families who received welfare that year.[43] In 1969, *all* AFDC families across the country averaged $60 per month in non-AFDC income, more than half of which was labor earnings. Among those AFDC families with non-AFDC income, the average monthly non-AFDC income was $135. In those AFDC families with working mothers, the average monthly wage of these women was $176. Fathers in such families averaged $218 in earnings; children averaged $90.[44]

Not only does the "welfare economy" share the peripheral characteristic of instability, but the typical "rate" of welfare income in the United States is extremely low—the conventional wisdom about welfare and Cadillacs notwithstanding. In 1966, of the 3.1 million people who received public assistance, only 304,000 (less than 10 percent) were in families (cases) receiving more than $2,000 during the entire year; only 834,000 (a quarter of the total) received more than $1,000.[45] This little-known fact about the *magnitude* of the average welfare payment obtains in even the wealthiest urban areas. In New York City, for example, the average weekly welfare allowance in 1967 for a family of four was only $63.22 (during the same year, manufacturing workers in the city averaged $106.60 per week). Even the poorest-paying industry in the city—rubber and miscellaneous plastics—paid an average wage of $87.20, almost $25 a week above the welfare "rate."[46]

It is also possible to get a fix on the combined work-welfare possibilities for New York City. A sample survey conducted in June, 1964, revealed that "over twenty-five percent" of the city's welfare recipients "were earning hourly rates of less than $1.25" in the secondary labor market, "sixty percent [were] below $1.50, and all but a smattering [were] below $2.00." In 1966, 90 percent of all the jobs solicited by one Human Resources Administrator for welfare recipients paid between $1.25 and $1.75 per hour.[47] In the four principal ghettos of New York City, over the period July, 1967, to June, 1968,

> families headed by women drawing welfare allowances at some time during the year preceding the interview had a median income of $2,713 ... [S]uch a mother ... would need to have grossed $74 in weekly wages in order to earn what she would receive in welfare allowances, and to pay for work-related expenses ... [F]or employed poverty-area women heading households and working full-time, weekly gross earnings [in fact] averaged $84

43. Vietorisz and Harrison, *Economic Development of Harlem*, pp. 234–35.
44. U.S. Department of Health, Education and Welfare, National Center for Social Statistics, *AFDC: Selected Statistical Data on Families Aided and Program Operations*, NCSS Report H-4 (71) (Washington, D.C.: Govt. Prtg. Off., 1971), tables 60, 61.
45. U.S. Office of Economic Opportunity, "Survey of Economic Opportunity: 1966 Unweighted Counts" (mimeographed, 1969), p. 2.48.
46. Elizabeth Durbin, *Welfare Income and Employment* (New York: Praeger, 1969), p. 34.
47. *Ibid.*, p. 78.

per week during the survey period [but] close to one-third of these women earned less than $75.[48]

Workers' willingness to accept jobs paying less than, say, $1.30 to $1.60 per hour appears to depend upon the availability of supplemental forms of income—such as welfare. If workers refused to take such low-paying jobs, many firms would—predicts Bluestone—go bankrupt and many services would—in Herbert Gans's view—go unproduced. It is in this sense that the welfare system may be said to constitute a public subsidy for low-wage "secondary" employers.

The "Training Economy." The Johnson administration officially recognized that "a man may enroll in one of the training programs which pay stipends, in order to get funds to tide him over a lean period."[49] More recently, *New York Times* reporter John Herbers wrote that "a good many of the manpower training programs are tending to become more of a holding action to keep people out of the unemployed columns than a means of putting them permanently into the work force. There are reports of men going out of one training program into another."[50] In fact, at least one official program (USDL's STEP program) was designed explicitly for the purpose of providing "further training" for those program graduates unable to find work.

The training programs of the federal government have thus taken on the basic attributes of the peripheral segment of the economy: low "wages" and low stability. Cumulative figures from 1968 through January, 1970, show that, of 84,703 actual hires in the NAB-JOBS program (initiated by President Lyndon Johnson and Henry Ford II), 50,225 quit or were laid off. The high implicit quit rate is not surprising: jobs in the NAB-JOBS program paid low wages, the core employers participating in the program often segregated their "hard-core" workers from the "mainstream" force, and layoffs were (as indicated) highly probably. In fact, one steel firm reported to an investigating Congressional committee that, since layoffs are "an inherent part of the American economy," it used part of the Manpower Administration subsidies "in counseling for anticipated layoffs. Many of the trainees at this firm since have been laid off."[51]

Of the several components of the relatively new Public Service Careers Program, only the New Careerists receive a training stipend, which averaged

48. U.S. Department of Labor, Bureau of Labor Statistics, Middle Atlantic Regional Office, *Poverty Area Profiles: Working Age Nonparticipants*, Regional report no. 22, June 1971, p. 3.

49. U.S. Department of Labor, *1968 Manpower Report*, p. 94.

50. Quoted in Bennett Harrison, "National Manpower Policy and Public Service Employment," *New Generation*, Winter 1971, p. 4.

51. U.S. Congress, Senate, Committee on Labor and Public Welfare, *The JOBS Program*, 91st Cong., 2d sess., April 1970. For a more extended discussion of the JOBS program, see Chapter Six.

$2,819 per trainee in 1968.[52] The USDL recently reported that 40 percent of the New Careerists leave the program within the first six months of training.[53] Again, we see the combination of low earnings and high turnover which are the identification marks of the peripheral economy.

Sar Levitan and Robert Taggart III describe the government's principal program for young dropouts, the Neighborhood Youth Corps:

> Almost all are entry level positions requiring few skills. Men are usually assigned to maintenance and custodial work, while women typically work in clerical or health positions. Most [jobs] pay near the minimum wage [$1.60 an hour], with extra stipends for household heads with dependents. . . . Stripped of their titles, almost all the jobs were menial and unattractive. . . . A comprehensive follow-up of enrollees leaving the program between January and September, 1966, found that forty weeks after termination, less than two-fifths were employed [and] more than a fourth were not in the labor force.[54]

The USDL's Work Incentive Program (WIN) is the pilot for President Nixon's "Family Assistance Plan," or welfare reform program. WIN guarantees participating adult welfare clients a minimum $30 training stipend per month, plus their normal welfare payment (which we have already seen to be extremely small). All able-bodied adults are required by law to participate. Together, these flows still constitute a poverty level income. A major evaluation of the WIN program in 32 cities was completed recently.[55] The evaluators defined four measures of program output (or "impact"): job placement rates, the quality of the placements (e.g., wage rates, retention rates, and job satisfaction), training course completion rates, and the quality of trainee preparation (measured by such indices as perceived job prospects, perceived skill improvement, and enrollee satisfaction). Direct program inputs included training efforts, supportive services (such as day care), and the extent of inter-agency cooperation. "Non-program forces" included employee characteristics (such as pre-training occupation and wage, age, race, etc.) and a number of labor market variables; e.g., the unemployment rate, USES reports on local employment prospects, and community attitudes toward WIN clients.

Bradley Schiller served as principal investigator for the evaluation. He summarizes the results:

52. Bennett Harrison, "Public Service Jobs for Urban Ghetto Residents," *Good Government*, Fall 1969, p. 14; reprinted in U.S. Senate, Subcommittee on Employment, Manpower and Poverty, *Hearings*, 91st Cong., 2d sess., 1 April 1970, p. 1437.

53. U.S. Department of Labor, *1971 Manpower Report*, p. 43.

54. Sar Levitan and Robert Taggart III, *Employment of Black Youth in Urban Ghettos* (New York: Twentieth Century Fund, 1971), p. 101.

55. Pacific Training and Technical Assistance Corporation, *Effectiveness of Urban WIN Programs*, USDL contract no. 51-09-70-10 (Washington, D.C.: U.S. Department of Labor, Manpower Administration, 1972); and Bradley R. Schiller, "The Little Training Robbery: Part I" (mimeographed; Department of Economics, University of Maryland, May 1972).

Variations in local job placement rates cannot be explained by local training efforts. Program inputs alone account for less than 15 percent of [placement rate] variation; when non-program forces are included in the analysis the coefficient of determination jumps to 0.544. Apparently, WIN's ability to place clients on jobs is dictated more by non-program forces (e.g., local unemployment rates) than by program activities.

It is especially interesting to note the apparent insignificance of WIN training efforts. The central thesis of the WIN model is that more and better training will lead to greater employment success. Yet, local variation in the extent and quality of training activity has no significant impact on job placement rates.[56]

For the second output/impact measure—placement quality—program operations were again relatively weak predictors of employee success. This time, moreover, even the labor market variables were of only marginal significance. "Apparently, the type of job a WIN graduate obtains is not very much influenced by general labor market conditions. A tighter labor market enables him to get a job [the earlier result], but not necessarily a better job."[57]

Analysis of the third measure—course completion rates—lends further support to the hypotheses of this chapter. Again, enrollee and labor market variables are controlling. In particular,

a one percentage point rise in local unemployment rates alone can raise WIN completion rates by 8.5 percentage points. Apparently, the desire to stay in the WIN program is strongest when other employment opportunities do not beckon. In fact, many WIN enrollees express the view that program participation "provides something to do" . . . when no jobs are available.[58]

WIN *is* successful in contributing to workers' skills (or at least to workers' *perceptions* with respect to the augmentation of their human capital). The quality of WIN staff is the most important of the program inputs. However, as already indicated, real (or perceived) skill acquisition did not always or even often lead to placement in "primary jobs."

These findings lead Schiller to conclude that

job placement success at the local level appears to depend almost entirely on the level and structure of the demand for labor and on community attitudes toward WIN clients. [This, and the invariance of job quality,] contradict not only the expectations of many human capital theories, but also the common rationale for funding public training efforts. From the vantage point of this study, it appears that public training efforts are a combination of concealed income transfer and public employment. One is led to ask whether these objectives could not be attained more effectively.[59]

56. Schiller, "The Little Training Robbery," p. 8.
57. *Ibid.*, p. 10.
58. *Ibid.*, p. 12.
59. *Ibid.*, pp. 14–15.

These findings are easily explicable in terms of the dual labor market theory. If workers treat training programs as temporary sources of income, then we would expect their tenure to be more or less insensitive to changes in program elements but very sensitive to the availability of other means of acquiring income. Employers in the primary labor market will, for the most part, simply not hire the poor, regardless of the quality of the training they acquire,[60] while secondary employers—having no choice, and no pressing need for skilled labor—will hire them whether they have had training or not.

The "Hustle": Ferman's "Irregular Economy." Our analysis thus far indicates that a labor supply model which ignores the welfare and training economies as possible objects of part of the attention (and time) of the urban poor is clearly incomplete. And there is still another source of unconventional income available to ghetto dwellers, the existence of which confounds the neoclassical analysis even further. This is the set of activities which Ferman and (then) Fusfeld have named the "irregular economy."[61] "A man may have his own type of 'hustle'—an easy way to money, sometimes legitimate, sometimes partly not, that puts him in a quasi-entrepreneurial role."[62] A study of the Washington ghettos found this sector of the economy to be at least as highly structured as those other peripheral "markets" we have been discussing. "People employed in the crime economy, like those on the other side of the law, usually work in structured environments. They meet schedules, attain skills, compete with the opposition, seek promotions, work their way through a complex of hierarchies."[63]

60. Where typically secondary workers (such as urban blacks) *are* employed by primary firms—as, for example, in the NAB-JOBS program—they tend to be confined to jobs and promotion ladders not involving positions of status or authority (which is why the secondary labor market has been depicted in figure 24 as overlapping part of the core of the economy). Evidence for this has been presented by Doeringer and Piore, *Internal Labor Markets*; by EEOC; and by David P. Taylor, "Discrimination and Occupational Wage Differences in the Market for Unskilled Labor," *Industrial and Labor Relations Review*, April 1968. In fact, it has recently been shown that such *internal segmentation* within core firms is greatest in precisely those industries which pay the highest wages—the "leading edge" of the core. In other words, in those core firms where average black earnings are at a maximum, the black share of high-paying, high-status jobs is at a minimum. See A. A. Alexander, *Structure, Income and Race: A Study in Internal Labor Markets* (Santa Monica, Cal.: RAND Corporation, October, 1970), R-577-OEO.
61. Cf. Barry Bluestone, "Tripartite Economy"; Louis A. Ferman, "The Irregular Economy: Informal Work Patterns in the Ghetto" (mimeographed, Department of Economics, University of Michigan, 1967); Daniel Fusfeld, "The Basic Economics of the Urban and Racial Crisis," *Conference Papers of the Union for Radical Political Economics*, December 1968; David M. Gordon, "Class and the Economics of Crime," *Review of Radical Political Economics*, Summer 1971.
62. U.S. Department of Labor, 1968 *Manpower Report*, p. 94.
63. Paul W. Valentine, "Crime a Vital Prop to Ghetto's Economy," *Washington Post*, March 5, 1972, p. A1. Another study—this a set of in-depth interviews with hustlers in many large cities—also shows the "irregular economy" to be well structured. Moreover, many hustlers reported that they had held low-wage legal jobs in the past and expected to do so "from time to time" in the future. Frederick A. Siegler, "On Hustling" (preliminary draft, U.S. Department of Labor, Manpower Administration, contract no. 41-0-006-09, 1971). Two other papers which apply economic analysis to the "mod-

While all irregular activity is not illegal, it is the latter type of "work" which is undoubtedly the most controversial—and the most lucrative (although the high risk associated with narcotics distribution, grand theft, and other serious criminal activities probably induces the same kind of discontinuous work patterns found elsewhere in the periphery of the economy, with the result that annual income is still relatively low for all but a very few professional criminals). The aforementioned study of Washington, D.C.'s hustlers reports that "at any given moment, there are probably a minimum of 2,500 to 3,000 ghetto residents who are employed full-time in illegal livelihoods, an estimate based on interviews with police, attorneys and prisoners here," and that these hustlers "contribute heavily to the gross inner-city product—15 percent by some estimates."[64]

Stanley Friedlander's interviews in Harlem have led him to conclude that perhaps two-fifths of all adults in that ghetto had some illegal income in 1966, and that 20 percent appeared to exist entirely on money derived from illegal sources (it is, for obvious reasons, difficult to quantify this illegal income).

> The young people interviewed had little hope of significant increases in [legal] earnings, because they saw so little chance of an occupational breakthrough. At best, they expected marginal employment at wages which would allow them to "get by." . . .
>
> Hustling was often regarded as a logical and rational option. The market for gambling, numbers, prostitution, and narcotics is large and highly profitable, and the possibility of "being on one's own" competes powerfully with the opportunities available in the regulated middle-class world.
>
> Criminal activities and the possible handicap of an arrest record did not seem to present problems for these Harlem youth. . . . No great social stigma accompanies arrest, so far as the immediate neighborhood is concerned. Job opportunities are already limited by other barriers, so that the effect of an arrest record is not considered important. The probability of being apprehended is considered relatively small. And the penalty for a particular offense, if one is caught, can be calculated with reasonable accuracy.[65]

---

eling" of illegal markets are Christopher Clague, "The Operation of the Heroin Market Under Alternative Systems of Control" (mimeographed; Department of Economics, University of Maryland, March 1972); and Thomas C. Schelling, "Economics and Criminal Enterprise," *The Public Interest*, Spring 1967.

64. Valentine breaks down his (undoubtedly very crude) estimates of annual employment and earnings as follows: prostitution—$12 million, employing at least 3,000; numbers—$150 million, employing at least 500 bookies and runners; heroin—$110 million, sold to 15,000 addicts, at least a fifth of whom are also peddlers; fencing stolen goods—"100 to 150 full-time operators, each of whom sells and distributes stolen goods received from a cadre of 20 to 25 burglars," with a value "substantially higher than the estimated $107.8 million stolen by heroin addicts alone"; bootlegging—"a small and declining industry involving several hundred full- or part-time individuals. . . . Some net up to $35,000 a year." Valentine, "Crime a Vital Prop."

65. U.S. Department of Labor, *1971 Manpower Report*, pp. 98–99.

Friedlander also found that the unemployment rates in sixteen cities in 1966 correlated negatively with the crime rates in these cities, suggesting that, "the larger the sources of illegal income, the fewer the people in the slums who persist in looking for legitimate jobs (or the greater the numbers who report themselves as employed when they are not, in order to explain their style of life to the enumerators)."

Formally, the Friedlander model is:

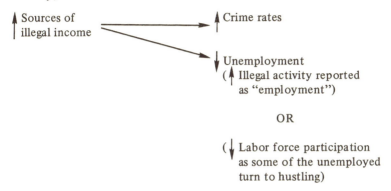

Of the two possible explanations of lower unemployment, there is now some evidence consistent with the second. LFPR's and crime (or at least arrest) rates for "economic" crimes committed by black men (e.g., auto theft, larceny, burglary, robbery) were found to be strongly inversely related in the country as a whole over the period 1952–67. With respect to robbery, for example, a 1 percent increase in LFPR's is associated with a 3.31 percent decrease in robbery arrest rates for black men.[66]

INTERSECTORAL MOBILITY

This study began with references to the elaborate mythology which has developed in America, according to which generations of immigrants were allegedly able to lift themselves out of poverty through education and training. During the "manpower decade" of the 1960s, moreover, billions of dollars were expended on the operation of public job placement institutions. It is therefore important to examine the extent to which upward mobility from the periphery to the core of the economy is facilitated (or hindered) by the school and job placement systems to which peripheral workers and their children have access.

We may begin with the school system; it is to this piece of the puzzle that the results reported in earlier chapters of this book are addressed. These

66. Llad Phillips, Harold L. Votey, Jr., and Darold Maxwell, "Crime, Youth, and the Labor Market: An Econometric Study," paper presented to the Annual Meeting of the Western Economic Association, August 1969.

studies compel us to conclude that the public education system does not—by itself, at any rate—promote the kind of intersectoral mobility for the peripheral worker which he or she has been led to expect. What effect *does* education have, then, particularly on ghetto blacks? For a small number, it probably does provide access to primary jobs. But the expectation certainly is otherwise. It follows that, with blacks crowded disproportionately into the secondary labor market, increasing education investments *ceteris paribus* may only increase the effective supply of secondary labor, which might then drive black wages down even further.

Two different explanations of this insufficiency of education may be proposed. From the point of view of conventional liberal theory (i.e., a racially discriminating but structurally integrated economy), a "market imperfection" (discrimination) is preventing the education system from functioning in its "normal capacity." In a non-discriminating economy, those ghetto workers who made the effort to "lift themselves up" by investments in their own "human capital" *would* be rewarded with higher incomes, fewer unemployment "spells," and higher status jobs.[67]

Bowles and Gintis, on the other hand, would argue that the "normal capacity" or true social function of the education system is not so much to develop job skills as to socialize young people to the roles they are most likely to play as adult workers, given their (and their parents') place in the class structure. By this interpretation, the low returns to education received by the urban poor of both races and particularly by blacks are not the result of improper or inadequate functioning of the ghetto schools. Quite the contrary; those schools are performing precisely the function they are "intended" to perform. Their indulgence of irregular behavior (within the classroom and in terms of class attendance) prepares their students for the peripheral lifestyle which the majority of them will probably be forced to adopt. The stifling of creativity and imagination reported so often by such educational critics as Edgar Friedenberg, Ivan Illich, Jonathan Kozol, and Christopher Jencks conditions ghetto children to accept the uncreative, routine kind of unskilled work which most of them will be required to perform after they "graduate." Most important of all, the failure of ghetto schoolteachers and

67. For example, Glazer and Moynihan assume that public education would help to improve the employment status of blacks if only the "serious obstacles to the ability to make use of a free educational system to advance into higher occupations" could be removed. Moreover, "there is little question where [these obstacles] must be found: in the home and family and community." Nathan Glazer and Daniel P. Moynihan, *Beyond the Melting Pot* (Cambridge, Mass.: Harvard University Press, 1963), pp. 49–50. Herman Miller, chief economist of the Census Bureau, has written that "it is entirely possible and indeed likely that productivity potentials of nonwhites have been raised, as suggested by the theory that correlates increases in years of schooling with additions to human capital, but [that] these potentials may not have materialized, owing to discrimination." Herman P. Miller, "Does Education Pay Off?" in *Economics of Higher Education*, ed. Selma J. Mushkin (Washington, D.C.: U.S. Department of Health, Education, and Welfare, 1962), p. 132.

education programs to acquaint their students with primary lifestyles, and the tendency of teachers and guidance counselors to "steer" their students into secondary jobs,[68] have the latent function of frustrating the development among lower-class youth of aspirations which might become socially destabilizing. That such aspirations are often formed anyway, and that the kind of schooling we are analyzing has not succeeded completely in preventing social tension, is due not so much to the inability of the schools to train productive workers because of discrimination as to the fact that the educational system does not operate in a vacuum. Other forces, over which the schools have little or no control (such as mass communication, the emergence of black pride and, in some places, volatile black nationalism) have—by this theory—interfered with the "normal function" of the schools. That function, to repeat, is to prepare lower-class students for secondary social and economic roles.

Another institution whose ostensible function is to promote upward mobility is the elaborate training/placement system developed over the last forty years. Students of the operation of these systems—some of which were developed explicitly for the purpose of "helping the poor" in the periphery of the economy—have concluded that placement programs have not made significant contributions to intersectoral mobility. Earl Main studied the institutional training programs financed under the MDTA, and concludes that the placement function has succeeded in helping the disadvantaged to find new jobs but not in increasing their wage incomes.[69] Doeringer's study of the poverty program in Boston came to a similar conclusion.[70] A comprehensive study of MDTA programs in four large urban areas—Boston, Denver, San Francisco, and Oakland—found that "the average enrollee who worked following training was still earning only at the rate of $3,000 per year."[71] Part of the explanation for these placement patterns appears to lie

68. I refer here to the common practice of advising lower-class students that they will be unable to obtain work in certain occupations and should therefore concentrate on other "traditional" positions. When such advice is taken, it amounts to self-fulfilling prophecy. It is important to note that not all the students in a predominantly lower-class school are treated this way. Many schools use an internal "tracking" system, in which students with "promise" are placed in substantially separate curriculums from those with less or no "promise." "Placement in these curriculums may determine the student's entire future life [and] it is known . . . that even very able boys from working-class homes who fail to make really good grades in the seventh and eighth grades are seldom advised to take a college preparatory course. This is not equally true of boys from white-collar homes." Patricia Cayo Sexton, "Education and Income: Senior High Schools," in Gordon, *Problems in Political Economy*, pp. 201–2. Lee Webb is currently attempting to explore the relationship between this fascinating internal segmentation of education "markets" and the labor market segmentation described in the text.

69. Earl Main, "A Nationwide Evaluation of MDTA Institutional Job Training," *Journal of Human Resources*, Spring 1968.

70. Doeringer *et al.*, "Low-Income Labor Markets."

71. Olympus Research Corporation, *The Total Impact of Manpower Programs: A Four-City Case Study*, vol. I: Summary of the Final Report, U.S. Department of Labor, Manpower Administration contract no. 43–8–008–47, Report MEL–71–05 (Washington, D.C.: Govt. Prtg. Off., 1971), p. 7.

in the MDTA requirement that training be offered only in occupations where there is a "reasonable expectation of employment." To meet this requirement while keeping per capita training costs low, MDTA administrators have chosen to train for jobs where openings occur because of high turnover, whether or not they are characterized by high demand.[72]

Together, these results imply that government placement programs simply *recirculate* the poor among a class of employers who tend to pay low wages. In a sense, public programs designed to promote mobility in fact serve as a recruiting instrument for employers in the secondary labor market. Recall our earlier discussion of the WIN Program, and the finding that WIN activities have no effect whatever on the probability of placement of a WIN graduate or on the quality of the jobs those "graduates" acquire. It has been suggested that this absence of upward mobility is attributable to a lack of personal motivation on the part of the trainees—and "peripheral" workers in general—rather than to their "confinement" by such public institutions as those analyzed here.[73] A study of "hard-core unemployed" trainees in Cleveland's Concentrated Employment Program strongly rejects the former hypothesis:

> . . . [P]ositive [trainee] attitudes toward work [i.e., motivation] were uncorrelated with higher job retention or job performance. . . . [T]he sole factor that differentiated successful from unsuccessful . . . persons at statistically significant levels was the degree of support within the immediate organizational context [where "support" refers to the behavior of peer workers and supervisors].[74]

To restate the thesis once more, public institutions ostensibly designed to facilitate intersectoral mobility seem instead to *recirculate* the working poor among the various segments of the periphery of the economy.[75]

This thesis is argued most forcefully by Stephan Michelson, who addresses himself to the U.S. Employment Service (USES), the government's principal placement institution:

> With local budgets often being a function of placements, local offices are discouraged from sending Negroes for jobs from which they will be auto-

72. "Manpower Programs in Four Cities," *Manpower*, January 1972. The quotation is from the Olympus Report, which this article surveys.

73. For a debate on this subject, see Robert A. Klitgaard, "Thoughts on the Dual Labor Market," *Monthly Labor Review*, November 1971; and Bennett Harrison, "Additional Thoughts on the Dual Labor Market," *Monthly Labor Review*, April 1972.

74. Frank Friedlander and Stuart Greenberg, "Effect of Job Attitudes, Training, and Organization Climate on Performance of the Hard-Core Unemployed," *Journal of Applied Psychology*, December 1971, p. 293.

75. Another institution which prevents intersectoral mobility is the police system. A recent study charges that "disqualification of job applicants because of arrest records . . . not involving convictions . . . is a 'national disgrace' that threatens a quarter of the population." William F. Clairborne, "Arrest Records Seen Bars to Employment," *Washington Post*, March 18, 1971, p. D6.

matically excluded. Thus, [US] ES tacitly aids the job discrimination which, with a different administrative procedure, it could confront.[76]

Recently, the Urban Coalition cosponsored a penetrating evaluation of USES, which supports the hypotheses presented previously about the de facto role of government job placement programs.

> The Employment Service today is an inflexible bureaucracy, absorbed in its own paper work, with a staff that is either incapable of or disinterested in committing the resources necessary to make the chronically unemployed self-supporting. The inability of the ES to provide meaningful assistance results in more individuals dropping out of the labor force, thereby contributing to the very problems the manpower programs were designed to solve. In 1970, despite a growing national work force and increased unemployment, only 11.5 percent of the work force sought out the service of the ES's 2,200 local offices. Those who actually received job placements as a result of ES assistance represented 5.3 percent of the work force.
>
> The jobs listed with the Service have decreased over the past five years and, for the most part, represent only the lowest levels of the economy. Almost half are considered unfillable by ES administrators because of low salaries, excessive job requirements or untenable working conditions. For their part, employers view the ES as the placement agency of last resort. Major employers, including state and local governments, conduct their own recruiting or rely on public advertising.[77]

More explicitly,

> The chief weakness of the ES with regard to minorities is that it mirrors the attitudes of employers in the community. The ES could provide a model of vigilance and aggressiveness toward affirmative action for equal employment opportunity. Instead, it is frequently a passive accessory to discriminatory employment practices; it is widely viewed in that light by the minority community.[78]

That USES placements are concentrated in what we have been calling the secondary labor market is illustrated by the fact that "over sixty percent of [non-agricultural USES] placements are in positions receiving less than $1.60 per hour."[79] Only 5 percent of USES placements in fiscal 1969 were in the

---

76. Stephan Michelson, "Incomes of Racial Minorities" (unpublished manuscript; Washington, D.C.: Brookings Institution, 1968), p. 8.23. In remarks to the Faculty Study Group on the State and the Poor at the Kennedy Institute of Politics in October, 1969, Michael Piore suggested that "the best operational definition of a secondary job is one which the Employment Service has in its files and is able to fill."

77. The Lawyers' Committee for Civil Rights Under Law and the National Urban Coalition, *Falling Down on the Job: The United States Employment Service and the Disadvantaged* (Washington, D.C.: National Urban Coalition, April, 1971), p. III.

78. *Ibid.*, p. 60.

79. *Ibid.*, p. 45. The Coalition's basis for this calculation is somewhat shadowy. However, in a private communication from a USES official, I learned that the incidence

professional, technical, or managerial categories.[80] That nonwhites are placed in the least desirable class of these generally undesirable jobs is exemplified by the fact that, again in fiscal 1969, between 80 and 100 percent of all domestic service placements among the largest states were assigned to non-whites.[81]

CONCLUSION

In this chapter I have presented one version of a model of labor market duality in the United States. Other versions are possible—and are appearing in print. For example, Frank Davis perceives the relationship between the (white) core and the (black) periphery of the American economy as one of explosive disequilibrium. Core products are increasingly subjected to oligipolistic pricing, but the core's demand for peripheral (largely unskilled) labor is income inelastic, so peripheral wages do not rise as the economy expands (in the rhetoric of some black "militants," black labor is rapidly becoming redundant). As a result of these forces, the "terms of trade" between the periphery (which exports labor to the core) and the core steadily worsen. Disequilibrium in the system gets *worse*. The presence of imperfect competition in the economy is at the root of the problem. Similar explosive disequilibriums describe the relationship between the agricultural and industrial sectors of the economy and between the rich countries of the West and the poor countries of the Third World.[82]

In a series of papers, Peter Albin has developed formal mathematical "unbalanced growth" models, in which the urban economy is divided into a leading sector consisting of those private industries and government agencies in which wages are growing and a lagging sector which includes private industries with zero (or lethargic) productivity and (therefore) wage growth.[83] Wage growth in the private leading sector is permitted by positive productivity growth there. Wage growth in the public sector is explained by the need of public employers to attract labor, i.e., to be competitive with the private leading sector, but is *not* accompanied by proportionate productivity growth; thus, the costs of public services rise over time.[84] Achievement of specified

---

of sub-minimum–wage job placements in the major labor market areas is "probably at least 40 percent." These are, of course, the areas with the *greatest* number of high-wage jobs.

80. *Ibid.*, p. 39.
81. *Ibid.*, p. 67.
82. Frank G. Davis, *The Economics of Black Community Development* (Chicago: Markham, 1972).
83. Peter S. Albin, "Unbalanced Growth and Intensification of the Urban Crisis," *Urban Studies*, June 1971; P. S. Albin, "Poverty, Education, and Unbalanced Economic Growth," *Quarterly Journal of Economics*, February 1970.
84. The assumption that service production is inherently less susceptible to technological change than goods production is a popular one; cf. William F. Baumol, "The Macroeconomics of Unbalanced Growth," *American Economic Review*, June 1967. There is in fact remarkably little empirical evidence to support this assumption. For

educational credentials constitutes a necessary and sufficient condition for intersectoral mobility.[85] Given an initial imbalance in sectoral wages (and, therefore, in the expected returns to educational self-investment) and differential access to the capital markets (the working poor have less access), the stratification of the economy "might be expected to persist for generations."[86]

Regardless of particular differences, all of these models have about them a "feel" which is decidedly unorthodox. They all assert the feasibility—indeed the inevitability—of chronic disequilibrium in the economic system, whether explosive, stable, slowly convergent, or of uncertain dynamic structure. Most important, all tend to lead the policy analyst to a similar set of recommendations which depart in important ways from traditional economic advice to American governments. That is, they lead to a call for comprehensive *economic planning.*

Locked out of existing primary jobs by discrimination, class bias and the institutionalized prerogatives of primary labor, and segregated into the peripheral economy with its secondary jobs and "irregular" means of supporting a family, the urban poor (and indeed the working poor everywhere) need *new jobs.* These jobs must offer adequate pay, promotional opportunities, and attractive benefits. They must be *stable* jobs, and this stability may be exactly what is needed to motivate the development among the disadvantaged of new attitudes toward the "world of work." Finally, the new jobs must be accessible to the poor, in terms of both location and skill requirements. In other words, we desperately need in the United States an explicit economic development policy. As Bluestone notes: "Funds for economic development—the creation of new jobs and new and expanded industries—were limited to a total of $508 million in 1969, less than a quarter of the budget for manpower programs"[87] and less than three-tenths of 1 percent of the $185 billion federal budget in that year.

---

public services, it is impossible to study the question by reference to the national income accounts; there—precisely because the measurement of public service productivity is so difficult in the absence of data on sales—output is defined as identical to the value of labor costs! One of Albin's examples offered in support of the assumption—that of the roughly constant student-teacher ratio in a school system over time—is incorrect; the output of an educational process is not measured by the number of students but rather by the extent of their education. One of the few extant econometric studies found that postwar productivity growth (estimated by the residual difference between value added and capital and labor compensation) was *not* significantly different between the private manufacturing and private nonmanufacturing sectors. See Phoebus J. Dhrymes, "A Comparison of Productivity Behavior in Manufacturing and Service Industries," *Review of Economics and Statistics*, February 1963. Moreover, between 1961 and 1970, in seven of the ten years of that decade, the annual percentage growth in output per man-hour was greater in nonmanufacturing than in manufacturing. U.S. Department of Labor, *1971 Manpower Report of the President*, p. 318.

85. The empirical results of Chapters Two to Four above rather strongly challenge this assumption.

86. Albin, "Unbalanced Growth," p. 141*n.*

87. Bluestone, "Tripartite Economy," p. 18.

Public service employment may be able to provide a major share of the new jobs that are needed. This is already the fastest growing sector of the economy. Federal subsidization in order to assure the continued expansion of this sector (as in the Emergency Employment Act of 1971, which provides $2.25 billion in public sector wages and benefits over a two-year period), and federal efforts to "broker" a share of these public service jobs for the poor (as in the OEO Project PACE MAKER),[88] constitute an essential part of what ought to be a concerted national effort to reduce the degree of segmentation in American labor markets. We shall return to the subject of public service employment in Chapter Seven.

It is important to realize that programs to move ghetto workers out of the narrow labor market into which they are presently "crowded" and into the wider metropolitan job market would result in penalizing those employers who presently benefit by the immobility of ghetto labor. At the very least, their implicit subsidies would be removed. For those firms whose existence has depended on the artificial monopsonistic power conferred upon them by the "dual market" system, the consequences could be more serious.

Generally, labor mobility and job development programs will create competition for the services of the secondary labor force. Those workers who actually move from secondary private to primary public employment, for example, will benefit directly.[89] Moreover, there is every reason to expect that those who are left behind will benefit from the upward pressure exerted on secondary labor market wages and benefits by the competition.[90] And in the process—as Harold L. Sheppard has tirelessly argued for many years[91]—the production and delivery of public services which are now in critically short supply will be expanded.

88. For a discussion of PACE MAKER and other federal experiments in opening up public employment to the poor, see U.S. Department of Labor, *1971 Manpower Report*, pp. 171–76; and Bennett Harrison, *Public Employment and Urban Poverty* (Washington, D.C.: Urban Institute, June, 1971), Paper No. 113–43.

89. Comparison of the existing wages of a sample of 15,000 ghetto workers with the entry-level salaries obtaining in municipal government indicates that those ghetto residents who can be moved into the public service agencies in their respective cities might expect to increase their wage incomes by a factor of between one and three times. *Ibid.*, p. 23.

90. For an elaboration of this argument, see Barry Bluestone, "Economic Theory, Economic Reality, and the Fate of the Poor," *Social Policy*, January–February 1972.

91. Harold L. Sheppard, *The Nature of the Job Problem and the Role of New Public Service Employment* (Kalamazoo, Mich.: W. E. Upjohn Institute, January, 1969), reprinted in U.S. Congress, House, Committee on Education and Labor, Select Subcommittee on Labor, *Hearings on H.R. 17, H.R. 29, and H.R. 3613—the Emergency Employment Act of 1971*, 92d Cong., 1st sess., 3 March 1971, pp. 156–88. See also Sheppard's testimony in the same volume, pp. 151–55 and 189–203. The highlights of this important paper will be reviewed in Chapter Seven.

We have yet to reach the point where our concern is for the
crises experienced by the Black ghetto dweller, for his frustration and despair. The "crisis of the cities" has been, and
largely remains, a euphemism for white middle-class financial
risks, esthetic distastes, inconveniences and discomforts, and
fears of physical violence.

— Robert H. Binstock

6.

URBAN
EMPLOYMENT
POLICY:
CURRENT
ORTHODOXY

INTRODUCTION

In this monograph, we have attempted rigorously to quantify the extent of the insufficiency of education and training as social instruments for increasing the economic well-being of ghetto—and especially nonwhite—workers.

Neoclassical economic theory posits a mechanism by which increased education (and other forms of "human capital") will increase personal income. Education is assumed to enhance an individual's skills. Given suitable and adequate complementary capital, the marginal productivity of a worker is then assumed to be an increasing function of his "stock" of skills. Finally, under a competitive allocation of resources, profit-maximizing employers are expected to pay the individual a wage which is proportional to his marginal productivity.

Differences between the incomes of blacks and whites could therefore arise because of real differences in productivity (part of which might be attributable to differential access to human capital of at least standard quality), because of "marginal imperfections" in the allocation process, e.g., elements of monopoly or racial discrimination, or because of a more fundamental segmentation of the labor force according to class as well as race and sex. The evidence accumulated in this study tends, I think, to support the last hypothesis. Preliminary assessments of the JOBS programs indicate that blacks perform about as well as whites on the job, in terms of absenteeism, turnover, learning rates, vandalism, and discipline. Task analyses by the USDL and several private research organizations show, moreover, that blacks seem to have acquired more than enough general education to competently perform (or learn) a much broader range of technical tasks than our economic system is presently permitting them to perform. Indeed, the degree of complexity of modern job tasks seems itself to have been vastly overstated.

A number of economists are presently engaged in the study of the processes of discrimination and labor market segmentation.[1] It is a central conclusion of this monograph that such studies are more likely to bear fruit than continued academic (and policy) emphasis on increasing the stock of non white human capital.

In the next two chapters, our concern is with urban employment policy. The empirical results developed in Chapters Two, Three, and Four, and the arguments presented in Chapters One and Five, suggest that policy should focus on the structure of the *demand* for urban—and particularly ghetto—labor. The current orthodoxy in this field has been ineffective because it is based upon fallacious assumptions about the responsiveness of the economic system to improvements in the supply of ghetto labor, and on unjustified optimism about private corporate demand for ghetto labor.

---

1. Of the various research projects presently under way, two of the largest are the Research Project on Labor Market Stratification, being conducted at the National Bureau of Economic Research in New York, and the Project on the Economics of Discrimination, an activity of the Department of Economics of the University of Maryland.

THE CURRENT ORTHODOXY I: IMPROVING THE SUPPLY OF GHETTO LABOR

Education and training are the conventional prescriptions for the alleviation of poverty. There are several problems with such a strategy. The skill requirements—and, therefore, the academic accomplishments—needed for many modern urban jobs have, as we saw earlier, been exaggerated by policy makers. This has led Ivar Berg to conclude that

> the fact that certain forces have generated a need for better-educated workers in some occupations . . . does not support sweeping generalizations about education as one of the major panaceas for the solution of urban economic ills . . . [T] he notion that most of the labor supply should be so treated is an unwarranted extrapolation of the facts regarding relatively few jobs in the city's economy.[2]

Indeed, the myth of the efficacy of education as the principal historical instrument for "bootstrap" improvement of minority welfare has itself been called into question by S. M. Miller:

> If job opportunities are improved, then perhaps in the next generation a greater number of the children of the new working classes may make real moves to improve their conditions. It is not sufficiently realized that former disprivileged ethnic groups did not improve their conditions mainly by education, but through assimilation by business and political employments. The Irish and Italians did not initially have a heavy emphasis on education as vehicles for improvements. It was usually after the parents had made some economic stake—frequently through business—that Irish and Italian youth began to go to college. The Jews were different in that more of their ascent was through education; the emphasis on literacy and learning among Jews has been noted as important in their movement. Ignored has been the fact that in the "old country" many of them were petty traders and small businessmen so that they came to this nation with more varied experience than do the new [black] working classes of today.[3]

The emphasis on education as preparation for nonspecialized work may, as Ribich suggests, even help to perpetuate poverty:

> Graduating from high school or college may . . . merely imply that employers have a preference for degree holders that, in turn, may be founded largely on a belief that graduates have demonstrated desirable ambition and persistence by the successful completion of a long course of study. If the graduates had not been available, nongraduates might have been hired at roughly the same rate of pay and have performed on the job at roughly

2. Ivar Berg, "Education and Work," in *Manpower Strategy for the Metropolis*, ed. Eli Ginzberg (New York: Columbia University Press, 1968), pp. 116–17.
3. Quoted in David R. Hunter, *The Slums: Challenge and Response* (Glencoe, Ill.: Free Press, 1964), pp. 140–41.

the same level of efficiency. Thus, while the individual may find a diploma useful in the scramble for high paying jobs, his gain may entail a commensurate loss for someone else.[4]

In any case, we now have evidence that "improved" ghetto labor is not in substantially greater demand than "unimproved" ghetto labor—particularly if that labor is nonwhite. In this monograph, we have learned that minority workers living in the urban slums have not been able to translate their additional schooling into more than token increases in hourly or weekly earnings. Indeed, in a substantial number of cases (and generally for unemployment), we were unable to find statistically significant evidence of any payoff at all.[5] In the central city poverty areas of the nation's twelve largest cities in 1965-66, a high school diploma had three times as high a marginal earnings payoff for ghetto whites as for ghetto nonwhites. For the latter, the present value of a high school diploma was estimated at about $6,000, a figure which is much smaller than previous estimates in the literature, and well below the returns available in any number of illicit "street activities" in the ghetto. Although education did contribute to improved occupational status for nonwhite ghetto dwellers, the effective range of prestige positions over which these workers were mobile was found to be exceedingly small. And while the white high school graduate from the ghetto could expect to be unemployed nearly 4 percent less often than the white ghetto dweller who never entered high school at all, we found no appreciable difference between the expected incremental unemployment rates of high school and grammar school nonwhites. Even attendance at college did not reduce the risk of nonwhite unemployment.

In the ten UES ghettos, the findings were essentially the same. A number of different earnings models yielded estimated returns of from three to nine cents per hour for each additional year of schooling, and—over the interval 9-12 years, with all interactions accounted for—estimated returns of no more than twenty-four cents per hour. The asymptotic maximum expected hourly wage rate, given education, was never more than about $2 per hour in any of the urban ghettos. Education again had virtually no effect whatever on expected unemployment.

---

4. Thomas I. Ribich, *Education and Poverty* (Washington, D.C.: Brookings Institution, 1968), p. 11.

5. This is an appropriate time to point out to the reader (if he or she has not already been aware of the fact) that we are evaluating only the direct and quantifiable *employment* "payoffs" to investments in human capital. Nothing in these concluding remarks should (or can) be construed as addressing the larger issues of the social and private value of education as a means of expanding the intellectual absorptive capacity of the population, creating an "enlightened citizenry" (the enlightenment of whom is usually considered to be a necessary condition for political democracy), increasing the "joy of living," and so forth. I confess that I find the Bowles-Gintis theory of education (presented in the previous chapter) to be rather convincing, in which case these "external benefits" of education have to be traded-off against what Gintis calls the opportunity cost of education "reflected in . . . an alienated and repressed labor force."

These findings lead me to agree with the position of S. M. Miller:

> In American life, it has been customary to offer "education" as the panacea for all problems, whether those of racial prejudice, sexual happiness or economic conflict. I have the feeling that to the problems of discrimination, inadequate economic functioning and poverty, we are again offering the reply of "education." In doing so, we are telling those who have the most strikes against them, that they have to do the most work to improve the situation. I am saying that schools and education cannot be expected to solve the blight of poverty and inhumanity—the entire society and economy are implicated. And, it may be, that by our stress on eliminating dropouts, we are not politicizing the important issues. At the same time, we may be giving people a confortable way to forget about the corrosive character of much of our social and economic life.[6]

Continued education should be an important objective of all those concerned with improvement in the lives of ghetto residents. Moreover, "equal education should be a goal in itself, not diminished for its failure to produce income for nonwhites."[7] But as a short-run antipoverty policy instrument, education without a supply of commensurate jobs—jobs which utilize and fully reward the capabilities of ghetto workers—is unlikely to have much impact. In the words of the EEOC:

> Obviously, minority groups should be given an equal chance for education and training. . . . But they must be given hope as well. . . . It is the expectation of reward—the anticipation of productive labor, money, status, and social acceptance—which enables men to endure the apprenticeship of training, education, and experience.[8]

Former President Johnson has put the matter even more succinctly:

> It will not be enough to provide better schools for Negro children, to inspire them to excel in their studies, if there are no decent jobs waiting for them after graduation.[9]

The essential objective of public policy must, I contend, be the explicit development of new and broader urban job markets into which the residents of the ghetto can then be invited. Two major opportunities in this regard are the development of a comprehensive program for "public employment of the disadvantaged" in new jobs involving the delivery of desperately needed urban services, and the support of ghetto development corporations, both in

6. Quoted in Hunter, *The Slums*, pp. 141–42.
7. Stephan Michelson, "Incomes of Racial Minorities" (Unpublished manuscript; Washington, D.C.: Brookings Institution, 1968), pp. 8–28.
8. U.S. Equal Employment Opportunity Commission, *Job Patterns for Minorities and Women in Private Industry–1966*, EEO report no. 1 (Washington, D.C.: Govt. Prtg. Off., 1969), vol. I, pp. 20–21.
9. Lyndon B. Johnson, "The Negro American—Introduction," *Daedalus*, Fall 1965, p. 744.

their avowed role as instruments for developing the political and commercial base of the ghetto, and in their potential role as suppliers of recruitment, "pre-vocational training," and placement services to employers outside of the ghetto.

Strategies which rely exclusively on attempts to place large numbers of core city blacks into suburban private industries, either through reverse commuting or large-scale subsidized residential integration, have little chance of success and are increasingly being questioned by the younger and more activist members of the ghetto population themselves. Existing jobs are going to open up to ghetto residents only under the direct pressure of the federal government—if then. The so-called "Philadelphia Plan" of the USDL, under which construction firms bidding for federal contracts must give evidence of genuine attempts to hire local nonwhites, is the most important current pilot program aimed toward changing the hiring practices of the private sector.

These are the policy issues to which we now turn our attention.

THE CURRENT ORTHODOXY II: SUBURBANIZATION OF GHETTO WORKERS

A central theme in the literature of urban economics is that the progressive decentralization of jobs from the late nineteenth century up to the present (with a brief interruption during the 1930s) has made suburban residence the optimal location in terms of maximizing urban employment opportunities. Nonwhites tend to be concentrated in the oldest neighborhoods of the central city, and it is this growing distance between place of residence and place of potential employment that is one of the principal causes of urban poverty. Kain, for example, writes:

> Low income white workers adapt their residential choices to their job locations and to available transit services. When their jobs are in suburban areas, an increasing trend, they invariably live in suburban areas. When Negro jobs are located in suburban areas, they must either be foregone [because of residential segregation] or they represent difficult, costly, and time-consuming trips from [the central ghetto out] to suburban work-places.[10]

Reverse Commuting. Short of actually relocating inner-city minorities to the suburbs, many economists and urban planners recommend a policy of "reverse commuting." The objective here is to transport workers from the urban core out to the suburban fringe where an increasingly larger number of the allegedly "decent" jobs are located. Many specific proposals have been made, including the reservation of parking or breakdown lanes for the unobstructed

10. John F. Kain, "The Big Cities' Big Problem," in *Negroes and Jobs*, ed. Louis A. Ferman *et al.* (Ann Arbor, Mich.: University of Michigan Press, 1968), p. 238.

use of special buses, extensions of the subway system (where such a system already exists), and the subsidization of car pools.[11]

Even as a short-term expedient, reverse commuting experiments have not met with much success in the municipalities where they have been tried—Boston, Detroit, Washington, D.C., and elsewhere.[12] In the capital, in fact, there is evidence that special buses running in both directions carry more suburbanites into the city than nonwhite ghetto dwellers out of the city. The figures below come from an interim evaluation of a two-year reverse commuting experiment being subsidized by the U.S. Department of Transportation.

Average Number of Passengers Riding Capitol
Flyer Buses, Week of March 9–13, 1970

	Per Bus[a]
D.C. *out* to Prince Georges County	7.0
D.C. *out* to Montgomery County	23.5
D.C. *out* to Fairfax County	3.3
Prince Georges County *in* to D.C.	23.1
Montgomery County *in* to D.C.	19.5
Fairfax County *in* to D.C.	28.6

Source: *The Washington Post*, April 2, 1970, p. F-1.
[a]Full capacity = 51 persons.

The only relatively successful run in the table is the ghetto-to-Montgomery County route, and this is largely attributable to the opening of a Health, Education, and Welfare building in the town of Rockville, Maryland, with virtual door-to-door service. Many such experiments have been undertaken during the last several years by the Departments of Transportation and Housing and Urban Development (HUD) under the authority of the Urban Mass Transportation Act of 1964.[13] The general conclusion of the sponsoring agencies is that

> improved transit will reduce unemployment only when there are job openings for the potential users of the service at wages high enough to cover

11. For example, a front-page article in the *Detroit Free Press* (September 2, 1968), "calls for a large-scale subsidized system of buses to transport inner-city Detroit Negroes to suburban employers." Joseph D. Mooney, "Housing Segregation, Negro Employment, and Metropolitan Decentralization: An Alternative Perspective," *Quarterly Journal of Economics*, May 1969, p. 311*n*. See also Oscar Ornati, *Transportation Needs of the Poor* (New York: Praeger, 1969).

12. Cf. Carol S. Greenwald and Richard Styron, "Increasing Job Opportunities in Boston's Urban Core," *New England Economic Review*, Federal Reserve Bank of Boston, January-February 1969, pp. 34 ff.

13. See Charles Haar, "Transportation and Economic Opportunity," *Traffic Quarterly*, October 1967.

commuting expenses . . . [T]ransportation arrangements, when geared to slum residents, should be subsidiary to a job development and placement program.[14]

To be sure, intrametropolitan transportation should be sufficiently well developed to permit efficient journeys-to-work for all residents of the area. Much further research on the costs of traveling from home to job is needed. To some extent, as Ornati[15] and others have shown, the central city ghetto *is* physically isolated from the suburban ring. Ornati shows that, even where mass transit is relatively abundant—as in New York City—antiquated routes may contribute to "effective isolation" of the ghetto. But the question of greatest priority is whether or not, given access to suburban jobs (however achieved), nonwhite economic opportunity is in fact increased. Before bringing the results developed in the earlier chapters to bear on this question, I should like to first examine the more ambitious policy proposal of "ghetto dispersal."

"Ghetto Dispersal"—Programmed Nonwhite Suburbanization. The full-scale strategy of moving ghetto workers into the wider private metropolitan job market is popularly referred to as "ghetto dispersal." Its most persuasive advocate among economists is John Kain. The "ghetto dispersal" strategy proposes a number of interrelated public actions: relocation of ghetto residents to areas in the suburbs which are closer to new, blue-collar industrial complexes, open housing and income or rent subsidies, and large-scale investment in Southern economic development in order to reduce the migration pressure on those Northern cities where "ghetto dispersal" has not been completed.[16]

For advocates of dispersal, the suburbanization of the kinds of jobs for which minorities are "best suited"—and the suburban residential segregation which prevents these minorities from relocating—constitute the principal causes of the "urban crisis." Kain, for example, estimates that "as many as 24,000 jobs in [suburban] Chicago [in 1956] and 9,000 jobs in [suburban] Detroit [in 1952] may [have been] lost to the Negro community because of housing segregation."[17]

14. U.S. Department of Labor, *1971 Manpower Report of the President* (Washington, D.C.: Govt. Prtg. Off., 1971), p. 104. Even such advocates of public investments in improved physical access to the suburbs as Kain and John R. Meyer admit that "virtually nothing has been done so far to establish a factual basis for evaluating the utility of improved transportation in reducing urban poverty and unemployment." Quoted in George M. von Furstenberg, "Place of Residence and Employment Opportunities Within a Metropolitan Area," *Journal of Economic Issues*, June 1971, p. 113n.
15. Ornati, *Transportation Needs.*
16. Cf. John F. Kain and Joseph J. Persky, "Alternatives to the Gilded Ghetto," *Public Interest*, Winter 1969.
17. *Ibid.*, p. 78.

Moreover, the high and growing concentration of blacks inside the central city exacerbates the problem, by stimulating the intransigence of newly "suburbanized" whites who are afraid that their former neighbors in the city will try to follow them out.

Some have proposed that it would be better to promote minority economic development within the central city than to challenge this intransigence of suburban whites.

> Recognition of high rates of Negro unemployment, low incomes and other undesirable conditions found in central city ghettos have led to widespread demands for corrective action. A majority of practical men [he may be referring especially to the late Robert F. Kennedy] seem to have concluded that residential integration is either impossible or will take too long. They contend the problems of the urban Negro are current and real and that while residential integration might be desirable as a long-range goal, such a course for the immediate future is uncertain, difficult and politically dangerous. . . .
>
> Proposals to patch up [or "gild"] the ghetto and make it a better place to live [in] and to create jobs there are heard with increasing frequency.[18]

Kain, however, opposes "ghetto-gilding." For one thing, such programs would "reduce pressure for residential integration and would tend to perpetuate existing patterns and practices of racial segregation." For another, the capital-absorption capacity of the ghetto is far too small to permit sufficient internal job development to make up the whole deficit, particularly if the amelioration of underemployment as well as outright unemployment is the goal. Another and

> . . . most telling objection is that such policies might well [aggravate the situation]. There are strong links between Northern ghettos and the still vast pools of rural, Southern Negroes. Ghetto improvement and particularly job-creation programs might well have as their principal result increased migration of Southern Negroes to Northern metropolitan areas. Growth rates of Northern ghettos might increase severalfold, greatly aggravating the problems . . . [T] he distortions of metropolitan growth would be magnified, and the goal of assimilating and integrating the Negro into urban society would be made far more difficult.[19]

Instead, Kain asserts that "there is no alternative [*sic*] but vastly increased suburbanization of Negro populations, if we are to avoid unnecessary economic waste and growing social political conflict." Public policy, "should emphasize the strengthening of the Negro's ability to break out of the ghetto

---

18. Kain, "Big Cities' Big Problem," p. 242.
19. *Ibid.*, pp. 242–43.

[by] (education and job training) and the expansion of suburban housing opportunities."[20]

I perceive at least six different assumptions underlying Kain's position.[21] First, the jobs which blacks are most capable of performing are believed to be suburbanizing most rapidly. This in itself is questionable. Charlotte Fremon of the Urban Institute found, in eight different SMSAs, that semiskilled and unskilled jobs were expanding almost as rapidly in 1965-67 in the central city as in the suburbs. The openings were being filled by suburban commuters—"while, we should add, manpower training programs were expanding."[22] In any case, Kain, himself, has admitted that his results may be biased: "the census data presented in . . . this paper may be providing a misleading picture of employment changes by focusing on those employment categories that are decentralizing most rapidly."[23] One sector in particular is omitted in all of Kain's tables: state and local government. According to the USDL, employment in this sector will grow by 42 percent between 1968 and 1980—faster than any other sector of the American economy. And most of this growth will take place inside central cities. Between 1958 and 1967, for example, "local governments provided nearly 100,000 new jobs for New York City's workers. This was nearly twice the number generated by the next 'best' sector, business services."[24] The subject of public employment will be taken up again in Chapter Seven.

Second, there is in Kain's argument the implicit assumption that those nonwhites who are able to "suburbanize" will in fact be hired, and that this suburban employment will improve their economic opportunities. In the next section of this chapter, I shall draw upon the findings of Chapter Four to challenge this assumption.

Third, Kain predicts an increase in Northern migration of Southern blacks in response to a ghetto job development program. This "negative feedback effect" will swamp any ghetto renewal effort. There are urban economists who disagree even with the premise. Anthony Pascal of the RAND Corporation suggests, for example, that

. . . a good deal of data now becoming available seem to indicate that migration behavior for the low-skilled and disadvantaged segments of the

20. *Ibid.*

21. For a much more detailed presentation of the evidence and policy inferences concerning suburbanization and its implications for minority well-being, see Bennett Harrison, *Metropolitan Suburbanization and Minority Economic Opportunity* (Washington, D.C.: Urban Institute, 1973).

22. Charlotte Fremon, *The Occupational Patterns in Urban Employment Change: 1965-1967* (Washington, D.C.: Urban Institute, June, 1971), paper no. 113-32.

23. John F. Kain, "The Distribution and Movement of Jobs and Industry," in *The Metropolitan Enigma*, ed. James Q. Wilson (Cambridge, Mass.: Harvard University Press, 1968), p. 30.

24. Bennett Harrison, "Public Service Jobs for Urban Ghetto Residents," *Good Government*, Fall 1969, p. 2.

population is significantly motivated by factors other than employment opportunities.[25]

Even if the premise is true, however—even if Southern blacks are responsive to Northern urban jobs programs—Kain's analysis of its implications is too static. It ignores the improvements in ghetto and city-wide political organization over time: changes in the "technology" of social organization which permit communities to absorb new immigrants, to find a place for them in the neighborhood social structure. It is these dynamic "self-help" institutions, from the Cooper Unions and Workmen's Circles of the Jews to the ghetto development corporations and civil rights organizations of the blacks, which can prevent immigration from necessarily constituting a "negative feedback."

Fourth, it is argued that it would be impossible to "create" nearly enough jobs within the ghetto to meet any meaningful employment target. This is quite true, but Kain attacks a straw man here, for no advocate of ghetto development has ever suggested that such a program would be feasible. On the contrary, it is Kain who is the "extremist," arguing that "inside" and "outside" development are mutually exclusive alternatives. There is no alternative to suburbanization, he writes. Surely, the appropriate attitude of an economist should be to ask, "What is the optimal mix?" rather than to assert the superiority of a corner solution. This, for example, was the position of the Kerner Commission, whose famous study of the 1967 "civil disorders" led it to conclude that ghetto development "must be an important adjunct to integration, for no matter how ambitious or energetic the problem, few Negroes now living in central cities can be quickly integrated. In the meantime, large-scale improvement in the quality of ghetto life is essential."[26]

Fifth, Kain asserts that investments in education and training in the ghetto will "strengthen the Negro's ability to break out," i.e., to "suburbanize."

Education . . . can be used to weaken the ties of the ghetto. Formal schooling . . . greatly enhances their ability to compete in the job market with the promise [*sic*] of higher incomes. As a result, large-scale programs of compensatory education can make important contributions to a strategy of weakening and eventually abolishing the Negro ghetto.[27]

There is little evidence in the pages of this monograph to support such an assertion. "Promise" notwithstanding, the *expected* value of education to a nonwhite urban ghetto dweller is a slightly higher (but still subsistence-level)

25. Anthony H. Pascal, "Manpower Training and Jobs," in *Cities in Trouble: An Agenda for Urban Research*, ed. Pascal (Santa Monica, Cal.: RAND Corporation, August, 1968), document no. RM-5603-RC, p. 71. For a review of some of the new data and research results referred to by Pascal, see Harrison, *Metropolitan Suburbanization.*

26. *Report of the National Advisory Commission on Civil Disorders* (New York: Bantam Books, 1968), pp. 22-23.

27. Kain and Persky, "Alternatives," p. 81.

wage, a somewhat "whiter" collar, and about the same risk of joblessness as that faced by the worker's dropout neighbor.

Finally, Kain assumes that residential integration is an explicit social and political goal in the United States, and he asserts that dispersal of the ghetto is consistent with that goal, but development is not. The assumption that a real commitment to integration exists in the United States will be addressed in the next paragraph. On Kain's assertion of a basic incompatibility between integration and ghetto development, it may be noted that several black and white scholars argue that genuine integration can only take place between groups who are cooperatively dependent on one another, i.e., groups of equal political status.[28] If William Grier, Price Cobbs, Charles Hampden-Turner, Gordon Allport, and Thomas Pettigrew are correct that "black power" is "a form of group therapy . . . a blueprint for psychosocial development," then "progress through an affirmation of identity is more likely to succeed in a large community in the present ghetto than in the proposed pocket ghettos of dispersal."[29] And, of course, there is the "definite political advantage to be gained from visibility of large numbers, in affecting the allocation of resources toward compensatory education or compensatory investment."[30] It is the desire to protect this advantage which forms the basis for Piven and Cloward's opposition to the formation of metropolitan area-wide super-governments which might become dominated by the representatives of the (lily-white) suburban communities at the expense of the (increasingly black) central cities.[31]

As for the "commitment" to integration, it is certainly difficult to perceive. After a decade of improvement in some neighborhoods during the 1950s, there has been an increase in residential segregation in American cities since 1960, in both absolute and relative terms. The numbers and proportions of blacks living in census tracts in which they were already highly concentrated in 1960 have risen, while the black proportions living in tracts which were predominantly white in 1960 have fallen (see table 13).

The incidence of blacks in the suburban rings of our metropolitan areas has actually been falling steadily since at least 1900. The proportion of sub-

28. Cf. Dale Hiestand, *Discrimination in Employment: An Appraisal of the Research* (Ann Arbor, Mich.: Institute of Labor and Industrial Relations, University of Michigan–Wayne State University, February, 1970), pp. 41–42.

29. Matthew Edel, "Development or Dispersal? Approaches to Ghetto Poverty," in *Readings in Urban Economics,* ed. Matthew Edel and Jerome Rothenberg (New York: Macmillan, 1972). See also Y. Amir, "Contact Hypotheses in Ethnic Relations," *Psychological Bulletin,* Summer 1969; and Charles Hampden-Turner, "Black Power: A Blueprint for Psycho-Social Development?" in *Social Innovation in the City,* ed. Richard S. Rosenbloom and Robin Marris (Cambridge, Mass.: Harvard University Press, 1969).

30. *Ibid.*

31. Frances Fox Piven and Richard A. Cloward, "Black Control of Cities: Heading It Off by Metropolitan Government," *New Republic,* September 30, 1967, Part I, and October 7, 1967, Part II; Piven and Cloward, "What Chance for Black Power?" *New Republic,* March 30, 1968. See also U.S. Commission on Civil Rights, "Metropolitanism: A Minority Report," *Civil Rights Digest,* Winter 1969.

Table 13

Percent of All Blacks Living in Census Tracts Grouped
According to Proportion Black in 1960 and 1964-68

(in percent)

SMSA	Year	All Census Tracts	75 Percent or More Black	50-74 Percent Black	25-49 Percent Black	Less than 25 Percent Black
Cleveland	1960	100	72	16	9	4
	1965	100	80	12	4	4
Memphis	1960	100	65	26	5	4
	1967	100	78	14	4	4
Phoenix	1960	100	19	36	24	21
	1965	100	18	23	42	17
Buffalo	1960	100	35	47	6	12
	1966	100	69	10	13	8
Louisville	1960	100	57	13	17	13
	1964	100	67	13	10	10
New Haven	1960	100	–	33	19	48
	1967	100	16	19	27	38
Rochester	1960	100	8	43	17	32
	1964	100	16	45	24	15
Sacramento	1960	100	9	–	14	77
	1964	100	8	14	28	50
Des Moines	1960	100	–	28	31	41
	1966	100	–	42	19	39
Providence	1960	100	–	23	2	75
	1965	100	–	16	46	38
Shreveport	1960	100	79	10	7	4
	1966	100	90	–	6	4
Evansville	1960	100	34	27	9	30
	1966	100	59	14	–	27
Little Rock	1960	100	33	33	19	15
	1964	100	41	18	22	19
Raleigh	1960	100	86	–	7	7
	1966	100	88	4	2	6
Trenton	1960	100	26	9	48	17
	1968	100	24	55	13	8

Source: U.S. Department of Commerce, Bureau of the Census, *Current Population Reports*, series P-23, no. 29, "The Social and Economic Status of Negroes in the United States, 1969" (Washington, D.C.: Govt. Prtg. Off., 1970), p. 10.

urbanites who were black was 8.9 percent in 1900, 6.5 percent in 1920, 5.5 percent in 1940, and 4.6 percent in 1960.[32] Early in 1971, the Bureau of the Census announced that—based upon a preliminary analysis of the 1970 Census—only about 5 percent of the nation's suburban population was found to be black, "approximately the same proportion as ten years ago."

32. *New Republic*, April 4/11, 1970, p. 22.

These are regarded as meager changes by the Census authorities, particularly for a decade which saw passage of a federal fair housing law, many similar local and state laws, and determined efforts by private groups to open suburbs to Negro homeowners.[33]

In February, the Bureau released a new—and lower—estimate of 4.5 percent.[34]

Where "suburbanization" of blacks *has* occurred, it appears to have led to—or perhaps been facilitated in the first place by—resegregation. In 1967, the proportion of black families living in "substantially integrated neighborhoods—defined as areas with a black population of at least ten percent and with positive net black *and* white inmigration—was equal in the suburbs and the central cities; this estimated proportion was only ten percent."[35] If the filtering theory of housing is correct, then resegregation may well be the *only* way that the market will permit blacks to purchase suburban property. This seems to be true even where recent black suburbanization has been substantial. Thus, for example, while more and more Negroes are moving to Washington, D.C.'s suburbs, most of them are going to areas where others have gone before, creating new enclaves of black segregation, especially in Prince George's County.[36] Perhaps the most extreme example is Philadelphia, where entire suburban towns (many of them old industrial enclaves themselves, with large stocks of aged housing) are becoming black ghettos. Some of these ghettos, such as those in the town of Ardmore, were traditionally reserved for the black servants who used to work in Main Line homes.[37]

The attitudes of white homeowners, realtors and planners do not seem consistent with the national commitment to integration perceived by Kain. In a study of two "new towns" in California, Dr. Carl Werthman asked residents how they interpreted 'planning' and how they would react to the development of "lower-priced" homes in the towns. His interviews with citizens of Foster City and James Conejo led him to the conclusion that "planning is thought to be a guarantee against . . . the lower-priced home sold to the lower-income person . . . [p]eople feared the introduction of low-income families partly because they thought this was synonymous with the introduction of Negroes."[38]

33. William Chapman, "Integration in Suburbs Found Slight in 1960's," *Washington Post*, January 16, 1971, p. 22.

34. "Desegregation Slight in '60's," *Washington Post*, February 11, 1971, p. A16.

35. Seymour Sudman, Norman Bradburn and Galen Gockel, "The Extent and Characteristics of Racially Integrated Housing in the United States," *Journal of Business*, January 1969, p. 62.

36. Andrew Barnes, "New Black Enclaves Forming in Suburbs," *Washington Post*, February 11, 1971, p. A1.

37. Lenora Berson, "Philadelphia," *City Magazine*, February 1971, pp. 40–42.

38. Quoted in Edmund P. Eichler, "Why New Communities?" in *Shaping an Urban Future*, ed. Bernard J. Frieden and William W. Nash (Cambridge, Mass.: MIT Press, 1969), p. 105.

But perhaps the most startling—and certainly the most demoralizing—discovery is the role that agents of the federal government have played in perpetrating and even reinforcing suburban residential segregation. Unquestionably, the worst offender has been the Federal Housing Authority (FHA).

Through the end of the 1940's, well into the postwar housing boom . . . and at least until President Kennedy's Executive Order of November, 1962, barring discrimination in federally aided housing . . . the FHA had a clear policy of discouraging new developments open to blacks as well as whites; and its "Underwriting Manual" advised appraisers to lower their ratings of properties in neighborhoods occupied by "inharmonious racial or nationality groups—often to the point of rejection." It even recommended a model racial restrictive covenant.[39]

More recently, the FHA has been accused of forcing the creation of a new black ghetto in the suburbs of Flint, Michigan. The Beecher school district had been one of the few successfully integrated suburban communities in America, with a 70-30 racial mix and joint white-black control of the school board. Under HUD's so-called "235 program" the FHA insures mortgages on new houses up to $24,000 and subsidizes the low-income buyer's monthly interest payments. "Hard hit by the 'tight money' recession in conventional home building, private developers have flocked to the program."[40] Despite the pleas of Beecher's citizens not to concentrate all of the region's low-income housing in their single community, "Thomas Hutchinson, the veteran FHA director in Flint, has made commitments to local builders to construct a total of 716 '235' . . . units in the tiny Beecher district—more than he allotted to all the other Flint suburbs [combined] in sprawling Genesee County (population 441,000)."

In an interview in the Flint FHA office, Hutchinson said he had no 'special guidelines' [from HUD] to do otherwise, except for vague talk of 'geographic dispersion.' The impact of housing—any housing—on a community's schools was not his business, nor was racial balance.[41]

"When I first got into this thing," reported a black community organizer in Flint, "I thought the opposition in Beecher was racial. But it isn't. The fact is that the FHA was running the program for the benefit of builders at the expense of the community."[42] Thus, even where Congress has appropriated money for the kinds of rent and mortgage subsidies advocated by Kain as instruments to facilitate nonwhite suburbanization, administrators have

39. George Grier, "Washington," *City Magazine*, February 1971, p. 47.
40. Peter Braestrup, "HUD's Biggest Housing Effort Runs into Trouble in Michigan," *Washington Post*, February 16, 1971, p. A3.
41. *Ibid.*
42. *Ibid.*

shown precious little commitment to integration as one of the "stated goals of American society."

Kain's insistence that ghetto dispersal and ghetto development are mutually exclusive antipoverty strategies ("there is no alternative but vastly increased suburbanization of Negro populations") is particularly unfortunate. Even Anthony Downs admits that

> it is not inconsistent to support *both* Black Nationalism and dispersal simultaneously . . . I believe dispersal programs should only be undertaken simultaneously with large-scale ghetto enrichment programs. The latter would provide comparable, or even greater, benefits for those "left behind" in central cities—who will undoubtedly comprise the vast majority of Negroes in our metropolitan areas for many years to come.[43]

Examination of the "development plans" of many community development corporations demonstrates the falsity of the dispersal-development dichotomy. Most of the more enlightened and responsible black and brown leaders understand perfectly well the infeasibility of totally autarchic development of the ghetto (their public rhetoric notwithstanding). Thomas Vietorisz and I addressed this issue in testimony before the U.S. Senate Subcommittee on Employment, Manpower and Poverty:

> The limitations of physical space within the ghetto need not bottle up development . . . [A]s long as the new activities are part of a comprehensive community development plan, their effectiveness need not be undermined by placing them in readily accessible outside locations. Examples from the . . . Harlem development 'plan' are the airspace over the South Bronx rail yards or the recently completed Brooklyn Navy Yard industrial park . . . [T]he plan may well include a downtown and even a suburban jobs component for ghetto residents, involving coordinated recruitment, pre-vocational training, placement, and follow-up support. If backed by negotiations of the community development organization for block placement of trainees with large corporations and government agencies, together with a restructuring of publicly-regulated fares for large-scale reverse commuting (e.g., from Harlem up to Westchester), such a component within a ghetto development plan may well be the most effective way of securing outside employment for ghetto residents. The example certainly demonstrates the potential complementarity of "inside" and "outside" job development programs.[44]

The dichotomy is doubly false if the prescription against development is meant to apply to the entire central city, as is implied in Kain's emphasis on

43. Anthony Downs, "Alternative Futures for the American Ghetto," in Downs, *Urban Problems and Prospects* (Chicago: Markham, 1970), pp. 63, 67.
44. Thomas Vietorisz and Bennett Harrison, "Ghetto Development, Community Corporations and Public Policy," *Review of Black Political Economy*, Fall 1971.

suburbanization of central city blacks as the *only* viable strategy for combatting urban poverty. Much recent research has been concerned with demonstrating that central city economies are by no means exhausted; that the decentralization of jobs has *not* resulted in the accelerating net job losses predicted by earlier studies based upon observations of recession years; that the availability of central city jobs now *exceeds* the supply of residential central city labor; and that employment decentralization has *not* been accompanied by a skill "mis-match" as was feared.[45]

As whites continue to leave the central city, more and more old but still viable housing will filter down to the expanding central city black population. It is popular among writers on this subject to portray this process as "the expansion of the core ghetto." However, as Peter Labrie points out, the ghetto qua slum represents "only one aspect of black urban life."

> Kain, instead of referring [exclusively] to the works of Kenneth Clark and Claude Brown to characterize the ghetto as "institutionalized pathology," would have done better to refer to the works of E. Franklin Frazier [whose] studies on the ecological settlement of the black population in Harlem and Chicago have revealed that neighborhood differentiation by family organization and socio-economic status tends to follow in broad outline the same general pattern within black residential areas as it does within white residential areas. . . . The hard-core slum ghetto is no more characteristic of black urban communities than skid row is of the white central city communities.[46]

Labrie goes on to predict that this differentiation among black neighborhoods will increase as blacks take over more and more of the central city in the wake of "suburbanizing" whites.

Even for the ghetto qua poverty area, a crucial distinction must be drawn "between the material manifestations of poverty and the culture of poverty." Oscar Lewis has written extensively on the example of "poor but relatively integrated, satisfying, and self-sufficient cultures with a high degree of social organization." One of his examples concerns a transformed modern urban slum:

> In 1947 I undertook a study of a slum in Havana. Recently [1965], I had an opportunity to revisit the same slum and some of the same families. The physical aspect of the place had changed little, except for a beautiful new nursery school. The people were as poor as before, but I was impressed to find much less of the feelings of despair and apathy, so symptomatic of the culture of poverty in the urban slums of the U.S. The slum was now highly organized, with block committees, educational committees,

45. Harrison, *Metropolitan Suburbanization.*
46. Peter Labrie, "Black Central Cities: Dispersal or Rebuilding (Part II)," *Review of Black Political Economy*, Winter/Spring 1971, pp. 83–84.

and party committees. The people had found a new sense of power and importance.[47]

The sheer physical magnitude of the task of "suburbanizing" central city blacks and other minorities is so enormous that it is easy to understand why many young black writers (Labrie, for example) believe the argument for exclusive reliance on a dispersal strategy to be disingenuous. Downs, in his research for the Kerner Commission (i.e., The National Advisory Commission on Civil Disorders), estimated that, in order for dispersal to take place over the period 1970-75 at a scale sufficient to keep the central city nonwhite population share constant at its 1970 level, "there would have to be an out-movement of 1.9 million Negroes into the suburbs. This amounts to 380,000 per year." That is the target. But in fact, "from 1960 to 1966, the Negro population growth in all suburban areas declined sharply to a rate of 33,300 per year [and] there was actually in-migration of Negroes from suburbs to central cities."[48] Reporting on the studies of George Schermer, Piven and Cloward write that

> ... in order to insure a 50-50 population balance in Washington, D.C. in the year 2000 [and] assuming that migration trends and birthrates remain constant, 12,000 nonwhite families would have to be dispersed to suburban areas and 4,000 white families induced to return to the District *every year until 2000* ... [T]o achieve integration neighborhood-by-neighborhood in Philadelphia by the end of the century 6,000 Negro families would have to go to the suburbs and 3,000 whites settle *exclusively in ghetto areas* each year. The numbers, of course, would be infinitely greater in cities like New York and Chicago, which have much larger aggregations of Negroes ... [emphasis in the original].[49]

The potential social and political costs of challenging these powerful vested interests and traditional fears may reasonably be assumed to be substantial. While this does not mean that such a challenge ought not to be one element in a larger urban antipoverty program, it does suggest that exclusive reliance on such a strategy would be foolish.

Empirical Findings on the Relative Insensitivity of Nonwhite Employment Opportunity to Intrametropolitan Residential Location. The distributions generated in Chapter Four—and especially the graphical displays of average earnings, unemployment, and occupational status in figures 17-19—indicate that nonwhite employment opportunities are rather insensitive to where in

47. Oscar Lewis, "The Culture of Poverty," *Scientific American*, October 1966, p. 22.
48. Downs, "Alternative Futures," p. 46.
49. Frances Fox Piven and Richard A. Cloward, "Desegregated Housing: Who Pays for the Reformers' Ideal?" in *Race and Poverty*, ed. John F. Kain (Englewood Cliffs, N.J.: Prentice-Hall, 1970), p. 177.

the metropolis the worker happens to live, as compared with the much greater intrametropolitan spatial sensitivity displayed by the figures for whites. Nor are the marginal returns to nonwhite education significantly greater in the suburbs than in the ghetto.

In general, for whites and nonwhites, education is associated with increased mobility into what are nationally considered to be higher-status occupations. For whites, this promise is realized; as education increases, whites move into new occupations where they receive higher earnings and face lower expectations of unemployment. Moreover, these improvements in white employment status are greater in the non-poverty neighborhoods of the central city than in the ghetto, and still greater in the suburbs. For nonwhites, however, the promise is not realized; as their education increases nonwhites move into new occupations, but their earnings are hardly affected at all by anything short of a college degree, and there is almost no effect on their chances of finding themselves without a job over the course of the year. Moreover, the effects are no greater outside the ghetto than inside—even for those nonwhites who have already been "suburbanized."

Thus, the "ghetto dispersal" strategy must be rejected as an exclusive approach to combatting urban poverty. In no part of the American city does the labor market "work" for nonwhites.

Only through a direct transformation of the demand for his labor can the ghetto dweller's economic situation be improved. Attempts to change the worker himself—whether to remedy his personal "defects," or to move him to a "better" environment—have not worked in the past, and there is no evidence that they will work in the future.

THE CURRENT ORTHODOXY III: HIRING THE "HARD-CORE" IN PRIVATE INDUSTRY

In Chapter One, we learned that—when they *have* experimentally lowered the barriers to hiring the disadvantaged—private employers have discovered to their admitted surprise that the poor are capable workers, when given the opportunity. Through the activities of the Urban Coalitions in cities across the country, and through USDL training subsidies offered to the member companies in NAB, the private sector was encouraged by Presidents Johnson and Nixon to involve itself in the "urban crisis" by hiring the poor and by investing in the ghetto.

The JOBS Program.[50] The National Alliance of Businessmen's Job Opportunities in the Business Sector program to employ the "hard-core" in primary

---

50. See Chapter One for a discussion of the origins of the NAB-JOBS program, the kind of subsidies offered by the government to private firms, and the eligibility criteria promulgated by the government.

("core") plants located outside the ghetto began to lose momentum in early 1969.[51] Member companies shut down their much publicized inner-city recruiting centers and laid off many of their recently hired ghetto workers. In January 1969, Leo Beebe (then Executive Vice Chairman of NAB) announced that some 120,000 people had been placed in jobs with USDL subsidies, and that 85,000 were still at work.[52] But by the end of March, the Alliance's momentum had slowed down considerably; only about 5,000 new workers had been hired. Altogether, these 125,000 new workers were distributed among some 12,500 companies, for an average of only ten new hires per company (between 15,000 and 20,000 firms had been asked for pledges).[53] By the middle of March, moreover, the Ford Motor Company was announcing the closing of two special hiring centers in central Detroit and the layoff of several hundred newly hired workers from the ghetto.[54]

At the same time, evidence began to emerge that the jobs for which NAB companies were "training" (for an average subsidy of $3,000) were often menial, relative even to the capabilities of the so-called "hard-core unemployed" in the ghetto. One of the critics was William Kaufmann, a former New York City NAB executive director, who called for "fewer, but better jobs . . . [I]t does no good to take a man who is leaning against a lamppost and lean him against a broom."[55] There was also some indication that firms were receiving subsidies for the provision of services (such as day care) which, in fact, were not provided. Then, in May of 1970, the president of the AFL-CIO Building and Construction Trades Department charged the Nixon Administration with aiding "one of the most flagrant corporate boondoggles in history." Specifically, the union was protesting a $600,000 JOBS grant to subsidize "extremely low wages . . . under the guise of training" for a California prefabricated housing producer. The units being built were too expensive to qualify as low-income housing, according to the union, and the trainees were paid "only $2 an hour, only half of it paid by the company."[56]

These suspicions, and a general dissatisfaction with the progress of the program, led the U.S. Senate Subcommittee on Employment, Manpower, and Poverty and the General Accounting Office (GAO) to conduct investigations of NAB-JOBS in 1969–70. These investigations uncovered a "lack of contract procedures, misuse of federal funds, and disappointing performance records

---

51. While it is true that any private enterprise program such as NAB-JOBS will inevitably be weakened by a national recession—and indeed, it is the recession of 1970 to which apologists for the program point in explaining its failure to meet its highly-publicized goals—the slowdown in JOBS hires began during the first quarter of 1969, at a time when the national unemployment rate was 3.3 percent, its lowest level since the Korean War.

52. Murray Kempton, "The Private Sector," *New York Post*, January 8, 1969, p. 34.

53. *Business Week*, March 8, 1969, p. 62.

54. *Business Week*, March 22, 1969, p. 66.

55. *Business Week*, November 1, 1969, p. 66.

56. "Prefab Labor," *Washington Post*, May 5, 1970, p. A7.

by many of the private firms in the [JOBS] program." One subcontractor submitted a bill for the rental of three large air conditioning units, none of which could subsequently be found at the training site. More seriously, the Senate Subcommittee charged many employers with "taking federal money for hiring people in low-paying jobs that require little or no training." One steel firm, for example, reported to the Subcommittee that, since layoffs are "an inherent part of the American economy," it used part of the Manpower Administration subsidies "in counseling for anticipated layoffs. Many of the trainees at the firm since have been laid off."[57]

Estimates of the number of jobs "created" under the contract (i.e., federally-subsidized) component of the program are given in table 14. These

Table 14

Cumulative[a] Performance Record of the JOBS Program
(Labor Department Contract Component)

		Number of Workers
Jobs pledged		129,169
Trainees hired		127,210
Trainees terminated		78,859
Quit	52%	
Discharged	32%	
Laid off	5%	
Other	11%	
Trainees on board		48,351
Number of companies pledging jobs[b]		26,671
Number of companies hiring[b]		15,501

Source: Comptroller General of the United States, *Evaluation of Results and Administration of the Job Opportunities in the Business Sector (JOBS) Program in Five Cities* (Washington, D.C.: General Accounting Office, 1971), pp. 13, 17.

[a]Through June 30, 1970.
[b]Includes both contract and noncontract components.

numbers are extremely crude, according to both groups of investigators. In marked contrast to the extensive and detailed publicity generated by the public relations experts representing NAB,[58] hard data on both contract and "noncontract" (voluntary) program performance have been difficult to validate: "Even with the contract employers, statistics may be more questionable than would be expected. . . . The fact is that statements . . . in a NAB booklet on the JOBS/70 program are simply not verifiable."[59]

57. *Washington Evening Star*, April 29, 1970, p. A20.
58. U.S. Senate, Subcommittee on Employment, Manpower, and Poverty, *The JOBS Program*, 91st Cong., 2d sess., April 1970, p. 119.
59. *Ibid.*, pp. 117, 119.

A second problem has been substantial underutilization of the appropriated federal subsidies. In fiscal 1968, Congress (at President Johnson's request) appropriated $104.7 million for the JOBS program; only $4.2 million was actually spent. In fiscal 1969, the figures were $153.8 million and $41.7 million, respectively. In fiscal 1970–long after "start-up"–the respective figures were $300.0 million and $59.4 million. USDL "obligations" were reduced in 1970 substantially below the Congressional appropriation; even so, "it seems relatively rare for a firm to collect the full amount obligated."[60]

One logical explanation for the very high quit rate shown in table 14 is the low average wage paid by NAB-JOBS employers (recall our analysis of the "training economy" in Chapter Five). The GAO studied the jobs pledged by 215 contract employers in five cities; 3,300 of the 6,300 jobs (52 percent) offered a starting way of $2 or less an hour. Moreover, the bulk of those jobs paying this low a wage were jobs which "historically had a high rate of turnover, did not provide for permanent employment," and, in the words of the Director of the California Department of Human Resources Development,

> are duplicates of traditionally low paying occupations that have been unacceptable for training purposes. . . . When you consider that the employer receives full reimbursement for wage loss during the time the trainee is not on on-the-job training, and fifty percent of the wage loss while the trainee is on on-the-job training, it would appear reasonable to insist upon an entry level wage which exceeds the poverty level.[61]

Even former Assistant Labor Secretary for Manpower, Arnold Weber, admitted that the average entry level wage across *all* NAB companies in 1970 was only $2.10 per hour.[62]

The overall assessment of both teams of investigators is captured in two succinct paragraphs in the GAO report to the Congress:

> The number of job pledges by some prospective employers were unrealistically high and not always consistent with their ability, or intention, to provide the jobs. . . .
>
> A significant number of the jobs provided by contractors paid low wages and appeared to afford little or no opportunity for advance-

60. *Ibid.*, p. 111.

61. General Accounting Office, *Comptroller General's Report to the Congress: Evaluation of Results and Administration of the Job Opportunities in the Business Sector (JOBS) Program in Five Cities* (Washington, D.C.: Govt. Prtg. Off., 1971), pp. 48–49.

62. U.S. Senate, *JOBS Program*, p. 169. A Labor Department analysis of the 1969 UES reveals that, of all sources of job training (e.g., institutional, armed forces, etc.), the "special manpower" programs–mainly NYC and JOBS–were the least successful in raising workers' earnings. In fiscal 1969, among all six UES areas, the average hourly wage of workers who had *never* completed a job training program was $2.16. For those who *had* completed some kind of program, it was $2.53. But for those who had completed NYC or JOBS training, it was–again–only $2.16. In the Detroit ghetto, where JOBS (and NYC) were more effective than in any other UES sample area, the respective figures were $2.57, $2.85, and $1.97. Roberta V. McKay, "Job Training Programs in Urban Areas," *Monthly Labor Review*, August 1971, especially table 1. Given that the JOBS Program was begun by Henry Ford II, this is a depressing discovery indeed.

ment. . . . In these cases, it appeared to GAO that very little was being accomplished under the JOBS program for the funds expended.[63]

Corporate Activities in the Ghetto. Immediately after the 1967 riots, many corporations hastily created "urban affairs" offices to "improve relations with the black community." Many companies lent out members of their staffs to "help out on community projects" (although less than half of a sample of firms doing so allowed this activity on company time).[64]

At about the same time, several large corporations were establishing branch plants in the ghetto, on the model of IBM's cable factory in Bedford-Stuyvesant. A study by the Center for Manpower Policy Studies of George Washington University, after analyzing industries that had already established subsidiaries in core city areas, concluded that "the experience generally has not been favorable and the business environment of ghetto areas does not seem to be profitable." The most highly publicized of the branch plants was Aerojet-General's tent manufacturing facility established in Watts in 1966. By May of 1969, and despite Labor and Defense Department subsidies and contracts totaling well over $2 million, the project had lost "several hundred thousand dollars" and employment had been cut back from 500 to 300 ghetto workers.[65]

Writing immediately after a two-year review of the Los Angeles riot areas including Watts—and then again in early 1969—Nathan Cohen of UCLA criticizes the superficiality of the corporate sector's "involvement" in the redevelopment of the inner city:

Efforts by private industry and private enterprise to develop corporate urban projects have been minimal and without great success. There is a question as to whether great expansion can be achieved without the government's underwriting the risks. President Nixon's campaign interest in "black capitalism" seems to have waned; it has not found articulation through government programs. Along similar lines, plans for banks to increase their ghetto lending await legislation that provides a mechanism through which government can underwrite a program of credit expansion. . . .

The cutbacks are the most distressing. For example, the Neighborhood Youth Corps project in Los Angeles is now training 89 young people, compared with 500 when it started five years ago.[66]

63. General Accounting Office, *Evaluation of the . . .(JOBS) Program*, p. 2.

64. Jules Cohn, *The Conscience of the Corporations* (Baltimore, Md.: Johns Hopkins Press, 1971), p. 20.

65. John Herbers, "Economic Development of Blighted Inner-City Areas Is Running into Snags," *New York Times*, May 4, 1969, p. 15. For a more detailed evaluation of these efforts, see Sar A. Levitan, Garth L. Mangum, and Robert Taggart III, *Economic Opportunity in the Ghetto: The Partnership of Government and Business* (Baltimore, Md.: Johns Hopkins Press, 1970).

66. Nathan Cohen, ed., *The Los Angeles Riot Study* (New York: Praeger, 1969), pp. 708–9.

As of 1971, the record of relative successes and failures was quite mixed. "One type of undertaking, direct investment by outside business in fully controlled [ghetto] installations, virtually ceased after 1968," to be replaced by joint ventures, technical and financial assistance to private or cooperative ghetto-based projects, and participation in government-sponsored housing construction and rehabilitation programs. "To date, these efforts have [with some exceptions, to be discussed below] had little over-all impact."[67]

The McKinsey & Co. Evaluation of Corporate Programs. The most definitive analysis of the attitudes of corporate executives toward "involvement" in the "urban crisis" was made by Jules Cohn in 1969–70, on the basis of a seven-month study of 247 companies. The study was sponsored by McKinsey & Company, a well-known management consulting firm.

"Of the 247 major companies studied," reports Cohn, "nearly one-third reported programs for the disadvantaged." Of the various types of firms in the sample, "labor-intensive industries" (which were beginning to face expensive manpower shortages by the late Sixties) "and those dependent on government favors and/or good-will" were the most likely to have special programs for the "hard-core unemployed." One executive told Cohn that "those on aerospace had to go out of their way to be good citizens simply to keep the government money flowing."[68] Moreover, "two-fifths of the companies interviewed adopted their programs in order to meet government equal opportunity requirements in employment and in the awarding of contracts. One executive said: 'Our policy against discrimination was arrived at in response to the law—not conscience, civic spirit, or sentiment.' "[69]

One of the most serious problems Cohn encountered was the lack of provision for upgrading:

> The evidence is far from encouraging for the long-term prospects of entry-level jobs offered by urban affairs employment programs. . . . Few companies provide upgrading opportunities for graduates of their own entry-level training programs, even though one of the major findings of the Kerner Report was that many rioters, though fully employed, felt locked into low-status, low-income, dead-end jobs.[70]

Cohn is particularly distressed at the kind of "technical assistance" being rendered to active corporations by research and consulting groups. The "urban orientation" materials distributed by many of these organizations are, in his view, "alarmist and sensational. They tend as much to provoke as to lessen prejudice. . . . These groups . . . have helped disseminate the notion

67. James K. Brown and Seymour Lusterman, *Business and the Development of Ghetto Enterprise* (New York: The Conference Board, 1971), report no. 517, p. iii.
68. Cohn, *Conscience of the Corporations*, p. 39.
69. *Ibid.*, p. 6.
70. *Ibid.*, p. 28.

that the behavior of the hard-core or disadvantaged worker will shock the sensibilities of allegedly well-adjusted, well-mannered, and properly motivated co-workers and supervisors."[71] Efforts are needed, Cohn concludes, "to reduce rather than exacerbate the anxieties of potential employers and co-workers about the special qualities of the disadvantaged" and "extraneous training costs [should] be pared."[72]

Cohn finds that, since 1969, "business support of urban programs is waning and that companies want to evaluate these activities to determine future directions." He offers four reasons for the change in corporate policy:

> After two "cool" summers, public and government pressure to develop urban programs has diminished.
>
> Urban programs have proved more costly than many corporate officials anticipated. . . .
>
> Planning and managing urban affairs programs requires more skills than many companies realized at the start.
>
> Some urban programs have affected the internal life of large companies in unexpected—and often unwelcome—ways.[73]

According to Cohn, "a dozen or so companies have pulled out of urban affairs completely; others are saying that they cannot handle training the hard-core, that perhaps it takes professionals with skills business doesn't have." And a member of the faculty of the Harvard Business School reported to Cohn that "corporations this year [1970] are not lionizing black MBA candidates the way they did in 1969. The heat from the executive suite is off." Local Urban Leagues also told Cohn that requests from companies for minority group workers are "down significantly."

Perhaps employers can still be induced through subsidy schemes as yet untried to hire and train ghetto workers, and to invest in new economic enterprises for the ghetto. But at least one urban consultant gave Cohn a more cynical appraisal: "If we really want business to stick its neck out, we should institutionalize the riots."[74]

SUMMARY

The current orthodoxy in urban policy consists of efforts to upgrade the "quality" of the supply of low-skilled inner-city labor through investments in human capital; to increase the physical access of low-income workers to

71. *Ibid.*, p. 49. The "auxiliary services" (e.g., "how to tie your tie") which these consultants advise corporations to undertake "in support of" their job development programs—and which are often required by the government as a condition for the receipt of subsidies (as in the JOBS program)—are, in Cohn's view, useless as well as potentially divisive.
72. *Ibid.*, p. 60.
73. "Is Business Pulling Out of the Ghetto?" *Business Week*, March 7, 1970, p. 23.
74. *Ibid.*

expanding job sites by means of transportation investments and suburban "open housing" programs; to induce large private corporations to hire what I have called "peripheral" workers for their "core" plants; and to subsidize the location of branch plants of those corporations within the ghetto itself.

Our survey suggests that none of these strategies has been especially successful. This is not to say that any of them should be totally discarded in a future attack on urban poverty. It does, however, strongly suggest that these approaches are—in and of themselves—*insufficient* to make a serious dent in the problem, so that new (that is to say, *additional*) strategies must be devised, and—to use a terribly hackneyed phrase—priorities must be reordered. A sample of new approaches will be proposed in the next chapter.

We Americans have suffered such losses of humane communality that we cannot allow ourselves to see the waste of life that stares us in the face. Our very sense of crisis is often nothing more than a refined technique of avoidance. Thus we have a "problem of the schools," and talk to each other solemnly about improved facilities, better methods of instruction, more supervision, ignoring all the while the painful truth that what children need most is for the lives of their elders to make sense.

— George Dennison

7.

URBAN EMPLOYMENT POLICY: NEW DIRECTIONS

NEW DIRECTIONS I: GHETTO DEVELOPMENT

We have found that most nonwhites in the ghetto have been unable to translate either education, "suburbanization," or participation in corporate social programs into greater economic opportunity. It seems appropriate to argue that the economic revitalization of the "black community"—as well as the other minority areas of our cities—will require the development of new demands for minority manpower. New labor markets must be created to which nonwhite workers may turn for relief.

But economic wellbeing for nonwhite Americans is probably not possible unless it is supported by broad-based black and brown political power, especially within the urban ghettos. By granting the minority communities a greater degree of autonomy, we will be recognizing their maturity and the validity of their own value systems. It is perhaps the only action we can still take to convince those in the ghetto that we do not, in the words of Elliot Liebow, think of them as "animals or children."[1] These are some of the issues bound up in what has come to be called "ghetto development."

Joel Bergsman of the Urban Institute notes that "ghetto development" means very different things to different people, so that discussants of the subject ought to be precise about their conception of the matter.[2] In my view, "ghetto development" refers to

> An overall social and economic transformation, with a large increase in the diversity of higher economic and institutional functions which ghetto residents are capable of sustaining, matched by a decisive improvement in the cohesion of the ghetto community. Specifically, we envisage the creation of a number of "inside jobs," acquisition by the community of assets both inside and outside the ghetto, a substantial expansion of existing black businesses (particularly through cooperative forms of ownership), the large-scale transfer of ghetto property to ghetto residents and/or the community *qua* community, emphasis on the provision of pre-vocational and skill training within these ghetto enterprises, and local control of community political institutions, e.g., schools, police, health facilities.[3]

While "ghetto development" is frequently portrayed as a competing and even an "extreme" alternative to "ghetto dispersal," I consider it rather as a necessary complement to the other strategies for minority development (such as suburban open housing enforcement). Without the former, I do not believe that the residents of the ghetto will be able to take full advantage of the latter.

1. Elliot Liebow, "No Man Can Live With the Terrible Knowledge That He Is Not Needed," *New York Times Magazine*, April 5, 1970, p. 66.
2. Joel Bergsman, *Alternatives to the Non-gilded Ghetto: Notes on Different Goals and Strategies* (Washington, D.C.: Urban Institute, June, 1971), paper no. 113-29, pp. 1-2.
3. Thomas Vietorisz and Bennett Harrison, "Ghetto Development, Community Corporations, and Public Policy," *Review of Black Political Economy*, Fall 1971, pp. 29-30.

The cornerstone of a ghetto development strategy might well be the creation of a network of community development corporations (CDC's), directed entirely by those energetic young activists inside the ghetto who are prepared to challenge existing conditions and who are responsive to the opinions and preferences of the residents of the ghetto. These community development corporations, of which a small number of innovators already exist,[4] might also be invited into the public business of creating new job markets for ghetto workers. This can be done in at least three ways: first, by hiring these corporations to perform outreach and recruiting functions for outside employers, both public (e.g., city hall) and private (e.g., the member companies in the NAB); second, by public investments in the nonprofit corporations themselves; and third, by giving federal public service employment grants (see pp. 186-96) directly to CDC's to produce and deliver public services in the community. The new jobs created within the ghetto by these activities, even if their numbers fall short of the need (as is almost inevitable), ought to pay a handsome social dividend, particularly if they are deliberately skewed toward young males in the community.

A truly comprehensive program of ghetto development might contain some of the following elements, suggested by Tom Hayden:

> ... public housing, administered and owned by a combination of tenants and community housing groups; community control of police: elected civilian review boards in each precinct, with powers to investigate, subpoena, and initiate proceedings for the removal of policemen convicted of brutality against the residents of the community; management of all local branch stores of national chains by local business groups; [and] taxation of all commercial property owned by non-residents, or revenue-sharing with the city and the state.[5]

HUD is in fact about to begin a limited experiment in "community control" of the public housing projects in 14 cities, involving the strengthening of tenant councils and the use of tenant managers. HUD Secretary George Romney described the agency's objectives:

> Hopefully, the end product of these three-year experiments will be improved management, reduced tension and frustration on the part of the tenants, lower operating costs, and greater acceptance of the concept of public housing on the part of the general community.[6]

4. Cf. Geoffrey Faux, *CDC's: New Hope for the Inner City* (New York: Twentieth Century Fund, 1971); and Howard Hallman, *Neighborhood Control of Public Programs: Community Corporations and Neighborhood Boards* (New York: Praeger, 1970).

5. Tom Hayden, "Colonialism and Liberation as American Problems," in *Politics and the Ghettos*, ed. Roland L. Warren (New York: Atherton Press, 1969), pp. 184-85.

6. Kirk Scharfenberg, "Plan Devised to End Public Housing Ills," *Washington Post*, March 19, 1972, p. C1. Another new HUD program—one receiving much greater publicity and financial support—may fail precisely because (so far, at least) it does *not* involve creative institutional change. In six cities, HUD will substitute housing allowances to poor families for government contracts to builders, in the hope that the construction and

Much has been written recently about the issue of community control of ghetto schools. Nearly all of these discussions (not to mention the many abrasive and occasionally explosive confrontations between white teachers and black and brown parents) have focused on the political aspects of control over the education system. One of the few minority leaders who is both sensitive to and articulate about the *economic* consequences and benefits of ghetto control of schools is Roy Innis, national chairman of CORE. Community-controlled schools could, Innis observes, develop curricula directly relevant to the demands of an economic development effort. Job training and work-study programs for adults would be easier to "sell" to the community (and infinitely easier to manage) if the "salesmen" and the "managers" were themselves residents of the community. Moreover, control of the schools would contribute to community economic development not only by providing a trained and motivated (politicized) labor force, but also directly, through the redirection of purchasing contracts. Innis estimates, for example, that "Harlem schools purchase over $100,000,000 in goods and services each year."[7]

Just as there is no logical incompatibility between "inside" and "outside" economic development, so community control of ghetto schools seems perfectly consistent with programs to facilitate integrated "outside" education for the children of those ghetto parents who want it, e.g., through "busing." In any case, the much-heralded benefits to black children of attending integrated schools now appear to have been exaggerated. A major new "re-view" of the Coleman Report, while it reaffirms some of the original conclusions with respect to the determinants of educational achievement, is critical of others.[8] In particular, according to Thomas Pettigrew,

> . . . the gains made by poor blacks in mostly white classes amount to "less than one-sixth of the difference between average Negro and White achievement. . . at grade 12."

---

maintenance industries will thereby provide more low-income housing services to the poor. Many urban economists believe that a number of cities already have a surplus of physical structures, that what is needed is rehabilitation and maintenance, and that those services can best be provided through decentralized private markets. Hence the idea of rent subsidies or housing allowances. "Housing Money That Goes to the People," *Business Week*, January 8, 1972, pp. 51–52. But without community control of the rehabilitation and maintenance activities, the new HUD program may be in for trouble. The Government Operations Committee of the U.S. House of Representatives has "found speculators making huge profits—as much as 60 or 70 percent in three months—on housing rehabilitation programs in Detroit; there is little reason to think they do not do it elsewhere." D. J. R. Bruckner, "The Housing Mess: Romney's Genius for Telling Truth," *Washington Post*, April 5, 1972, p. A24.

7. Quoted in Charles Tate, "Brimmer and Black Capitalism," *Review of Black Political Economy*, Spring/Summer 1970, p. 89. For a broad discussion of these issues by the CORE chairman himself, see Roy Innis, "Separatist Economics: A New Social Contract," in *Black Economic Development*, ed. William F. Haddad and G. Douglas Pugh (Englewood Cliffs, N.J.: Prentice-Hall, 1969).

8. *On Equality of Educational Opportunity*, ed. Frederick Mosteller and Daniel P. Moynihan (New York: Random House, 1972).

Thus . . . the average achievement test deficit of lower-class black high school seniors would be cut [by integration] from about 4 years below the white middle-class norm to about $3\frac{1}{3}$ years below.[9]

Another important activity which CDC's might pursue is the provision of child day care. Some ghetto areas, such as Bedford-Stuyvesant, have few official (i.e., government subsidized) day-care facilities, and these are not widely distributed among the blocks of the ghetto. Other areas, such as Harlem, have a large number of centers which are dispersed throughout the ghetto. Even in the latter case, however, the capacity of these centers is far below the existing and potential demand for space. In the 1968–69 UES conducted in the ghettos of New York City, 75 percent of those women not in the labor force because of "child care problems" reported that no day-care center was located nearby, or that those that were accessible were filled.

The majority of these women said they would use such a center, were it available. During the survey period, the capacity of the day care centers located in or near the poverty areas where the survey was conducted was less than the number of women who said they would use such facilities.[10]

To return for a moment to the development-versus-dispersal controversy, it is important to confront what has (at least among professional economists) been the most persuasive criticism against the former strategy: the relative inefficiency of investment in the ghetto, due to the high costs of "doing business" (especially in the form of labor turnover) and the allegedly low capital-absorption capacity of such areas. Comparative studies of the marginal efficiency of investment inside and outside the ghetto have led many analysts to forecast "red ink for ghetto industries."[11]

Such criticisms are themselves subject to three kinds of rebuttals. In the first place, they ignore the external economies associated (at least potentially) with community control of the development process. For example,

. . . proponents of community industries . . . argue that turnover rates would be lower given indigenous management, different labor relations practices, and greater identification of workers with the success of the business. . . .

9. Laurence Feinberg, "All in the Family? New Study Shows Schools Less Vital Than Home," *Washington Post*, March 12, 1972, p. A1. Columnist Joseph Alsop's rather cynical appraisal of the new study is that, "educationally, desegregation by busing in fact appears to make no significant difference for the black students. Socially, in regard to aspirations, self-image and so on, desegregation by busing further appears to do a certain amount of harm." Joseph Alsop, "Harvard Swallows Hard," *Washington Post*, March 20, 1972, p. A21.

10. U.S. Department of Labor, Bureau of Labor Statistics, Middle Atlantic Regional Office, *Poverty Area Profiles: Working Age Nonparticipants*, Regional Report no. 22, (Washington, D.C.: Govt. Prtg. Off., 1971), p. 4.

11. Cf. John T. Garrity, "Red Ink for Ghetto Industries," *Harvard Business Review*, June-July 1968.

Early experience with black-owned businesses suggests this may be true. Warner and Swasey, for example, reported less problem of turnover in their Hough subsidiary than among nonwhite participants in training programs at their main plant. EG & G Roxbury, Inc. had about fifty of its initial sixty-four trainees still working after nine months. A survey of small businesses in Oakland reported minority employees, particularly Blacks, tended to remain longer with a single employer of their own racial or ethnic groups than white workers stayed with white-owned firms.[12]

This phenomenon has been subsumed under the concept of " 'greenhouse industries,' in which sympathetic nonwhite foremen can train ghetto workers on the job and in a familiar environment until their attendance levels, work performance and preferences warrant 'promotion' (which may involve placement into jobs outside of the ghetto altogether)."[13] It is difficult to imagine any institution other than the community corporation which would be willing and able to accept the reduced profit margins and unorthodox operating procedures (with respect to standards of work and discipline, schedules, and so forth) necessarily associated with such an experiment. "Investment in the slums," as even David Rockefeller admits, "is a bad business risk."[14]

In *The Economic Development of Harlem*, Thomas Vietorisz and I argue that ghetto economic development is

. . . far more than a mechanism for allocating resources efficiently, organizing production, generating profit streams, or even creating jobs. Moreover, jobs created outside the ghetto are incommensurable in their overall social welfare effects with jobs created inside the ghetto as part of an overall development effort. Economic development, wherever it takes place, acts as a catalyst of social and political change. Jobs created inside the ghetto are the instruments as well as the objects of this change, contributing to a reduction in psychological and social pathology, an improvement in the 'technology' of community organization, increased skill levels, and re-enforcement of the community's political base and potential. Conventional economic analysis treats these social effects as external –incidental to, and not very important in light of overall economic activity. We believe, however, that economic development of the ghetto is vital because of the social externalities that it can generate—social benefits far in excess of the mere creation of even a considerable number of otherwise sterile work places.[15]

12. Matthew Edel, "Development vs. Dispersal: Approaches to Ghetto Poverty," in *Readings in Urban Economics,* ed. Matthew Edel and Jerome Rothenberg (New York: Macmillan, 1972), p. 323.

13. Vietorisz and Harrison, "Ghetto Development, Community Corporations, and Public Policy," p. 32. Technically, we are arguing that investments in ghetto-based and locally controlled industries can generate an external economy in the form of a *joint product*: an output (whether good or service) and a trained work force.

14. Quoted in Hayden, "Colonialism and Liberation."

15. Thomas Vietorisz and Bennett Harrison, *The Economic Development of Harlem* (New York: Praeger, 1970) p. 66.

Matthew Edel gives us a concrete example of such externalities from his South American experience:

> In Colombia . . . Community Action Boards formed originally for rural construction projects have a tendency to continue activity into other areas . . . (charity, recreation, agricultural improvement, literacy training, cooperative stores, and advocacy of community interests).[16]

Moreover, according to Edel, "a somewhat similar progression of activities has been observed for neighborhood community development groups in India."

The second problem is that the advocates of development and dispersal operate from radically different assumptions and in terms of significantly different objectives. As Bergsman has observed, one implication of this lack of consistency in the debate is that the *efficiency* of economic development is of limited relevance to the more militant developers, who assume

> . . . that poor minorities will continue to exist as groups or classes for some time, that political and economic power are inextricably linked and cannot exist independently of each other, and that power can be created and exploited only through *institutions* which organize and exercise the more basic sources of power such as money, votes, etc. These assumptions imply that if poor minorities want power . . . there must be economic development of their community . . . based on autonomous institutions controlled by the poor minorities, in the economic as well as the political sphere.[17]

Bergsman contrasts this position with that of the "liberals," whose advocacy of ghetto dispersal and rejection of development as being marginally inefficient is seen to be based upon the acceptance of "existing institutions and the structure of power," and central concern for "helping individuals" by "ameliorating the symptoms or results of the status quo."[18] As between the two "schools,"

> The liberal package has a natural attraction for economists, who at least in this country, are taught to concentrate. on technical matters such as efficiency and to avoid ethical or value problems such as redistribution. This asceticism is often expressed in the 'liberal' package by analyzing proposals in terms of costs and benefits to the society as a whole, and ignoring who pays the costs and who gets the benefits. Since transfers are an essential goal of many programs, such analysis is often not very relevant. Much economic analysis also falls short in considering only marginal changes, in one variable at a time, within a static framework. Real progress in solving problems of poor minorities may well require fairly large changes in certain variables and institutions, and may depend on complex interactions in

---

16. Edel, "Development vs. Dispersal," p. 316.

17. Bergsman, *Alternatives to the Non-Gilded Ghetto*, p. 6.

18. *Ibid.*, p. 8. This distinction is also drawn by Gerson Green and Geoffrey Faux, "The Social Utility of Black Enterprise," in Haddad and Pugh, *Black Economic Development.*

which progress in one dimension depends on progress in others. Considering such complex and larger-scale phenomena is not one of the strong points of most economic analyses.[19]

This is precisely my argument: progress in achieving economic equity for ghetto residents requires the development of political power within the ghetto. *Institutional change* is critical if urban minorities are to be able to deal with society as equals. This—the importance of group development relative to individual development—lies at the center of the confrontation between liberals who advocate "ghetto dispersal" and those radicals advocating "ghetto development." While the former are concerned with efficiency in achieving the goal of integration, the latter are probably more concerned with questions of distributive justice (or equity) and institutional change through collective action.

Finally, any consideration of the development-dispersal controversy at the present time must take into account the promise and the failure of recent public programs designed to achieve integration in employment, if only to appreciate the growing cynicism of young blacks in the ghetto. A single example will suffice. Writing in mid-1968, at the birth of the NAB-JOBS program, Robert A. Levine (then affiliated with OEO, now a member of the research staff of the RAND Corporation) predicted that full integration in employment was possible and that JOBS was the answer: "through programs like JOBS, very large parts of business have made a much tougher commitment to . . . positively encourage the bringing of black people and other minorities into their plants." Besides, "the locus of real power and real money in American business has shifted out of the returns to ownership anyhow [so that] the whole ghetto economic development approach was pretty badly conceived to begin with. As fast as black people can be trained to be managers, the real route to economic power will be open. . . . [T]he competition for black executives seems as tough as any such competition in American economic history."[20] Unhappily, as we have seen, Levine's prediction has not been realized—and those in the urban ghetto know it.

NEW DIRECTIONS II: PUBLIC EMPLOYMENT

The prevalence of involuntary part-time employment and substandard wages, in conjunction with the findings of low returns to education, strongly suggests that existing urban labor markets underutilize ghetto workers—do not permit these workers to realize their potential productivities. The prin-

19. Bergsman, *Alternatives to the Non-Gilded Ghetto*, p. 9.
20. Robert A. Levine, "Black Power, White Style," (mimeographed, U.S. Office of Economic Opportunity, June, 1968), p. 20. This view of the "real route to economic power" for blacks is shared by a number of prominent black economists, including Andrew Brimmer and Sir W. Arthur Lewis.

cipal remedy must be sought in opening up new urban job markets to the ghetto poor, markets whose jobs are physically accessible to ghetto residents, whose availability is made known to them, and whose entry level wages and promotional possibilities will in fact lead to a significant improvement in their levels of living.

At the same time, and quite apart from the problems of the ghetto, Harold Sheppard has noted

> . . . a need for more workers in what has been called "public service employment." Unfortunately, this need has been obscured by the use of such terms as "government as employer of the last resort," which implies that such employment should be advocated and provided only after private enterprise has failed to employ everyone; that these jobs with government agencies are only temporary, pending the rise in demand for workers in private enterprise; and that such jobs are not very desirable for the individual or useful and worth while to the community.

> But government is more than an employer: more accurately, its function is to provide services to citizens—such as education, health protection, national defense, park and recreation facilities, waste disposal, water services, construction and maintenance of highways and other transportation facilities, police and fire protection, etc.

> In living up to these and other obligations, the government obviously employs persons in jobs which are vital to the functioning of the society and the economy. The main point here is that the need for the services to be provided is the underlying justification for public service employment.

> . . . the present level of services in all these categories is inadequate to meet public needs; an expansion of services would provide more jobs. Furthermore, it can be argued that these public services facilitate growth in the private sector, and that if the latter is to prosper, it requires an 'infrastructure' of the public service facilities, provided by public service employees.[21]

Thus, a promising strategy for moving the ghetto poor out of the limited job market to which they are presently confined is the development of public service jobs for urban ghetto residents. Such a program would, as indicated by Sheppard, be based not only on the income requirements of the poor themselves, but also and more fundamentally on the growing needs of all the residents of urban areas for expanded public services. Growing shortages in the supply of these "social overheads" penalize urban businesses as well as individual consumers. Moreover, our earlier analysis of the NAB-JOBS program strongly suggests that purely private enterprise "solutions" to urban poverty have little chance of success, at least in the short run.

There are many precedents for the proposal to use an entire sector of the urban economy as the vehicle for minority advancement. "It is," says

---

21. Harold L. Sheppard, *The Nature of the Job Problem and the Role of New Public Service Employment* (Kalamazoo, Mich.: W. E. Upjohn Institute, 1969), pp. 19-20.

Anthony Pascal, "difficult to think of a minority in the United States or elsewhere that did not utilize occupational specialization and, to some extent, dominance, as a ladder to assimilation." Pascal goes on to suggest that

> ... interest in public employment as an occupational ladder stems from the fact that its encouragement would be capitalizing on a process that is already underway. The government sector, especially at state and local levels, is growing rapidly. Also, Negroes are forming increasingly large fractions of the populations of many cities and will constitute a majority in several within the next decade. The urban population changes and consequent politicization of Negroes, when combined with the growth industry aspects of the public services, would together seem to present a target of opportunity.
> A precedent for the use of public employment to improve opportunities of a special group exists in the case of veteran's preferences on civil service examinations. A similar and even more meaningful preference system might be implemented for the benefit of the poor.
> The recommendation explored here should be distinguished from proposals that the government act as an "employer of the last resort." Examples of public employment proposed would be policemen, firemen, teachers, social workers, and clerks—not leaf rakers or cleaning women.[22]

Pascal argues that the public sector is a logical target for minority job developers. There is evidence that it is also likely to be a more equitable employer of nonwhites. The statistical models developed in Chapter Two can be used to compare the returns to education enjoyed by white and nonwhite ghetto dwellers employed by public and private employers. The results are shown in table 15. Education does indeed have more "punch" for nonwhites in government jobs than for nonwhites in private industry, after removing the effects of age, sex, training experience, and city of residence. For example, ghetto nonwhites working in state and local government earn an additional $1.79 per week and face a 0.7 percent lower risk of annual unemployment for each year of schooling completed. For a black high school graduate, these figures translate into substantial returns of an additional $21.48 in weekly earnings and an 8.4 percent smaller chance of annual unemployment, relative to a similar worker employed in the private sector. Table 15 identifies twelve private industrial categories, in addition to the two public sector classes. Among *none* of these fourteen groups is the payoff to white education affected significantly by industry. In other words, the marginal effect of education on the wages and unemployment rates of ghetto whites is independent of whether they are employed by the public or the private sector.

Within the metropolitan areas of the United States in 1969, the large majority of black families (79 percent) and nearly 60 percent of those house-

22. Anthony H. Pascal, "Manpower Training and Jobs," in *Cities in Trouble: An Agenda for Urban Research*, ed. Pascal (Santa Monica, Cal.: RAND Corporation, 1968), document no. RM-5603-RC, pp. 77-78.

Table 15

Education-Industry Interaction Terms in
Central City Poverty Areas in Twelve SMSAs

Industry	Earnings Effect ($/wk)		Unemployment Effect (*percent*)	
	Whites	Nonwhites	Whites	Nonwhites
Manufacturing (durable goods)	.14 (.14)	−.10 (.21)	−.08 (.21)	.54 (2.12)[a]
Manufacturing (nondurable goods)	.48 (.58)	.15 (.42)	.14 (.45)	.13 (.64)
Transportation	−3.95 (1.46)	−.56 (.56)	−.99 (1.00)	.27 (.50)
Communications	1.22 (.64)	–	−.71 (1.02)	–
Utilities and sanitation	.78 (.19)	.48 (.34)	−.14 (.09)	.48 (.62)
Wholesale	1.90 (1.03)	.90 (.73)	−.39 (.58)	−.52 (.78)
Retail	−.82 (1.05)	−.59 (1.74)	.01 (.04)	−.03 (.14)
Finance, insurance, real estate	1.17 (1.71)	−.74 (.93)	−.55 (1.31)	−.31 (.22)
Business and repair services	2.51 (1.86)	−.67 (.84)	−.21 (.41)	−.40 (.93)
Personal services	−.95 (.83)	−1.29 (4.42)[b]	–	−.85 (5.37)[b]
Entertainment and recreational services	–	–	–	–
Professional services	−.90 (1.10)	−.85 (.77)	−.05 (.09)	−.77 (1.22)
Federal government	2.57 (1.78)	2.94 (5.85)[b]	.11 (.20)	−.14 (.50)
State and local government	.99 (.79)	1.79 (3.60)[b]	−.21 (.43)	−.69 (2.55)[a]

Note: t - statistics in parentheses.
[a] Significantly different from zero at the 0.05 level.
[b] Significantly different from zero at the 0.01 level.

holds (of all races) with incomes below $4,000 lived inside the central city. It is useful, therefore, to inquire about the intrametropolitan location of public employers. Are these federal, state and local government offices accessible to central city low-income households, or do they tend to be located in the suburbs, requiring extensive (and probably expensive) "reverse commuting" which only a relatively small number of disadvantaged central city workers will find it profitable to undertake?

In an interesting research project conducted about a decade ago, Louis K. Loewenstein attempted to chart the location patterns of eight major employment sectors within thirty-nine large metropolitan areas. Using land use maps from the master plans of each city, Loewenstein created a graph for each major sector, showing the "typical" location propensities of each. These are represented in figure 27.[23]

23. Using land-use maps, Loewenstein divided each metropolitan area into five concentric rings. The center of the innermost ring was fixed on the major intersection of the central business district, while the "radius of the outermost circle was determined by a

Figure 27

Intraurban Location Patterns of Eight Major Employment
Sectors in Thirty-nine Metropolitan Areas, 1960

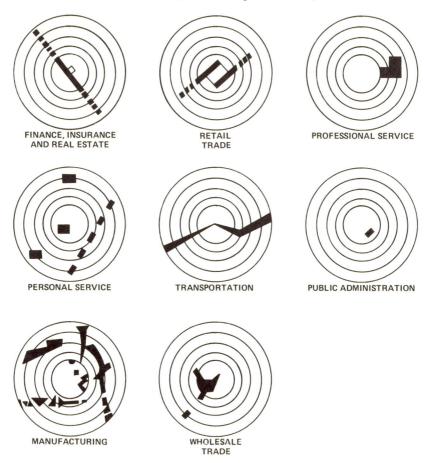

FINANCE, INSURANCE AND REAL ESTATE	RETAIL TRADE	PROFESSIONAL SERVICE
PERSONAL SERVICE	TRANSPORTATION	PUBLIC ADMINISTRATION
MANUFACTURING	WHOLESALE TRADE	

Source: Louis K. Loewenstein, "The Location of Urban Land Uses," *Land Economics*
November 1963.

It is clear that land allocated to "public administration" is located almost
entirely within the innermost part of the central city. Thus, for example,
"manufacturing activities typically tend to be dispersed away from the core,
while governmental activities tend to congregate at or toward the center."

_____

point which averaged the four directional limits of the metropolitan areas as depicted in
the base maps." Louis K. Loewenstein, "The Location of Urban Land Uses," *Land
Economics*, November 1963, p. 409.

Loewenstein also constructed a "concentration index" based upon the proportion of the total area in each ring allocated to a given use. This index varies between −1.000 for complete dispersion through zero for uniform spatial distribution to +1.000 for complete concentration. The manufacturing index (lowest of the eight) displayed a value of 0.2800. The government index (highest of the eight) was three times larger: 0.8400. These differences in relative concentration were found to be statistically significant in an analysis of variance.

Census data by place of work confirm Loewenstein's somewhat impressionistic observations. In a 1966 sample of fourteen large metropolitan areas, an average of two-thirds of all (federal, state and local) urban public jobs were found to be located within the central city. In half of the SMSAs in the sample, central cities contained at least 70 percent of all SMSA public sector jobs.[24] This finding stands in marked contrast to the private sector patterns identified by Kain and reported earlier.

The public sector would not be such an enticing object of interest for minority job developers, even given the apparent locational advantage, were it not for the fact that this is also a rapidly-growing "industry." In fact, for the nation as a whole, services have become a more important source of new jobs than manufactured goods. Almost the entire increase in total U.S. employment between 1947 and 1970 was in the service sector. In 1947, U.S. nonagricultural employment totaled 43.9 million jobs. By 1970, the number had risen to 70.7 million. Almost the entire increase (82 percent) occurred in the industries (especially government) which provide services, e.g., banks, hospitals, schools, transportation, rather than in industries which produce goods, e.g., steel, chemicals, paper.[25]

The increase alone in employment in education between 1950 and 1960 exceeded total employment in steel, copper, and aluminum combined in either year. Between 1950 and 1960, the change alone in employment in the health industry was larger than the total number of automobile workers in either year. And between 1953 and 1963, manufacturing employment actually fell by better than 4 percent nationally, while among the principal components of the service sector—business services, medical and health, and state and local government—employment increased over the same period by 131 percent, 73 percent, and 77 percent, respectively.[26]

Service employment is now the fastest growing source of jobs in all of the nation's cities, and an increasingly important source of incomes. And of the various "industries" producing these urban services, government is the most

24. Bennett Harrison, *Public Employment and Urban Poverty* (Washington, D.C.: Urban Institute, 1971), paper no. 113−43, table 1.

25. U.S. Department of Labor, *1971 Manpower Report of the President* (Washington, D.C.: Govt. Prtg. Off., 1971), table C−1. A third of the new service jobs developed between 1947 and 1970 were in government.

26. Victor Fuchs, "The New Society: The First Service Economy," *Public Interest*, Winter 1966.

important of all. Between 1958 and 1967, local governments in New York City provided nearly 100,000 new jobs for the region's workers. This was nearly twice the number generated by the next "best" sector: business services (such as secretarial agencies). During the same period, New York City lost nearly 160,000 manufacturing jobs. In 1967, services accounted for two-thirds of all employment in Baltimore. A quarter of these were in the public sector. In Columbus, nearly 70 percent of the city's people worked in the service industries, and nearly a third of these service jobs were in government. In cities as diverse in character and as far apart as Portland, Oregon; Nashville, Tennessee; and Boston, Massachusetts; over 10 percent of total personal income in 1962 came from public employment .[27]

Every expert predicts that this phenomenal growth in our urban public service "industries" will continue into the future, generating greater and greater demands for personnel. Between 1964 and 1975, according to the USDL, public demand for new workers in education will grow by 42 percent; in health by 70 percent; in housing by 92 percent; in sanitation by 86 percent. Between 1964 and 1975, according to the National Planning Association, public demand for new librarians will have grown by 102 percent; for welfare and recreation workers by 97 percent; for office-machine operators by 117 percent; for hospital and prison attendants by 144 percent; and for firemen and policemen by 78 percent.[28] These projections are probably more reliable than those which economists make for private employment, due to the extraordinary secular stability of public service employment. During three of the four recessions experienced in the United States since World War II, total private employment actually fell. Public employment, on the other hand, has *never* fallen below its previous annual average. During 1970—also a recession year—private employment in the United States rose at the weak rate of seven-tenths of one percent over its 1969 level. Government jobs, however, expanded at a rate of 3.3 percent.[29] Between March of 1970 and March of 1971, state and local government employment rose by 4.4 percent and 4.2 percent, respectively. [30]

In the spring of 1968, the National Urban Coalition asked the mayors of fifty large cities to estimate the number of additional personnel needed now in order to assure the adequate delivery of public services in their cities. The questionnaires were analyzed by the W. E. Upjohn Institute. Using the responses of thirty-four of the mayors as a base, Upjohn's Dr. Harold Sheppard estimated that the nation's 130 largest cities could usefully absorb about

27. Bennett Harrison, "Public Service Jobs for Urban Ghetto Residents," *Good Government*, Fall 1969, pp. 2–4.

28. *Ibid.*, pp. 5–6.

29. U.S. Department of Labor, *1971 Manpower Report*, table A–11.

30. U.S. Department of Labor, Bureau of Labor Statistics, "State and Local Government Employment and Payrolls," Statistical Series M/L 328, May 1970 and June 1971.

280,000 new workers now, for everything from antipollution enforcement to parks departments. Moreover, if those cities were willing to lower existing barriers to employment of the disadvantaged (such as refusing to hire workers with police records), then (according to the mayors) another 140,000 poor workers could usefully be employed in the public service.[31]

All together, the USDL projects an increase of 15.3 million new jobs in the service industries between 1968 and 1980, as against 3.4 million new jobs in the goods producing industries. And government alone is expected to contribute nearly a third of the new service jobs.[32]

Will new jobs in the public sector help the ghetto families we have been studying? An examination of the respective wage and salary levels indicates a clearly affirmative answer. In general, ghetto workers who can be moved into (or vertically within) the public service agencies in their respective cities can expect to increase their wage incomes by a factor of between one and three times.[33]

Female clerical workers living in Harlem and heading families earned about $260 a month in 1966. According to Public Personnel Association documents, New York City government clerk-typists start at between $363 and $480 per month. In Baltimore, they start at $377 and progress after five years to $478.

Male household heads living in the North Side ghetto of St. Louis earned wages of about $296 a month in 1966. As computer operators for any one of a number of St. Louis's local governments, they could double their incomes— St. Louis pays $512-$622 per month for computer operators.

"Welfare mothers" in the slums of New Orleans who gambled by taking a job averaged wages of only $140 per month in 1966. As nursing assistants for the City of New Orleans, they would start at $358 a month—over two and one-half times what they are earning now.

Mexican-born fathers in the Mission-Fillmore slum of San Francisco earned only $328 a month in 1966. As recreation leaders for the City of San Francisco or the State of California—perhaps working right in their own neighborhood—they could double their earnings; recreation leaders in San Francisco government earn anywhere from $653 to $795 per month.

In designing a relevant public jobs program, it is important to recognize that there are really three (and perhaps four) "jobs problems" in our core cities, and not just one.[34] A third of those metropolitan area residents who

31. Sheppard, *Nature of the Job Problem.*
32. U.S. Department of Labor, *1971 Manpower Report,* table E–11.
33. The following four paragraphs are based upon calculations from the 1966 UES data file studied in Chapter Three and c   public sector wage figures published in Harrison, "Public Service Jobs."
34. The following discussion is based upon Anthony Downs, *Who Are the Urban Poor?* (New York: Committee for Economic Development, October, 1968), supplementary paper no. 26.

live in poverty areas are in households headed by men who do work, but who receive only the substandard wages described earlier. These workers require better jobs at higher wages.

Over half of all the poor living in metropolitan areas are in households whose head is presently unable to work, either because he is too old, or because he is physically (or psychologically) disabled, or because the head is a female with children. Of this group, only a small portion (consisting primarily of the "welfare mothers") are likely to be responsive to a jobs program, and the President of the United States does the nation no service by exaggerating this potential. Anthony Downs of the Real Estate Research Corporation estimates that about 190,000 "welfare mothers" might be brought into the urban labor force through "new careers" type jobs. Of course, we will also need to establish adequate day-care centers and transportation for them.

The remaining one-seventh of all metropolitan area poor people live in households headed by non-disabled men under age sixty-five who can work, who have tried to find work, but who are now unemployed. This is where we must look to find the so-called "hard-core" unemployed. These men require new jobs—about 570,000 of them, according to Downs.

Actually, we might talk about yet another class: teenagers. They are scattered throughout all three of the above categories, and many of them need good jobs—especially part-time jobs. For many young students from the ghetto, a good summer job may make it possible for them to return to school and fight for a career.

A systematic, comprehensive public service jobs program can address itself to each of these categories of need. Such a policy will, as indicated previously, simultaneously address itself to the growing personnel requirements of public service agencies in the nation's cities. Bold, new approaches will be needed in the area of recruitment, prevocational training, placement, and especially in the design of relatively culture-free examinations and performance tests. One issue in public manpower planning which will have to be addressed is the relevance of so-called "career ladders." Most "new careers" programs advocate the development of such ladders.[35] But there are analysts who believe that the concern for "careers" has been overdone. Elliot Liebow, for example, argues:

> The job of the lathe operator, the assembly-line worker, the truck driver, the secretary, these tend to be dead-end jobs too, but they are not bad jobs because of it. Not everyone in our society is career-oriented. We have a large and relatively stable working-class population which does not aspire to moving up a career ladder. The working man who earns a living and supports his family by doing work that everyone agrees is socially useful does not necessarily want to become a foreman, or plant manager, or

35. Cf. Arthur Pearl and Frank Riessman, *New Careers for the Poor* (Glencoe, Ill.: Free Press, 1965).

office executive. If he is dissatisfied, it is probably because he wants more of what he has, and wants to be more certain of keeping what he has, not because he wants something different.[36]

Thus, the emergence of what Victor Fuchs calls "the service economy" creates an unparalleled opportunity to broaden the employment possibilities of ghetto workers. It will not be easy to open the public service to the residents of the slums. In what is perhaps a not untypical attitude of employers toward nonwhite workers who do acquire skill and experience, the U.S. Civil Rights Commission reports that "the director of finance for the city of Baton Rouge, when asked if he would hire a Negro certified as qualified by his city's civil service commission, replied: 'Would you steal a million dollars?' "[37] Many public agencies are presently as exploitative of the poor and the nonwhite as is the private sector, particularly with respect to ghetto dwellers. Nonwhite men living in urban poverty neighborhoods are presently underrepresented in government jobs, relative to all urban nonwhite men.[38] Moreover, there are real and imaginary administrative obstacles to be overcome (an example of the latter is the mistaken belief that civil service examinations must, by law, be written).

As was reported in Chapter One, educational requirements for jobs in America are greatly inflated, relative to the actual technical tasks required for average performance. A public employment program in the cities could, therefore, be "fruitfully preceded by the reduction of educational requirements for large numbers of jobs in the public sector, and [given] wide publicity when success follows."[39] In the State of Pennsylvania alone, a single review of entry requirements in 1969 "resulted in the elimination of high school graduation as a requirement in various entry-level classes of work involving about 20,000 positions. The review is continuing on an on-going basis."[40]

In fact, limited experiments along these lines are already underway. The National Civil Service League has undertaken the task of stimulating public employment of ghetto residents under merit principles at state and local levels, under the sponsorship of the Model Cities Program of HUD and other

36. Liebow, "No Man Can Live," p. 132.

37. U.S. Commission on Civil Rights, *For All the People . . . By All the People* (Washington, D.C.: Govt. Prtg. Off., 1969), p. 3.

38. In 1967, 15.9 percent of all nonwhite males living in central city poverty areas worked for federal, state or local governments. Of the remaining nonwhite male urban population, 23.9 percent were government employees. Hazel M. Willacy, "Men in Poverty Neighborhoods: A Status Report," *Monthly Labor Review*, February 1969, table 3.

39. Ivar Berg, *Education and Jobs: The Great Training Robbery* (New York: Praeger, 1970), p. 135.

40. Private communication from Mr. Henry C. Adams, Jr., Chief, Fair Employment Division, Bureau of Personnel, Office of Administration, Commonwealth of Pennsylvania, May 5, 1970.

programs of OEO and USDL. USDL has, for two years, operated an experimental "Public Service Careers Program." OEO finances technical assistance to state and local public agencies seeking help in developing minority manpower programs, under "Project PACE MAKER." The 1971 Emergency Employment Act requires state and local governments to address themselves to civil service barriers to the employment of the disadvantaged as a condition for receipt of a grant from the $2.25 billion fund created to subsidize public employment.

Much further effort is needed, however. Our cities are faced with the twin problems of ghetto underemployment and a growing shortage of public services. Each of these problems may carry the solution to the other.

NEW DIRECTIONS III: PUBLIC SANCTIONS ON THE HIRING PRACTICES OF PRIVATE EMPLOYERS

While the growth of public service jobs presents exciting possibilities for expanding the employment opportunities of minorities, it is still the case that between three-and four-fifths of the labor force presently work in the private sector. The federal government has created three agencies whose manifest function is to attack discriminatory practices among private employers and labor unions.

By an Executive Order of March 7, 1961, President Kennedy directed the federal government to assume responsibility for the promotion of "the full realization of equal employment opportunity."[41] An Office of Federal Contract Compliance (OFCC) was created within the USDL, and was granted the authority to initiate investigations to determine whether discriminatory practices exist, to terminate government contracts in excess of $1 million to private firms convicted of discrimination on the basis of sex or race, and to "require employers to take 'affirmative action' to remedy past discrimination." Unfortunately, the power of the OFCC has rarely been used. Firms with "contacts" in the Congress and the Executive Offices have usually been able to avoid prosecution, and some government agencies (such as the Department of Defense) have been unwilling to upset the "orderly procurement" of privately produced goods and services by bringing sanctions against discriminatory contractors. According to Bradley Schiller: "The power of the OFCC remains on paper. As yet, no contract has ever been terminated or cancelled to enforce equal opportunity."

Title VII of the Civil Rights Act of 1964 made discrimination by companies and unions illegal. The enforcement of the law was delegated to an Equal Employment Opportunity Commission. EEOC issues guidelines, con-

41. This and the following paragraph are drawn from Bradley R. Schiller, *The Economics of Poverty and Discrimination* (Engelwood Cliffs, N.J.: Prentice-Hall, 1972), chap. 14.

ducts research, monitors the racial and sexual composition of the work force of large companies, and often gives legal advice to individuals and groups suing for redress under the 14th Amendment and Title VII provisions. Unfortunately, however, the EEOC is not equipped to take any direct action itself. Its Congressional mandate authorizes the Commission to "endeavor to eliminate any [discriminatory] employment practice by informal methods of conference, conciliation, and persuasion." EEOC has no power to impose sanctions, nor may it issue cease and desist orders, and periodic attempts by some Congressmen to give it such powers have consistently failed. In fact, EEOC is not even permitted to "make public the fact that discrimination is being practiced" in a particular industry. Individuals with grievances must initiate a sworn complaint to the Commission. "If the complaint appears well-founded, the Commission then approaches the offending employer, union, or employment agency for 'conference, conciliation, and persuasion.' If conciliation is not attained, the complainant may seek redress in the courts." This process is time-consuming and expensive for the complainant, and is for those reasons especially likely to prevent justice from accruing to the poor.

The third program—probably the most well-known (if not the most successful)—is the so-called "Philadelphia Plan," designed to compel large construction unions to integrate their work forces. Launched in 1969 in the city of Philadelphia (from where it acquired its name), the program has gradually been extended to other labor market areas, whose firms and unions have been asked by the USDL to formulate so-called "home town plans." But the Philadelphia Plan, "which can compel the hiring of members of minority groups on Federal projects totaling $500,000 or more . . . has not begun to produce even minimal gains toward its modest goal of breaking the color barrier in six construction trades. As a result, the Department of Labor is moving to sue a number of contractors."[42]

On March 8, 1971, the U.S. Supreme Court handed down what may well prove to be a landmark decision. In *Willie S. Griggs et al.* vs. *Duke Power Company*, black employees in a class action brought suit to prevent the employer from allegedly violating the Civil Rights Act of 1964 by requiring a high school diploma and achievement of a "satisfactory intelligence test score" for certain jobs. The jobs in question had been previously limited to white employees. The plaintiffs alleged that the requirements of a high school diploma and a "satisfactory" score on the intelligence test had the effect of preserving the "effects of the employer's past racial discrimination." Chief Justice Warren Burger set forth the unanimous opinion of the court:

> . . . [T]he Civil Rights Act prohibits an employer from requiring a high school education or passing of a standardized general intelligence test as a condition of employment in or transfer to jobs when:

42. *New York Times,* July 20, 1970, p. 1.

1. neither standard [high school diploma or passing of a general intelligence test] is shown to be significantly related to successful job performance;

2. both requirements operate to disqualify Negroes at a substantially higher rate than white applicants; and

3. the jobs in question formerly had been filled only by white employees as part of a long standing practice of giving preference to whites.[43]

The court went on to say that the congressional intent or objective in enacting Title VII of the Civil Rights Act of 1964 "was to achieve equality of employment opportunities and remove barriers which operated in the past to favor an identifiable group of white employees over other employees. Practices, procedures, or tests neutral on their face, and even neutral in terms of intent, cannot be maintained if they operate to freeze the *status quo* of prior discriminatory practices." In that regard, the court stated that "good intent or absence of discriminatory intent does not redeem employment procedures or testing mechanisms that operate as 'built-in headwinds' for minority groups and are unrelated to measuring job capability." The court held that the employer has the burden of showing that a "given requirement has a manifest relationship to the employment in question," and that Section 703 (h) of the Civil Rights Act of 1964 was properly construed by the EEOC in its *Guidelines on Employee Selection Procedures* (29 CFR Secs. 1607.1– 1607.14), as permitting the use of only job-related tests.

It should be noted that the court did not proscribe the use of testing or measuring procedures per se. What is proscribed is giving these devices and mechanisms controlling force unless it can be demonstrated that they measure job performance. "If an employment practice which operates to exclude Negroes cannot be shown to be related to job performance, the practice is prohibited." A showing of "business necessity" is required to establish the validity of an employment practice in these cases.

A large and growing number of suits are being brought against both private and public employers, with *Griggs* being invoked as a precedent. For example, in *Carter* vs. *Gallagher* (Case No. 4–70 Civ. 399, United States District Court, Fourth Division of Minn., 1971), the court was presented with statistical data that showed that only six out of a total of 24 blacks who had taken the firefighters examination since 1948 had passed; and for various reasons none of the six who had passed were ever hired. The complaint further alleged that the test and testing method used by the Civil Service Commission for firefighters discriminated against certain minority groups, in that it denied said groups an equal employment opportunity. The court enjoined (prohibited) the use of the current firefighters examination until it can be validated according to the guidelines issued by the EEOC; required that references in

43. *Griggs* v. *Duke Power Co.*, 91 U.S. 849 (1971).

applications for employment regarding "arrests," as such, be eliminated (such reference must now refer to "convictions" as opposed to mere "arrests," and the circumstances surrounding any conviction must be considered); eliminated the requirement for a high school diploma for "entry level" firefighters positions; required affirmative action in the recruitment of minorities; and required that the next twenty firefighting positions that become vacant be filled by minority applicants without regard to their place on the list of eligibles.

So far, however, the White House itself has been unwilling to take a strong public position against discriminatory practices in employment. At an urban problems conference at the RAND Corporation in 1967, Lester Thurow proposed a strong equal employment program, which would: (1) Permit the OFCC to impose heavy fines upon employers who are not in compliance; they should be large enough to jeopardize the profitability of a contract. (2) Give the EEOC the power to issue cease and desist orders enforceable in federal courts. (3) Shift the burden of proof in both EEOC and OFCC complaints from the complainant, where it now seems to rest, to the defendant. (4) Specifically outlaw hiring and promotion criteria which cannot be shown to be causally linked to job performance on the job for which the applicant is hired. (5) Require government contracts to be let with a clause which specified that after the date the contract went into effect, some fairly large percentage of all new hires would have to be selected from low-income groups and/or poverty area residents. These individuals must be trained for regular jobs, but the costs of doing so could be included in the contract bid. (6) Place minority group hiring quotas on all government agencies. Of these frankly radical proposals, Thurow says: "If they are politically impossible, large minority group employment gains are politically impossible."[44]

NEW DIRECTIONS IV: COMPREHENSIVE REDEVELOPMENT OF THE CENTRAL CITY

One of the more interesting findings in Chapter Four was that the neighborhoods outside the ghetto but inside the suburbs comprise the part of the metropolis where the most successful nonwhites tend to live. These individuals and their organizations will surely come to dominate central city populations—and politics—within our lifetime. They clearly have a stake in the economic redevelopment of central cities.

The task of redevelopment will itself be the source of an enormous number of jobs (thus, for example, black organizations in the District of Columbia periodically succeed in halting construction of the new regional subway [Metro], demanding a significant share of the jobs and construction contracts

44. Lester Thurow, "Raising Incomes through Manpower Training Programs," in *Contributions to the Analysis of Urban Problems*, ed. Anthony H. Pascal (Santa Monica, Cal.: RAND Corporation, August, 1968), document no. P–3868, p. 101.

created by this project). The ultimate payoff, however, is a revitalized commercial-industrial sector within the urban core. Perhaps no city in the United States has greater need for such revitalization than New York, and few cities have undertaken a more rigorous analysis of the problem:

> An example of city planning and action for industrial renewal is pro-
> vided by New York City, where efforts in this direction date from 1967.
> The New York program aims at creating at least 100,000 new industrial
> jobs by 1980 to keep industries employing blue-collar workers in the
> central city and thus provide more and better jobs for low-skilled workers.
> It is hoped that a maximum number of jobs can be provided through
> intensive utilization of scarce industrial land, by means of new multistory
> industrial construction in places with good access to mass transit facilities.
>   Between 1960 and 1965, the city lost an estimated 20,000 jobs a year
> in manufacturing and other industries with a blue-collar work force and
> 7,000 annually between 1965 and 1970. While blue-collar jobs were de-
> creasing, a steady flow of unskilled workers entered the labor market. As
> of 1970, half the city's labor force had not completed high school. City
> planning officials felt that efforts to increase educational attainment
> should be accompanied by programs to provide employment for those
> who had left school early.
>   Natural business turnover seems to result in piecemeal, small-site devel-
> opments. The assembly of sizable plots of land is nearly impossible with-
> out public intervention. The city, on the other hand, can acquire sites as
> they become available and then combine them into plots suitable for larger
> plants. The initial New York City Planning Department survey located
> more than 500 vacant or underused parcels of industrial land in the city,
> with possibilities for immediate development. From this total, 200 prime
> sites, each covering more than one acre and located within a half mile of a
> subway station, were identified as most suitable for acquisition and leasing
> to desirable manufacturing concerns.
>   Although land in New York is costly, the competition for it is fierce.
> City planners hope to have an opportunity to chose companies carefully
> for industrial renewal projects. According to selection criteria developed
> by the planning department, the ideal company is one that pays high
> wages, uses relatively little floor space per worker, provides seasonally
> stable employment, is willing to hire minority workers, and makes avail-
> able training to upgrade the skills of the labor force.[45]

Given the strong historical trend toward dispersal or "suburbanization" of blue-collar-intensive industry and (white) population discussed earlier, it becomes apparent that a major long-run issue in urban economic planning is whether to develop the central city, or to encourage continued dispersal of center city residents (of all races) to the suburbs or exurbs. At the turn of the century, architect Frank Lloyd Wright foresaw the current development-

45. U.S. Department of Labor, *1971 Manpower Report*, pp. 105–6.

versus-dispersal controversy when "he predicted that the future would involve a race between the elevator and the automobile, and the wise man would bet on the automobile."[46]

Partly because of the automobile, other changes in transport technologies, and government subsidization of suburban real estate, dispersal has indeed been the norm. However, new technological developments make it at least technically feasible to redevelop the core.[47] These are bound up in what Irving Hoch of Resources for the Future calls "the three dimensional city":

> Perhaps, as a residual of agricultural applications, there is a tendency to think of land in terms of two dimensions—as the surface of the earth. But land in urban areas is a three-dimensional resource, in practice as well as principle. . . .
>
> The multiple use of urban "land," the lease or sale of air rights, and the purchase of apartments in condominiums can then be viewed as particular topics under the general heading of land seen in the broad as space.[48]

The basic idea of three-dimensional city planning is to so imaginatively exploit vertical space as to restore the comparative advantage of high density central city living. Lyle Fitch gives an example of integrated three-dimensional central city development. His "megastructure" (the term is commonly known and used by modern architects and planners) embodies a mix of planning principles, from Jane Jacobs's advocacy of functional diversity through mixed zoning[49] to Wright's original identification of the trade-off between vertical and horizontal transport technologies:

> The upper half of future skyscraper cities might well be residential, the middle zone institutional, the lower zone commercial and manufacturing. In such an urban structure, daily commutation would involve a vertical trip of thirty stories instead of a horizontal trip of many miles.
>
> The skyscraper of the future should be served by aerial streets at every eight or ten stories. In office buildings, these aerial streets would offer the range of amenities and services required for a business district—restaurants, cafes, bars, specialty shops. . . . Public and private transportation—wheeled

46. Irving Hoch, "The Three-Dimensional City," in *The Quality of the Urban Environment*, ed. Harvey S. Perloff (Baltimore, Md.: Johns Hopkins Press, 1969), p. 129.

47. John F. Kain says: "I know of no good statement of why these trends should be reversed. It is not obvious that a reduction in central area employment and population densities is detrimental." Kain, "Distribution and Movement of Jobs and Industry," in *The Metropolitan Enigma*, ed. James Q. Wilson (Cambridge, Mass.: Harvard University Press, 1968), p. 37. Apart from the previous evidence that suburbanization is of little value to nonwhites, I would suggest that it is a matter of tastes. If direct human interaction is preferred to communication between humans through intermediary mechanical or electronic devices, then agglomeration (the essential economic characteristic of cities) is necessary and desirable.

48. Hoch, "Three-Dimensional City," p. 89.

49. Jane Jacobs, *The Death and Life of Great American Cities* (New York: Random House, 1961).

traffic of all sorts—would be carried by special streets at some intermediate plane, e.g., at the thirtieth floor for a group of forty-five-story sky-scrapers.[50]

Virtually the entire technology necessary to permit high-density development without crowding and with ample provision for Ms. Jacobs's "casual interaction" already exists. One industrial example of an imaginative technological solution to the urban space shortage is the design by a Chicago firm of a prototypical "high-rise industrial building" with capability for vertical materials-handling, truck access to every floor via graded roadways which circle the building, and subterranean parking and loading areas.[51]

These concepts all imply even greater concentration of economic activity than now exists in central cities. However, as Kenneth Patton recently explained to a Congressional committee on urban growth,

> ... [I]t is important to distinguish concentration from congestion ... [I]n New York City ... the least congested place ... is perhaps the most densely developed, and that is Rockefeller Center. Rockefeller Center has a very functional separation of pedestrian activity, automotive activity, and mass transit, all surrounding a very important amenity, and the density of development is enormous. By contrast, perhaps the most congested part of New York City is Chinatown, which is probably one of the least densely developed places.[52]

Patton, who (as director of New York City's Economic Development Administration) is one of the most progressive and dynamic economic developers in the United States, notes also that high density central city development has important ecological implications. "The city," he told the Congressmen, "is a conservation device in the best sense of environmental conservation. It is a concentration of activity in an efficient place, using mass transit and elevator systems to provide for human interaction in a way that is very sympathetic with the need to preserve the environment."[53]

All of these techniques are being combined by planners into an exciting new strategy for central city redevelopment: the construction of "new towns in-town."[54] Several economists have advised decision-makers to discount the

50. Quoted in Hoch, "Three-Dimensional City," p. 131.

51. John H. Alschuler and Irving M. Footlik, "Industry Can Cut Costs with Multi-Story Buildings," *Mid-Chicago Development Study* (Washington, D.C.: Economic Development Administration Technical Assistance Project, 1966), vol. 1.

52. D. Kenneth Patton, statement before the Ad Hoc Subcommittee on Urban Growth of the Committee on Banking and Currency, U.S. Congress, House of Representatives, *Hearings on Industrial Location Policy* (Part 3), 91st Cong., 2d sess., 6 October 1970, p. 188.

53. *Ibid.*

54. Harvey Perloff, "New Towns In-Town," *Journal of the American Institute of Planners*, May 1966.

often extravagant claims made (especially by private builders) for the social value of exurban "new towns" such as Columbia, Reston, and Jonathan. One of the arguments made by these critics is that the minimum scale of activity needed to bring operating costs down to levels which the poor would be able to afford (or which it would be politically feasible to subsidize) is—because of the relative physical isolation of these projects—greater than anything currently contemplated by public and private new-town planners. Moreover, the construction of these new centers beyond the suburban rings of large cities weakens (or fails to exploit) existing economic and technological linkages, such as subway lines and utility-sharing arrangements.[55]

The "new town in-town" concept was developed to accommodate such criticisms. Central city "new towns" are complexes containing apartments, offices, factories, schools, shops, parks, and internal transportation systems linked to the distribution systems of the city as a whole. Figure 28 is a sketch by architects Conklin and Rossant of one view of Battery Park City, a "new town in-town" being constructed at a cost of $1 billion "off a one-mile stretch of decaying, south Manhattan waterfront."[56] Note the application of the "three-dimensional space" planning concept. The developers of Battery Park City (whose target population for 1983 is 55,000) have pledged not to dislocate low-income families; this remains to be seen. It is a requirement of the federal legislation which is providing the "seed" money: Title VII of the 1970 Housing and Urban Development Act. Other "new towns in-town" are planned for downtown Minneapolis (Cedar-Riverside), Washington, D.C. (Fort Lincoln), Philadelphia (Franklin Town), and—again—New York (Welfare Island).[57]

In short, redevelopment of an employment base within central cities now seems technically feasible. It represents a long-term agenda for public policy, one of whose most important "side effects" would be the creation of enormous new demands for minority labor, both in the construction and—subsequently—in the operation of the "three-dimensional city."

55. Cf. William Alonso, "What Are New Towns For?" *Urban Studies*, February 1970; and Harvey A. Garn, *New Cities, New Communities, and Growth Centers* (Washington, D.C.: Urban Institute, March, 1970), paper no. 113–30. Advocates of conventional new town development often point to the "lower" price of exurban land. The cost items that really matter over the long run, however, are not land and taxes but labor, transportation, and services. These tend to be more expensive outside than inside the city, on a unit cost basis. And, in many cases, speculation is rapidly eroding even the land rent differential.

56. *Newsweek*, July 19, 1971, pp. 44–45.

57. The Fort Lincoln project has been a complete administrative debacle. The fault—at least in this case—appears to lie not with the planners but with the conflicts among different political groups and the White House. For an excellent discussion of the obstacles to creative planning in America (or at least in its big cities), see Martha Derthick, *New Towns In-town: Why a Federal Program Failed* (Washington, D.C.: Urban Institute, May 1972), paper no. S94-112-21.

Figure 28

Battery Park City: Three-Dimensional Planning for a New Town In-Town

An architectural and urban planning commission carried out jointly by Conklin & Rossant with Harrison and Abramovitz/Philip Johnson and John Burgee. Rendering by James S. Rossant.

SYNTHESIS: A COMPREHENSIVE URBAN EMPLOYMENT POLICY

The programs we have been examining in detail can—and should—be part of a larger, concentrated effort to eliminate urban poverty and underemployment. The "crisis of the cities" is a crisis of the deterioration of the human and physical resources of the cities. It will be enormously expensive to arrest and reverse this process. Existing American political and economic institutions will be strained to the limit in doing so. Some of these institutions will undoubtedly collapse. Many experimental new ones will have to be designed to replace them. Without such planned institutional change, it is folly to believe that urban blight, poverty, underemployment, and social pathology can be eliminated.

A concentrated attack on these problems should be our most important national priority. In the concluding section of Chapter Five, a program for restructuring the "secondary labor market" was proposed. An agenda for the last quarter of the twentieth century might include the following additional elements:

Permanent, i.e., institutionalized federal revenue-sharing with states and cities, with pass-through allocation formulas designated by the Congress. "Permanency" may require a Constitutional amendment to guarantee sub-federal jurisdictions a minimum share of each annual national tax return. A fixed portion of each city's annual "share" should, by law, pass through to the community development corporations and neighborhood boards which would be chartered and provided "seed" capital by the federal government, along the lines defined by the Community Corporation Act of 1970 (a creative and important piece of legislation which was never even reported out of committee). The financial independence which such a policy would give to the CDC's would allow them to evolve according to the wishes of their constituencies and the particular circumstances in each location. Some would—hopefully—evolve into actual sub-municipal governments, with direct control over various public services (e.g., education, police, sanitation). *This*, however, should probably not be legislated by Washington, but rather allowed to develop spontaneously (hence the use of the word "evolve").

To arrest the physical deterioration of central cities and to provide attractive living and working environments, governments should undertake extensive development of "new towns in-town" and central city industrial parks. Research and development on new construction, distribution, traffic control, and pollution control techniques for these projects would provide employment to the thousands of scientists and engineers whose displacement from defense industries has made it so difficult for manpower planners to be able to afford to give much attention to the poor. Hundreds of thousands of construction jobs, jobs in the industries which sell to construction, and profits for new and existing contractors (including the rapidly proliferating minority contractors) would also be created. Technological innovations will bring costs down to a minimum, making the subsidization of rents politically and economically feasible. Such subsidization, together with *rigorous* enforcement of open-housing statutes, will ensure that these developments do not *necessarily* become preserves for the upper-middle and upper classes. There is no reason why such "new towns in-town" could not be built in suburban areas as well as in the urban core. The critical technical requirement is direct linkage to the urban center; many exurban new towns lack this vital characteristic. Wherever such projects are located, it will be necessary to legislate government controls on the acquisition and uses of land. It may even be necessary ultimately to nationalize urban land, as was first done in Stockholm in the seventeenth century to prevent speculation and the sprawl which it engenders. Judicious government stockpiling of land might be a useful executive policy instrument. The rationale for this admittedly radical proposal is to extract the profits from the increased value of land undergoing development, in order to apply these profits to social rather than to private use. It is important to note that the resulting lower costs of land and the things constructed on it would benefit *all* classes of the urban population, not just the very poor. To give but one example, reduced land costs mean that one dollar of new federal spending on housing would create more jobs.[58]

Even without the renewal of cities, urban transportation systems need to be redesigned and rebuilt. Renewal, of course, especially in the form of a network of central places such as "new towns in-town" and large (but environmentally "clean") "three-dimensional" industrial complexes, will require an enormous expansion of these systems. Again, there is a substantial job-creation potential here, at all skill levels. Large, transportation-oriented, high-technology firms now suffering from defense cutbacks could be contracted to participate in the design and construction of new mass-transit systems, "clean" short-range private vehicles, and so forth. Many thousands of *existing* jobs would thus be saved.

The single most serious social pathology in the central cities of the United States is undoubtedly drug addiction. "A study of heroin addiction by census

---

58. Speculation in urban land has driven the price of even ghetto property so high that the provision of low-cost housing has become nearly impossible. In the Shaw ghetto of Washington, D.C., for example, land now sells for more than $640,000 an acre. Because of this, "low-income town houses in Washington . . . will end up costing a minimum of $52,200 each. The houses will have no air-conditioning, washers or dryers, and 34 of them are only 16 feet wide and 29 feet deep." Land accounts for more than half of the total cost. Eugene L. Meyer, "Low-Income Housing: $52,200 Each," *Washington Post*, April 9, 1972, p. A1. A task force of the American Institute of Architects has endorsed the concept and strategy of "land banking" by urging "the local, state and federal government [to] immediately purchase one million acres of land in 58 fast growing metropolitan areas" as a first step toward "public control of land for the nation to grow on." Wolf Von Eckardt, "Plan for America the Crowded," *Washington Post*, February 13, 1972, p. B1.

tract in Washington [D.C.] indicates that in some inner-city neighborhoods, addicts represent as much as 10 percent of the total population."[59] There can be little doubt that this is the phenomenon which lies at the root of many serious urban crimes (New York City Police Commissioner Patrick Murphy believes that at least 70 percent of the crimes in his city are drug-connected).[60] Addiction, while perhaps not the cause of alienation and anomie (we have already proposed other causes: repressive schooling for all and lack of jobs for the poor), surely reinforces these attitudes and behaviors. Narcotics addiction can be fought only with a massive and *balanced* attack, including the experimental legalization of all drugs (to deflate their costs, undermine the organizations which distribute them, and reduce the incidence of violent robbery),[61] the provision (mainly through the community corporations and boards) of treatment and rehabilitation services and vocational guidance (possibly including a guaranteed job), and strong federal assaults on organizations distributing narcotics.

To the extent that the jobs created by these various programs provide decent wages and working conditions, workers in the "secondary labor market" will be bid away from "secondary jobs." This socially desirable attrition of the secondary labor market could be reinforced by public service employment programs, and by capital subsidies to secondary employers to facilitate *their* "upgrading." For those employers whose low-wage businesses failed as a result of these programs, the government could, as suggested in Chapter Five, provide income transfers and retraining.

Finally (at least for this particular "list"), governments must learn how to engage in true educational and manpower *planning.* Job possibilities (and their technical requirements) would inform the development of the prevocational (as distinguished from the liberal arts) curricula of the schools, rather than (as we seem now to have it) the other way around. Community "con-

---

59. Bart Barnes, "1 of 10 Addicted in Parts of Inner City," *Washington Post*, April 4, 1972, p. C1.

60. Stewart Alsop, "The Road to Hell," *Newsweek*, March 6, 1972, p. 84.

61. "A blue-ribbon committee of the American Bar Association, including Edward Bennett Williams, Joseph Califano, and New York District Attorney Frank Hogan, has unanimously come to essentially the same conclusion." *Ibid.* Alsop himself reluctantly endorsed this strategy (*ibid.*, and Stewart Alsop, "The City Disease," *Newsweek*, February 28, 1972, p. 96) until convinced of its infeasibility by three Washington addicts and two local narcotics treatment officials who argued that a heroin addict is literally insatiable, so that only constantly increased dosages—culminating in death—could possibly have the desired effect on social order. Unlike heroin, a substitute synthetic drug like methadone does not escalate the addict's demands. "After a certain dosage level is reached, the craving for heroin is blocked, and there is no craving for more methadone. Addicts on methadone sweat a lot, and some have trouble with constipation. But they can hold a job and live like normal human beings." Stewart Alsop, "To Save Our Cities," *Newsweek*, April 10, 1972, p. 96. The average annual per-addict cost of methadone maintenance is $2,000. At this price, "a federally financed methadone maintenance program for the nation's half million addicts . . . might cost $1 billion—about the price of an aircraft carrier. Our cities are worth a lot more than that." *Ibid.*

trol" would consist of management of the local system and modification of the labor-market-wide guidelines to suit local tastes and needs. Education services should be *continuously available*, i.e., day and night, year-round and (through government-subsidized educational leaves of absence, a benefit already enjoyed by many white-collar workers) throughout a person's lifetime. Again, it is instructive to consider the enormous number and diversity of jobs which such a program would create.

These remarks indicate both the interdependence among, and, at the same time, the primacy of a particular one of these social and economic programs. Without massive job development, drug control cannot possibly be successful. Without drug control, "law and order" cannot be restored to the streets of American cities (unless we are willing to create a police state). Without revenue sharing, cities will be unable to take the renewal and redevelopment measures necessary to retain a healthy mix of residential social classes. But without job development, i.e., "full employment," the federal government will be unable to generate sufficient revenues to share with other jurisdictions without running politically unacceptable deficits. Unless we utilize the economic (and social) advantages of "agglomeration," as embodied (for example) in the "new town in-town" concept, urban redevelopment will be prohibitively expensive. But central-place-oriented development requires (while at the same time, it actually makes easier) the planning of efficient passenger and freight transportation. Both programs assume and require that there be freight and people to transport, in other words, that there be "markets" for these services. *That* will depend on the existence of rising consumer incomes—which of course depends on the availability of jobs. Finally, the enforcement of EEO legislation without job development will at best lead to the substitution of a random for a racist distribution of poverty.

Job development is, therefore, clearly the central program element in a strategy to reduce urban blight, poverty, underemployment, and pathology. Planned job development should be our number one national priority.

CONCLUSION

In Chapter One, I said that I would—for the purposes of this study—accept the basic assumption of the theory of human capital, i.e., that a worker's potential productivity is enhanced by investments in his education and training. Under that assumption, we found that nonwhites living in the nation's largest metropolitan areas have not received returns—measured in earnings or probabilities of unemployment—commensurate with their acquired stocks of human capital, especially when compared with whites living in the same parts of the city. These returns are particularly low—and in the case of reduced joblessness, virtually nonexistent—in the urban ghetto. The validity of the white results (measured by their similarity to a number of previously published benchmarks) strengthens our confidence in the quality of the data, and therefore, in the validity of these nonwhite results.[62]

Berg challenges the human capital assumption itself and, therefore, the results of this study as well as others in the field. He accuses the neoclassical economists of failing to "study education in relation to the intervening variable of productivity," of "jump[ing] over it and deal[ing] only with income."[63] Indeed, he produces direct evidence that education and productivity are either not well correlated or, in some cases, are inversely related.[64] His productivity measures are valid, "since they were constructed from piecework or analogous earnings for each employee."[65] These researches lead Berg to agree with Richard Eckaus that the very term "human capital" is useful "... only when it is used in a loose way, to denote an idea, an analogy, without any implication that educated people should be handled as physical capital...,"[66] and with Erik Lundberg that "... market imperfections may have more to do with income distribution than the maximizing behavior attributed to a firm under perfect competition."[67]

It follows from Berg's critique that any rate of return analysis which assumes a positive correlation between education and productivity will impart an upward bias to the estimates of the monetary returns to that education. For my regressions, Berg's argument therefore means that my estimates of the earnings and employment returns to education and training are, if anything, overstated. Under the circumstances, this must be considered a comforting conclusion.

We have, in the previous pages, alluded to a different kind of bias. In his foreword to Berg's book, Eli Ginzberg of Columbia University writes that, more or less coincident with the introduction of John F. Kennedy's "New Frontier,"

62. That my results are so very much lower than most of those reported in the literature may well be attributable not only to differences in the populations being studied, but also to aggregation bias in many previous studies. My data were completely disaggregated, while other studies of the returns to education have generally (although not invariably) been aggregated: by tract, SMSA, state, industry, occupation, etc. W. S. Robinson suggested long ago that correlations using aggregated data will normally overstate the underlying micro-relation, and that the greater the degree of aggregation, the more severe the overstatement. See "Ecological Correlations and the Behavior of Individuals," *American Sociological Review*, June 1950, p. 356. Theil's discussion of aggregation bias has similar implications. Only when aggregate explanatory variables are constructed as weighted indices of the micro-variables, with the micro-slopes used as weights, will all aggregation bias be removed. Henri Theil, *Linear Aggregation of Economic Relations* (Amsterdam: North-Holland Publishing Co., 1965), pp. 137, 171–73, *et passim.*

63. Berg, *Education and Jobs*, p. xii.

64. *Ibid.*, chap. 5. Other researchers are beginning to come to the same conclusion. Cf. Daniel E. Diamond and Hrach Bedrosian, *Industry Hiring Requirements and the Employment of Disadvantaged Groups* (Washington, D.C.: Govt. Prtg. Off., 1970).

65. Berg, *Education and Jobs*, p. 89.

66. *Ibid.*, p. 38.

67. *Ibid.*, p. 34.

. . . public leaders and academic economists were giving birth to a new ideology. They proclaimed that the key to economic development is liberal expenditures for education, which, by improving the quality of labor, are the heart of productivity increases. From the President down, the leadership proclaimed throughout the land: "Education pays; stay in school."[68]

This proclamation, says Ginzberg, reflects the "profound bias inherent in American life and thought that makes us look at a malfunctioning of the labor market in terms of the personal failings of workers in search of jobs."[69]

Some psychologists are also becoming aware of this bias, and are attempting to alert their fellows. According to Friedlander and Greenberg, for example,

> Since most [hard-core unemployment] programs focus on changing the [trainee] to adapt to the predominant white middle-class structure, they would seem to proceed on the assumption that the culture of the [trainee] is defective and that [he] is accordingly deviant.
>
> [In fact] the very concept of "training". . . places the complete burden for change on the [trainee] —and eventually on the culture that he represents. [The authors prefer] a change process based on mutual adaptation, through an integration of attitudes and values of the predominant white middle-class culture and the [trainee's] culture.[70]

At the 1970 professional meetings of the American Psychiatric Association, Dr. Seymour Halleck of the University of Wisconsin urged that, "instead of helping patients adapt to society, psychiatrists should become 'deeply involved' in changing the society."[71]

The elitist presumption that the inability to "make it" in American society—or at least in the labor market—is the direct result of personal incapacities on the part of workers constitutes one of our most unfortunate national myths. If the returns to the education and training of ghetto workers are less than we would expect from previous studies on the subject, then the answer may lie in the *attitudes and institutions*—including institutional racism—of those who must employ or work beside the black and the poor. Far more significant than Coleman's "finding" that blacks "lag" whites with equivalent years of schooling is a remark made by a New Orleans cab driver to a Volunteers in Service to America (VISTA) volunteer:

68. *Ibid.*, p. xi.
69. *Ibid.*
70. Frank Friedlander and Stuart Greenberg, "Effect of Job Attitudes, Training, and Organization Climate on Performance of the Hard-Core Unemployed," *Journal of Applied Psychology*, December, 1971, p. 294.
71. "Psychiatrists Diagnose America and Pronounce It a Sick Society," *Washington Post*, May 12, 1970, p. A3.

I don't know why they say white people are prejudiced. Those nigguhs got everything they want. But they been tryin' to get jobs with Yellow Cab, and they can't. They even sent people down from Washington to find out why, but they couldn't get anything. Never been a nigguh driver for Yellow Cab—never will. How do we do it? We have our ways, lady, we have our ways.[72]

No group in American society has suffered more as the victims of this myth than those in the urban ghetto. And the myth governs even our most "progressive" legislation. A new civil rights bill was hastily passed by Congress in the wake of the assassination of Dr. Martin Luther King, according to which

> ... all law enforcement personnel are made exempt from prohibitions against violating the civil rights of citizens; a riot is defined as a public disturbance involving three or more people together with either an act or threat of violence (so that it becomes a crime to defend rebellion as a right); [and] the penalties for any of the above are more severe than those which might be imposed on a realtor if he is found guilty of discrimination in the sale of housing.[73]

The interest of the Nixon Administration in addressing these issues has been even more short-lived than the President's greatest critics could have expected. Thus, for example,

> ... the Urban Affairs Council ... is the unit ... which Mr. Nixon announced with fanfare in the first week of the new Administration to replace the previously "haphazard, fragmented and often woefully short-sighted manner" of U.S. policy-making toward urban concerns. ...
>
> After a few strong initiatives involved the Administration in controversy, however, the Urban Affairs Council was downgraded. While still technically on the books, the President doesn't meet with it anymore. Its former staff has been scattered to other safer and less meaningful work.[74]

As a direct result, there is a growing number of young blacks, Puerto Ricans, Indians and Chicanos who share Tom Hayden's stark belief that "the only way out of underdevelopment is through revolution. The haves will not help the have-nots." Thus,

> the failure of the government to deliver change, the violence of the police, and other signs of American racism, are showing black people the need for unity and struggle in a more concrete way than any nationalist ideology

72. Genevieve Ray, "Big Easy," *Vista Volunteer*, Fall 1969, p. 9.
73. Hayden, "Colonialism and Liberation," p. 177.
74. "More Than A Telethon Is Needed to Alleviate the Youth Crisis," *Washington Post*, May 14, 1970, p. A19.

could do. It is likely that united political organizations of a coalition character will develop in urban areas. These . . . will serve as institutional centers for protest and service in the community. They will teach people organizing skills and will develop programs for change.[75]

In this concluding chapter of a very long monograph, I have set out what to me seem to be the major policy options available to us in terms of the objectives of urban minority economic development in general, and the reduction of nonwhite underemployment in particular. Although the point was never made explicitly, it is surely a corollary to my strong advocacy of direct governmental intervention in urban markets that an expansionary fiscal and monetary policy is a necessary (but apparently not a sufficient) condition for expanding minority economic opportunity. The Manpower Administration has stated this need for a *balanced* development strategy especially well:

> . . . [T] hree general directions of action are called for . . .[:] upgrading workers' skills and employability through improved education and training, overcoming discrimination and other barriers to their employment, and achieving greater economic and employment growth within the geographic and occupational reach of inner-city workers. It is essential that efforts be made simultaneously in all three directions in order to be effective. Thus, gains in education and training will not succeed in integrating most of those currently disadvantaged into the Nation's economic life, unless these are tied to effective job development efforts. More and better jobs must become accessible to those currently unemployed or underemployed—not solely through national or local economic development programs but also by restructuring existing jobs and overcoming the numerous artificial barriers to employment of the disadvantaged.[76]

There is, however, another strategy which I have not mentioned. This is the strategy to press even greater numbers of ghetto workers into the very labor market in which they are now so dreadfully underemployed. In congressional hearings on employment policy, Representative Charles A. Vanik (D–Ohio) questioned former Labor Secretary George Shultz on a provision of the Nixon Administration's proposed welfare reform legislation according to which non-disabled adults in the ghetto whose families are presently receiving public assistance would be threatened with cessation of the transfers if they did not accept jobs procured for them by the federal and state employment services. The Secretary's unfortunate reply, after the usual caveats about being "on the lookout" for "better" jobs if possible, brings us directly back to the central theme of this study: ". . . a fact of the nation's economy is that many jobs pay low wages and 'we are not going to be remaking the economy in this program. . . . We can only put people in the jobs that ex-

75. Hayden, "Colonialism and Liberation," pp. 179–82.
76. U.S. Department of Labor, *1971 Manpower Report*, p. 108.

ist.' "[77] Yet "remaking the economy" is precisely what our task must be. Our objective can be nothing less than the reconstruction of the urban economy, to make a place in it for the minority workers who so far have been kept outside.

But the Philadelphia Plan, the Public Service Careers Program, and indeed the nascent and underfinanced ghetto development projects underway in several cities are all small-scale, hesitant, stopgap measures. Fundamentally, we as a society have yet to make a commitment to the total elimination of urban poverty. Should this lack of will continue, what consequences can we expect? Despite their low expectation of material payoff, blacks and other nonwhites will probably continue to increase their investments in themselves. If the circumstances which constrain their search for a decent job are not changed, therefore, then we should expect to see "more black schooling, migration, and, in the absence of reward for those accomplishments, greater frustration."[78] We have already experienced the direct results of minority frustration in the streets of our cities. This is a condition which cannot—which *must* not—remain unresolved indefinitely.

77. "Work Program in Welfare Plan Is Defended," *Washington Post*, October 17, 1969, p. A2.
78. Stephan Michelson, "Rational Income Decisions of Negroes and Everybody Else," *Industrial and Labor Relations Review*, October 1969, p. 18.

VARIABLES
AND
MODELS

CONSTRUCTION OF THE OCCUPATIONAL STATUS INDEX

In 1947, the National Opinion Research Center (NORC) asked "a sizable sample of the U.S. population" to rate the prestige of ninety occupational titles as "excellent," "good," "average," "somewhat below average," or "poor."[1] There are a number of problems associated with this widely used index: (a) The rated occupations encompassed (in 1950) less than half of the U.S. labor force; (b) "It has been found repeatedly in studies of prestige that respondents are less willing to make or are less expert in making negative judgments."[2] Thus, the NORC scores are probably biased upward, and the lower-level rankings for each occupation are probably relatively more ambiguous than the upper-level ones; (c) Only forty-five of the ninety NORC occupations correspond directly to Census occupational titles; (d) "There is a strong indication that the forty-five occupations for which the equation predicting NORC ratings was derived are much better known to the public than a great many occupations not on the NORC list."[3]

In 1959, Otis Dudley Duncan developed a method for using the NORC scores to derive a complete status rank-ordering for all 425 Census occupations. Briefly, his strategy was to relate a transformation of the NORC score for each of the forty-five Census-compatible occupational titles to the education and income of the set of workers in that occupation in 1950, using the 1950 Census. The resulting estimated equation was then used to "project" scores for all the other Census occupations, with education and income within each of those occupations as predictor variables. Finally, the model was tested for predictive efficiency and intertemporal stability.

Specifically, the NORC score biases enumerated above were partly overcome by focusing only on the relatively less ambiguous (although probably overly represented) "excellent" and "good" scores, and only on males. Duncan used these variables in fitting the model:

$$\emptyset_i^{1947} = \beta_{i0} + \beta_{i1} E^{1950} + \beta_{i2} Y^{1949} + \epsilon_i$$

for i = 1, 2, . . . , 45 occupational titles

where

$\emptyset_i$ = percent of NORC respondents who rated the prestige of occupation i in 1947 as "excellent" or "good." Thus, $0 \leqslant \phi_i \leqslant 100$.

E_i = percent of males in occupation i in the 1950 Census with at least 12 years of school.

1. National Opinion Research Corporation, "Jobs and Occupations: A Popular Evaluation," *Opinion News*, September 1947.
2. Otis Dudley Duncan, "A Socioeconomic Index for All Occupations," in *Occupations and Social Status*, ed. Albert J. Reiss, Jr. (Glencoe, Ill.: Free Press, 1961), p. 117.
3. *Ibid.*, p. 129.

Y_i = percent of males in occupation i in the 1950 Census whose family income was at least $3,500 in 1949.

ϵ_i = random disturbance term for the ith occupation.

In addition, Duncan developed an interoccupational age adjustment, to control for the finding that—within each occupation—younger workers tended towards having relatively less income but relatively more education. The fitted regression equation was:

$$\hat{\phi} = -6.00 + 0.59E + 0.55Y; \quad R^2 = 0.83.$$

Subsequent tests by Gordon in 1968 indicate that other variables "such as job training . . . and [other] labor force phenomena [such as] number of hours worked per week . . . are relatively unimportant in the explanation of the variation of socioeconomic status."[4] Duncan, himself, used the estimated equation to predict the status of sixteen other Census titles which "closely approximate" sixteen other (out-of-sample) NORC titles.

> The socioeconomic indexes computed for these sixteen occupations estimate the NORC prestige rating with reasonable effectiveness. . . . In fact, the root-mean-square of the errors of estimate is 15.3 points, only a little higher than the root-mean-square of the errors for the initial forty-five occupations, 13.0 points.[5]

A further "test" conducted by Duncan involved the examination of this question: How representative of all 425 occupational titles in the 1950 Census were the 45 used to estimate the model? For the set of 45, $r_{E,Y}$ = 0.72 and dE/dY = 0.60. For all 425 occupations in the 1950 Census, $r_{E,Y}$ = 0.78 and dE/dY = 0.68. From this he concludes that the sample was "probably representative."

Using 1950 education and income as predictors, Duncan then went on to generate ordinal scores for all 425 Census occupational titles. Each score is an ordinal rank in the interval 0–96 (there were no "predicted" scores above 96).

Subsequent tests were conducted by Duncan, Blau, Reiss, Hodge, Siegel, and Rossi, using the 1960 Census.[6] These tests indicated that the prestige ratings are "remarkably close to invariant with respect to (a) the composition and size of the sample of raters; (b) the . . . form of the rating scale; (c) the . . . notion of 'general standing'; and (d) the passage of time."[7]

4. Jerome B. Gordon, "Socioeconomic Status: A Re-examination of its Dimensions," *Journal of Human Resources*, Summer 1969, p. 356.

5. Duncan, "A Socioeconomic Index," p. 125.

6. Cited in Otis Dudley Duncan, "Measuring the Trend in Social Stratification," (mimeographed, December 31, 1967); Peter M. Blau and Otis Dudley Duncan, *The American Occupational Structure* (New York: Wiley, 1967), p. 119n.

7. Blau and Duncan, *American Occupational Structure*, p. 119.

Particularly important is the question of intertemporal stability. On this issue, Duncan and Blau write:

> We now have a detailed study of temporal stability in occupational prestige ratings. The results are astonishing. . . . A set of ratings obtained as long ago as 1925 is correlated to the extent of 0.93 with the latest set available, obtained in 1963. [Hodge, Siegel, and Rossi] conclude, "There have been no substantial changes in occupational prestige in the United States since 1925." . . . [I]nformation available in the Censuses of 1940, 1950, and 1960 points to a comparably high order of temporal stability. . . . [8]

In fact, Duncan and Blau have re-estimated scores for the 446 occupational titles in the 1960 Census. These scores, however, are unpublished. Given their findings on the intertemporal stability of the published 1950 scores, I have relied entirely on these in constructing the status variable used in the text.

For our purposes, what is the meaning of $(\Delta\phi/\Delta E)_i$ for the ith worker? If $(\Delta\phi/\Delta E) > 0$ and statistically significant, then we will infer that education does facilitate movement into what is nationally considered to be a higher status occupation. Whether this is in fact a "move up" for the ith worker depends upon the values and significance of $(\Delta w/\Delta E)$ and $(\Delta u/\Delta E)$. The closer these parameters approach zero, the greater the likelihood that discrimination within the occupation is taking place. This would constitute evidence calling for some modification of Barbara Bergmann's "crowding" hypothesis.[9] If, as she believes, most blacks are indeed crowded into relatively few occupations in which their excess supply then forces wages down, $(\Delta\phi/\Delta E)$ should be quite small. Evidence that $(\Delta\phi/\Delta E) > 0$ while $(\Delta w/\Delta E)\sim$ $(\Delta u/\Delta E)\sim 0$ would suggest that blacks do move into a broader range of occupations than is hypothesized by Ms. Bergmann, but that they meet with discrimination once they get there.

SPECIFICATION OF THE GENERAL REGRESSION MODELS

The theoretical relationship which will link our variables together is essentially captured in a recent statement by the Advisory Commission on Intergovernmental Relations: "Education largely determines occupation and occupation, in turn, largely determines income."[10] Duncan provides a more elaborate discussion of this relationship:

> . . . [F]rom a functional standpoint, education may be considered in large measure as a preparation for the pursuit of an occupation, or as the

8. *Ibid.*, pp. 120–21.
9. Barbara R. Bergmann, "The Effect on White Incomes of Discrimination in Employment," *Journal of Political Economy*, March/April 1971.
10. Advisory Commission on Intergovernmental Relations, *Metropolitan Social and Economic Disparities: Implications for Intergovernmental Relations in Central Cities and Suburbs* (Washington, D.C.: Govt. Prtg. Off., 1965), p. 163.

acquisition of qualifications for an occupation. Hence, there is both a functional nexus and a temporal order in the relationship of occupation to education. For most persons, the bulk of the income received consists of compensation for rendering the services of their occupations. Income and occupation, therefore, are functionally related. While we may think of income as being received more or less simultaneously with the pursuit of an occupation, it is true that most of the income received from an occupational pursuit accrues subsequent to the entry into, and identification with, that occupation. There is a sense, then, in which occupation may be considered logically or temporally prior to income, as well as functionally related thereto. Consideration of the various contingencies of actual work histories would enrich and complicate this simple model, but would not alter its basic relationships. We have, therefore, the following sequence: a man qualifies himself for occupational life by obtaining an education; as a consequence of pursuing his occupation, he obtains income. Occupation, therefore, is the intervening activity linking income to education. If we characterize an occupation according to the prevailing levels of education and income of its incumbents, we are not only estimating its "social status" and its "economic status", we are also describing one of its major "causes" and one of its major "effects."[11]

These remarks, and the studies by Weiss and Duncan-Blau, have led me to posit a sequential employment process the central element of which is the possibility of race, sex and class discrimination at every stage: in entering the labor force via some occupation, in getting a job in which to practice that occupation, and in being assigned (or negotiating) a wage within the job. The hypothesized (essentially recursive) process is as follows:

education (E), training (T) (except on-the-job training [OJT]), race (R), sex (S) → occupation (O)

occupation, race, sex → job title (J)

job, complementary capital (K), OJT (learning how to use the capital on the job) → productivity (P)

productivity, race, sex, competitive structure (V)

$$\to \begin{cases} \text{wage rate (w)} \\ \text{unemployment (u)} \end{cases}$$

Symbolically,

(1) $O = f(E, T, R, S)$

(2) $J = F(O, R, S)$

(3) $P = g(J, K, OJT)$

(4) $w = h_1(P, R, S, V)$
        $= h_1[g(J, K, OJT), R, S, V]$
        $= h_1[g[F(O, R, S), K, OJT], R, S, V]$
        $= h_1[g[F(f(E, T, R, S), R, S), K, OJT], R, S, V]$

(5) $u = h_2[g[F(f(E, T, R, S), R, S), K, OJT], R, S, V]$

---

11. Duncan, "A Socioeconomic Index," pp. 116–17.

If indeed the system is recursive, then expressions (4) and (5) can be collapsed to their reduced forms:

(6) $w = w(E, T, R, S, K, V)$
(7) $u = u(E, T, R, S, K, V)$

Since the structure of the employment process must be assumed to vary over time and space, it is crucial to account for these sources of variation. Age (A) is an appropriate proxy for structural change through time, since workers of different ages will (by the above assumption) encounter different labor market structures. Two location variables will also be specified. Let L_1 represent a vector of dummy variables for the sixteen different cities where our 50,000 workers lived in 1966. L_2 will serve as an indicator of intrametropolitan residential location: inside a core city poverty area, somewhere in the remainder of the central city, or somewhere in the suburban ring.

There are at least two important institutional and economic factors reflected in (V): union affiliation and degree of industrial concentration. The data we are using do not indicate whether or not the worker is a union member.[12] The 1966 SEO does, however, contain a 425-category industrial attachment variable (I). I am using this (aggregated after extensive experimentation to 15 categories) as a proxy for (V). The complementary capital variable (K) is also very important. It may well be that the only differences between two industrial floor polishers who receive unequal wages is that one works with a modern, electrical polishing machine while the other must work on his or her hands and knees with rags and a can of wax. Even aggregative capital data are difficult to acquire; it is quite impossible to find microdata that would fully suit our purposes. Given the contents of the SEO, the best we can do is to attempt to capture this source of variation with the industry group variable (I). Certainly, the structure of capital stock varies from one industry to another.

Since we are interested in three measures of the payoff to investments in human capital, we may bring this discussion on model specification to a close by reformulating the three general single-equation models to be estimated:

(8) $w = w(E, T, R, S, A, L_1, L_2, I); \ w \geqslant \$1.00$
(9) $u = u(E, T, R, S, A, L_1, L_2, I); \ 0 \leqslant u \leqslant 1$
      or $0\% \leqslant u \leqslant 100\%$
(10) $\emptyset = \phi(E, T, R, S, A, L_1, L_2); \ 0 \leqslant \emptyset \leqslant 100$

---

12. The 1967 SEO file indicates both union affiliation and hourly wages. But it does not include any training data. I chose to work with the 1966 file because of the central importance of the latter variable to this study. Unfortunately, as may be seen in Chapter Two, the training data in the 1966 SEO were found (after extensive analysis) to be rather weak.

where ($\emptyset$), the Duncan-NORC ordinal prestige score, is used as a proxy for occupation (O), and (T) in (10) excludes on-the-job training.

But can these relationships be validly estimated with single-equation models? Occupation was not specified in models (8) and (9) because the hypothesized employment and income-determination process was assumed to be recursive. But if occupation and education are positively intercorrelated, the exclusion of $\emptyset$ creates the possibility that my estimates of the returns to education ($\Delta w/\Delta E$ and $\Delta u/\Delta E$) will be biased upward. Similar remarks apply to the estimation of the T-coefficients. If this problem *does* exist, then some kind of simultaneous equation system will be needed to model the employment and income-determination process described earlier.

The operational question is whether the system is indeed recursive. We can examine this assumption with the following truncated models:

(11) $w = a + \beta E + \epsilon$

(12a) $w = a + bE + c\emptyset + u_1$

(12b) $\emptyset = a' + b'E + u_2$

In equation system (12), the estimated returns to education will be equal to

$$\frac{\Delta w}{\Delta E} = \hat{b} + \hat{c}\hat{b}'$$

If system (12) is recursive, i.e., if $\text{cov}(u_1 u_2) = 0$, then this estimate will be equal to the estimate generated by model (11):

$$\hat{\beta} = (\hat{b} + \hat{c}\hat{b}')$$

Moreover, if system (12) is indeed recursive, then the addition of $\emptyset$ to a model regressing w on E will not significantly reduce residual variation. We can make use of this property to form a significance test. The null hypothesis—recursiveness of system (12)—can be stated as:

$$(\Sigma\epsilon^2 - \Sigma u_1^2) = 0$$

The test was conducted on a sample consisting of 3,756 whites and non-whites living in the central city poverty areas of the twelve largest SMSAs (in this sample, w = annual earnings). The results were as follows:

$$w = 1966.88 + 135.18E; \qquad \Sigma\epsilon^2 = 2167.6 \times 10^7$$
$$w = 1944.66 + 84.09E + 22.36\emptyset; \Sigma u_1^2 = 2105.9 \times 10^7$$
$$\emptyset = 0.99 + 2.29E$$
$$\hat{\beta} = 135.18$$
$$\hat{b} + \hat{c}\hat{b}' = 133.29$$

Null hypothesis: $[\Sigma\epsilon^2 - \Sigma u_1^2] = 0$

If $F = \left[\dfrac{\Sigma\epsilon^2}{\Sigma u_1^2}\right]_{n-1,\ n-2\ \text{d.f.}} > F_{.05}$, reject the null hypothesis.

$F = 1.03 \not> 1.08$, so we cannot reject the null hypothesis.

Thus, we conclude that the single-equation estimation procedure used in the subsequent chapters is valid.

MODELS AND RESULTS ON THE SEO "GHETTOS"

SCHOOL COMPLETION RATES IN THE UNITED STATES

Table B-1

Proportion of the Population Aged 25 or More Having Completed
at Least 12 Years of School in 1960, 1966, and 1969:
United States and All SMSAs, by Race and Area

Area and Race	Year	Percent with 12 or More Years of School	Source
United States			
Total	1960	41.1	a
Total	1966	50.0	b
Total	1969	54.0	a
White	1960	43.2	a
White	1966	52.2	b
White	1969	56.3	a
Black	1960	20.1	a
Black	1966	27.8	b
Black	1969	32.3	a
All SMSAs			
Total	1960	44.0	c
Total	1969	58.0	a
White	1960	46.0	c
White	1969	60.2	a
Nonwhite	1960	26.0	c
Black	1969	37.0	a
Central cities (all SMSAs)			
Total	1960	43.0	c
Total	1969	52.7	a
White	1960	45.0	c
White	1969	55.8	a
Nonwhite	1960	26.0	c
Black	1969	38.1	a
Suburban rings (all SMSAs)			
Total	1960	44.0	c
Total	1969	62.6	a
White	1960	45.0	c
White	1969	63.6	a
Nonwhite	1960	27.0	c
Black	1969	36.3	a

[a]U.S. Department of Commerce, Bureau of the Census, *Current Population Reports*, series P-20, no. 194, "Educational Attainment, March 1969" (Washington, D.C.: Govt. Prtg. Off., 1970), Tables A and 2.

[b]National Industrial Conference Board, *Economic Almanac* (New York: Macmillan, 1967), p. 11.

[c]Advisory Commission on Intergovernmental Relations, *Metropolitan Social and Economic Disparities: Implications for Intergovernmental Relations in Central Cities and Suburbs* (Washington, D.C.: Govt. Prtg. Off., 1965), p. 13.

Table B-2

Proportion of the Population Aged 25 or More Having
Completed at Least 12 Years of School in 1960
in 17 SMSAs, by Race and Area

(in percent)

SMSA	Entire Metropolitan Area		Central City		Ring	
	Total[a]	Nonwhite[b]	Total[c]	Nonwhite[c]	Total[c]	Nonwhite[c]
Atlanta	42	20	40	21	48	10
Boston	50	40	45	36	57	48
Baltimore	33	20	28	20	41	19
Chicago	42	30	35	29	52	27
Cleveland	39	29	30	28	55	34
Detroit	36	27	34	26	47	26
Houston	45	25	45	26	46	19
Los Angeles	53	45	53	44	54	45
New Orleans	36	15	33	15	43	10
New York	40	32	37	31	52	30
Philadelphia	34	24	31	24	46	23
Phoenix	48	17	49	24	46	19
Pittsburgh	37	25	35	25	43	23
St. Louis	30	23	26	24	41	18
San Antonio	42	31	37	30	55	45
San Francisco	52	43	49	36	58	41
Washington, D.C.	51	33	48	34	65	25

[a]Weighted average of columns (3) and (5).

[b]U.S. Office of Education, "Profiles of Fifty Major American Cities" (mimeographed, Washington, D.C.: U.S. Department of Health, Education, and Welfare, May, 1968).

[c]Advisory Commission on Intergovernmental Relations, *Metropolitan Social and Economic Disparities: Implications for Intergovernmental Relations in Central Cities and Suburbs* (Washington, D.C.: Govt. Prtg. Off., 1965), Tables B1 and B2.

SPECIFICATION OF THE REGRESSION MODELS

The first experiments embody continuous and discontinuous specifications of (E) without allowing for interactions:

$$(13) \quad w = \beta_0 + \beta_1 E + \sum_{i=2}^{11} \beta_i T_{i-1} + \beta_{12} S + \beta_{13} A + \sum_{i=14}^{28} \beta_i I_{i-13}$$

$$+ \sum_{i=29}^{40} \beta_i C_{i-28} + \beta_{41} F + \epsilon$$

$$(14) \quad w = \beta_0 + \sum_{i=1}^{6} \beta_i E_i + \sum_{i=7}^{16} \beta_i T_{i-6} + \beta_{17}S + \beta_{18}A + \sum_{i=19}^{33} \beta_i I_{i-18}$$

$$+ \sum_{i=34}^{45} \beta_i C_{i-33} + \beta_{46}F + \epsilon$$

where

w = individual weekly earnings

E = years of school completed

$$E_1 = E_{0-7 \text{ years}} \quad = \begin{cases} 1 \text{ if individual completed less than 8 years of school} \\ 0 \text{ otherwise} \end{cases}$$

$$E_2 = E_{8 \text{ years}} \quad = \begin{cases} 1 \text{ if individual completed exactly 8 years of school} \\ 0 \text{ otherwise} \end{cases}$$

$$E_3 = E_{9-11 \text{ years}} \quad = \begin{cases} 1 \text{ if individual completed some but not all high} \\ \quad \text{school} \\ 0 \text{ otherwise} \end{cases}$$

$$E_4 = E_{12 \text{ years}} \quad = \begin{cases} 1 \text{ if individual completed high school} \\ 0 \text{ otherwise} \end{cases}$$

$$E_5 = E_{13-15 \text{ years}} \quad = \begin{cases} 1 \text{ if individual completed some but not all college} \\ 0 \text{ otherwise} \end{cases}$$

$$E_6 = E_{16+ \text{ years}} \quad = \begin{cases} 1 \text{ if individual completed at least 4 years of college} \\ 0 \text{ otherwise} \end{cases}$$

$$T_1 \quad = \begin{cases} 1 \text{ if individual completed a private institutional} \\ \quad \text{training program since 1956} \\ 0 \text{ otherwise} \end{cases}$$

$$T_2 \quad = \begin{cases} 1 \text{ if individual started but did not complete such} \\ \quad \text{a program} \\ 0 \text{ otherwise} \end{cases}$$

$$T_3 \quad = \begin{cases} 1 \text{ if individual completed an apprenticeship since} \\ \quad 1956 \\ 0 \text{ otherwise} \end{cases}$$

$$T_4 \quad = \begin{cases} 1 \text{ if individual started but did not complete an} \\ \quad \text{apprenticeship} \\ 0 \text{ otherwise} \end{cases}$$

$$T_5 \quad = \begin{cases} 1 \text{ if individual completed an OJT program of at} \\ \quad \text{least 6 weeks duration since 1956} \\ 0 \text{ otherwise} \end{cases}$$

$$T_6 \quad = \begin{cases} 1 \text{ if individual started but did not complete such} \\ \quad \text{a program} \\ 0 \text{ otherwise} \end{cases}$$

$$T_7 \quad = \begin{cases} 1 \text{ if individual completed an armed forces voca-} \\ \quad \text{tional program since 1956} \\ 0 \text{ otherwise} \end{cases}$$

$$T_8 \quad = \begin{cases} 1 \text{ if individual started but did not complete such} \\ \quad \text{a program} \\ 0 \text{ otherwise} \end{cases}$$

$$T_9 \quad = \begin{cases} 1 \text{ if individual completed a government training} \\ \quad \text{program, e.g., MDTA training, Job Corps} \\ 0 \text{ otherwise} \end{cases}$$

$$T_{10} \quad = \begin{cases} 1 \text{ if individual started but did not complete such} \\ \quad \text{a program} \\ 0 \text{ otherwise} \end{cases}$$

$$S \quad = \begin{cases} 1 \text{ if individual is male} \\ 0 \text{ otherwise} \end{cases}$$

$$A \quad = \text{ individual's age (in years)}$$

$$I_1 \quad = \begin{cases} 1 \text{ if individual is employed in the construction} \\ \quad \text{industry} \\ 0 \text{ otherwise} \end{cases}$$

$$I_2 \quad = \begin{cases} 1 \text{ if individual is employed in the manufacture of} \\ \quad \text{durable goods} \\ 0 \text{ otherwise} \end{cases}$$

$$I_3 \quad = \begin{cases} 1 \text{ if individual is employed in the manufacture of} \\ \quad \text{non-durable goods} \\ 0 \text{ otherwise} \end{cases}$$

$$I_4 \quad = \begin{cases} 1 \text{ if individual is employed in transportation} \\ 0 \text{ otherwise} \end{cases}$$

$$I_5 \quad = \begin{cases} 1 \text{ if individual is employed in communications} \\ 0 \text{ otherwise} \end{cases}$$

$$I_6 = \begin{cases} 1 \text{ if individual is employed in utilities or sanitation} \\ 0 \text{ otherwise} \end{cases}$$

$$I_7 = \begin{cases} 1 \text{ if individual is employed in wholesale trade} \\ 0 \text{ otherwise} \end{cases}$$

$$I_8 = \begin{cases} 1 \text{ if individual is employed in retail trade} \\ 0 \text{ otherwise} \end{cases}$$

$$I_9 = \begin{cases} 1 \text{ if individual is employed in finance, insurance} \\ \quad \text{or real estate} \\ 0 \text{ otherwise} \end{cases}$$

$$I_{10} = \begin{cases} 1 \text{ if individual is employed in business and repair} \\ \quad \text{services} \\ 0 \text{ otherwise} \end{cases}$$

$$I_{11} = \begin{cases} 1 \text{ if individual is employed in personal services} \\ 0 \text{ otherwise} \end{cases}$$

$$I_{12} = \begin{cases} 1 \text{ if individual is employed in entertainment and} \\ \quad \text{recreation services} \\ 0 \text{ otherwise} \end{cases}$$

$$I_{13} = \begin{cases} 1 \text{ if individual is employed in professional and} \\ \quad \text{related services} \\ 0 \text{ otherwise} \end{cases}$$

$$I_{14} = \begin{cases} 1 \text{ if individual is employed in federal government} \\ 0 \text{ otherwise} \end{cases}$$

$$I_{15} = \begin{cases} 1 \text{ if individual is employed in state or local} \\ \quad \text{government} \\ 0 \text{ otherwise} \end{cases}$$

$$C_1 = \begin{cases} 1 \text{ if individual lives in Baltimore} \\ 0 \text{ otherwise} \end{cases}$$

$$C_2 = \begin{cases} 1 \text{ if individual lives in Chicago} \\ 0 \text{ otherwise} \end{cases}$$

$$C_3 = \begin{cases} 1 \text{ if individual lives in Cleveland} \\ 0 \text{ otherwise} \end{cases}$$

$$C_4 \quad = \begin{cases} 1 \text{ if individual lives in Detroit} \\ 0 \text{ otherwise} \end{cases}$$

$$C_5 \quad = \begin{cases} 1 \text{ if individual lives in Houston} \\ 0 \text{ otherwise} \end{cases}$$

$$C_6 \quad = \begin{cases} 1 \text{ if individual lives in Los Angeles} \\ 0 \text{ otherwise} \end{cases}$$

$$C_7 \quad = \begin{cases} 1 \text{ if individual lives in New York} \\ 0 \text{ otherwise} \end{cases}$$

$$C_8 \quad = \begin{cases} 1 \text{ if individual lives in Philadelphia} \\ 0 \text{ otherwise} \end{cases}$$

$$C_9 \quad = \begin{cases} 1 \text{ if individual lives in Pittsburgh} \\ 0 \text{ otherwise} \end{cases}$$

$$C_{10} \quad = \begin{cases} 1 \text{ if individual lives in St. Louis} \\ 0 \text{ otherwise} \end{cases}$$

$$C_{11} \quad = \begin{cases} 1 \text{ if individual lives in San Francisco} \\ 0 \text{ otherwise} \end{cases}$$

$$C_{12} \quad = \begin{cases} 1 \text{ if individual lives in Washington, D.C.} \\ 0 \text{ otherwise} \end{cases}$$

$$F \quad = \begin{cases} 1 \text{ if individual worked at least 35 hours per week} \\ \quad \text{for at least half of the weeks he or she worked} \\ \quad \text{in 1965} \\ 0 \text{ otherwise} \end{cases}$$

Separate regressions were run for whites and nonwhites. In all runs, (E_1), (I_1), (C_7) were deleted in order to avoid singularity.[1]

Notice that participation in the five types of training programs has been specified in such a way as to emphasize the institutional factor of certification. Following the discussion in Chapter One, it is hypothesized that the contribution of training to earnings comes through the social acceptability which, once determined, is then manifested in credentials. Education is simi-

---

1. On the avoidance of linear dependence in working with dummy variables, see Daniel B. Suits, "The Use of Dummy Variables in Regression Equations," *Journal of the American Statistical Association*, 52 (1957). Since the regression results are completely independent of which variables are deleted, the choice of (E_1), (I_1), and (C_7) is quite arbitrary.

larly specified in the second equation to emphasize the passage of institutionally significant milestones such as high school graduation. In other words, institutional considerations are assumed to impose discontinuities on the $w(T)$ and $w(E)$ relations.

I considered the possibility that the policy variables (E) and (T) might be collinear, in which case the simultaneous inclusion of both in the same regression would distort the very parameter estimates whose precise identification is the central objective of this study. To test for this possibility, I computed the simple correlation coefficients between (E) and each of the ten (T)s in each of six subsamples: (i) central city poverty area whites, (ii) central city poverty area nonwhites, (iii) whites in the rest of the SMSA, (iv) nonwhites in the rest of the SMSA, (v) whites in the suburban ring, and (vi) nonwhites in the suburban ring. Only twenty-nine of these sixty correlation coefficients were significant (at $\alpha = 0.05$). Then, to determine how serious this might be in distorting the standard errors of the (E) and (T) coefficients, I compared each of these simple correlations (r) with the appropriate coefficient of multiple correlation (R) from the six regressions generated by fitting the first model to each subsample. Following a rule of thumb suggested by Lawrence Klein, "multicollinearity is said to be 'harmful' if $r_{ij} \geqslant R_y$."[2] In every one of the sixty comparisons, I found that

$$r_{E_j T_{ij}} < R_j; \quad i=1,\ldots, 10 \text{ categories of training}$$

$$j=1,\ldots, \text{ 6 subsamples}$$

Thus, I concluded that collinearity between the policy variables was not sufficiently strong to vitiate the use of models in which both (E) and (T) appear together.

The next experiment reported in the text concerns the interaction model

$$(15) \quad w = \beta_0 + \beta_1 ES + \beta_2 EA + \sum_{i=3}^{14} \beta_i EC_{i-2} + \sum_{i=15}^{29} \beta_i EI_{i-14}$$

$$+ \beta_{30} AS + \sum_{i=31}^{45} \beta_i SI_{i-30} + \beta_{46} F + \epsilon$$

fitted, again, to the white and then to the nonwhite samples. The training variables have been deleted for reasons explained in the text.

Unemployment equations of the form

$$(16) \quad u = \beta_0 + \beta_1 E + \sum_{i=2}^{11} \beta_i T_{i-1} + B_{12} S + \beta_{13} A + \sum_{i=14}^{28} \beta_i I_{i-13}$$

$$+ \sum_{i=29}^{40} \beta_i C_{i-28} + \beta_{41} F + \epsilon$$

2. Cited in Donald E. Farrar and Robert R. Glauber, "Multicollinearity in Regression Analysis: The Problem Revisited," *Review of Economics and Statistics*, February 1967, p. 98.

$$(17) \quad u = \beta_0 + \sum_{i=1}^{6} \beta_i E_i + \sum_{i=7}^{16} \beta_i T_{i-6} + \beta_{17} S + \beta_{18} A$$

$$+ \sum_{i=19}^{33} \beta_i I_{i-18} + \sum_{i=34}^{45} \beta_i C_{i-33} + \beta_{46} F + \epsilon$$

were then fitted, for poverty area whites and nonwhites. In these models,

$$u = \text{unemployment rate} = \left\{ 1 - \frac{\text{weeks worked in 1965}}{\begin{array}{c}\text{weeks in the labor}\\\text{force in 1965}\end{array}} \right\} \times 100$$

and all other variables are defined as before. Again, variables (E_1), (I_1), and (C_7) were excluded to prevent linear dependence in the $[X'X]$ matrix. The corresponding interaction model has the form

$$(18) \quad u = \beta_0 + \beta_1 ES + \beta_2 EA + \sum_{i=3}^{14} \beta_i EC_{i-2} + \sum_{i=15}^{29} \beta_i EI_{i-14}$$

$$+ \beta_{30} AS + \sum_{i=31}^{45} \beta_i SI_{i-30} + \beta_{46} F + \epsilon$$

Finally, we estimated white and nonwhite occupational status regressions of the form

$$(19) \quad \emptyset = \beta_0 + \beta_1 E + \sum_{i=2}^{9} \beta_i T_{i-1} + \beta_{10} S + \beta_{11} A + \sum_{i=12}^{23} \beta_i C_{i-11} + \epsilon$$

$$(20) \quad \emptyset = \beta_0 + \sum_{i=1}^{6} \beta_i E_i + \sum_{i=7}^{14} \beta_i T_{i-6} + \beta_{15} S + \beta_{16} A + \sum_{i=17}^{28} \beta_i C_{i-16} + \epsilon$$

Notice that only eight of the T-variables appear in these specifications. The effect of education on occupational status occurs in at least two temporally distinct stages of job acquisition: initial entry into the labor market, and subsequent movement into other occupations. The greater the relative importance of the entry stage (and—for the poor at least—I suspect that entry assignments are fairly permanent in terms of status), the more would the inclusion of post-entry training constitute a specification error. Thus, OJT is excluded from these models. As usual (C_7) (New York) is also excluded. Since we are concerned here primarily with entry phenomena, the variable (F) is deleted as well.

When interactions in the occupational-determination process are modeled, training is again deleted from the interaction specification:

$$(21) \quad \emptyset = \beta_0 + \beta_1 ES + \beta_2 EA + \sum_{i=3}^{14} \beta_i EC_{i-2} + \beta_{15} AS + \epsilon$$

The additive regression results are presented in table B-3.

Table B-3

Additive Regressions: Central City Poverty Areas[a]

Policy Variable		Payoff Variable and Race					
	Equation Number	Earnings ($/week)		Unemployment[b]		Occupational status[c]	
		Nonwhites (13) (14)	Whites (13) (14)	Nonwhites (16) (17)	Whites (16) (17)	Nonwhites (19) (20)	Whites (19) (20)
Education:							
E		1.81	4.05	0.0	-0.6	2.0	2.7
E_8							
E_{9-11}			14.80			2.9	
E_{12} (H.S. completion)		8.33	24.88	-0.4	-3.5	10.2	15.8
E_{13-15}		14.39	16.99		-4.9	17.4	24.1
E_{16+}		41.36	61.36		-5.4	40.4	37.9

	(1)	(2)	(3)	(4)	(5)	(6)	(7)	(8)	(9)	(10)	(11)	(12)
Institutional												
Completed												
Incompleted												
Apprenticeship												
Completed									3.3	3.0	3.9	7.3
Incompleted												
Private OJT												
Completed			30.61	30.46								
Incompleted			} n.a.							} n.a.		
Armed Forces voc.												
Completed	28.71	27.01										
Incompleted												
Government Program												
Completed					7.9	7.8						
Incompleted	−12.51	−11.26										
R^2	.352	.361	.280	.287	.221	.231	.129	.135	.149	.203	.260	.309
F	49.21	45.80	10.38	9.68	26.27	23.54	4.58	4.36	26.67	32.19	15.42	16.24
Sample sizes	2935	2935	821	821	2935	2935	821	821	2935	2935	821	821

[a] For the entries shown, the chances are 95 in 100 that, in repeated sampling from the same population, the marginal effect of (E) or (T) on the payoff variable would not be larger than the coefficient given in the table. Equation numbers are given in parentheses in the column headings.
[b] [1−(weeks worked in 1965÷weeks in the labor force in 1965)] × 100.
[c] Duncan-NORC ordinal ranking of 0–100.

233

CONSTRUCTION OF THE STEP-FUNCTIONS (FIGURES 5 AND 6)

Table B-4 shows *all* the education regression coefficients. Those intraracial *differences* which are significant at the 0.10 level or better are displayed in the graphs in the text.

Table B-4

Marginal Returns to White and Nonwhite Education
in the Central City Poverty Areas of Twelve SMSAs, March, 1966

Measure of Payoff	Years of School Completed					R^2	F	Sample size
	8	9–11	12	13–15	16+			
Weekly wages ($)								
Whites								
Levels	+2.47	+14.80[a]	+24.88[a]	+16.99[a]	+61.36[a]	.287	9.68	821
Differences		+12.33[b]	+10.08[c]	−7.89	+44.37[b]			
Nonwhites								
Levels	+2.33	+1.00	+8.33[a]	+14.39[a]	+41.36[a]	.361	45.80	2935
Differences		−1.33	+7.33[c]	+6.06[c]	+26.97[b]			
Absolute difference between white and nonwhite levels	0.14	13.80[d]	16.55[d]	2.60	20.00[e]			
Annual Unemployment (%)								
Whites								
Levels	+0.4	+0.5	+3.5[a]	−4.9[a]	−5.4[a]	.135	4.36	821
Differences		+0.1	−4.0[b]	−1.4[c]	−0.5[c]			
Nonwhites								
Levels	−0.6	+0.3	−0.4[a]	−1.9	−1.1	.231	23.54	2935
Differences		+0.9	−0.7[c]	−1.5	+0.8			
Absolute difference between white and nonwhite levels	1.0	0.8	3.1[d]	3.0[d]	4.3[e]			

Table B-4 (Continued)

Measure of Payoff	Years of School Completed					R²	F	Sample size
	8	9–11	12	13–15	16+			
Occupational Status *(rank order)*								
Whites								
Levels	+2.8	+3.7	+15.8[a]	+24.1[a]	+37.9[a]	.203	16.24	821
Differences		+0.9	+12.1[b]	+8.3[b]	+13.8[b]			
Nonwhites								
Levels	+1.7	+2.9[a]	+10.2[a]	+17.4[a]	+40.4[a]	.309	32.19	2935
Differences		+1.2	+7.3[b]	+7.2[b]	+23.0[b]			
Absolute difference between white and nonwhite levels	1.1	0.8	5.6[e]	6.7[e]	2.5[d]			

Source: Author's calculations from unpublished 1966 Survey of Economic Opportunity data files.

[a]Regression coefficient is significant at the .05 level.
[b]Difference is significant at the .05 level (the standard error of the difference between two coefficients β_i and β_j within a regression is estimated by $\sqrt{\mathrm{Var}_i + \mathrm{Var}_j - 2\,\mathrm{Cov}_{ij}}$).
[c]Difference is significant at the .10 level.
[d]Interracial difference is significant at the .10 level (determined by pooling the racial samples, adding education-race interaction terms for each education class, and conducting t-tests on the coefficients associated with each of these education-race dummies).
[e]Interracial difference is significant at the .05 level.

APPENDIX **C.**

MODELS AND RESULTS ON THE UES "GHETTOS"

SCHOOL COMPLETION RATES IN THE GHETTO

Table C-1

Years of School Completed—Roxbury, 1966

		Age 20+				Age 20–24			
		Black	White	Spanish-surname	Total[a]	Black	White	Spanish-surname	Total[a]
Number reporting		1,897	858	91	2,919	282	85	22	393
Years of school completed									
0–7	no.	327	151	36	535	9	6	10	25
	%	17.2	17.6	39.6	18.3	3.2	7.1	45.5	6.4
8	no.	187	141	19	355	9	4	3	17
	%	9.9	16.4	20.9	12.2	3.2	4.7	13.6	4.3
9–11	no.	522	199	18	747	103	23	6	133
	%	27.5	23.2	19.8	25.6	36.5	27.1	27.3	33.8
12	no.	677	254	16	977	132	32	3	168
	%	35.7	29.6	17.6	33.5	46.8	37.6	13.6	42.7
13	no.	184	113	2	305	29	20	0	50
	%	9.7	13.2	2.2	10.4	10.3	23.5		12.7
Percent with 12 or more years of school		45.4	42.8	19.8	43.9	57.1	61.2	13.6	55.5
Median years completed		11.5	11.1	8.5	11.3	12.2	12.3	8.3	12.1

Source: Author's calculations from the *1966 Urban Employment Survey*.
[a]The difference between the total and the sum of the three racial tallies is attributable to "Chinese, American-Indian, and others."

Table C-2

Years of School Completed—Central Harlem, 1966

		Age 20+				Age 20–24			
		Black	White	Spanish-surname	Total[a]	Black	White	Spanish-surname	Total
Number reporting		2,501	139	308	2,958	214	17	49	280
Years of school completed	0–7 no.	548	47	121	719	6	3	11	20
	%	21.9	33.8	39.3	24.3	2.8	17.6	22.4	7.1
	8 no.	228	13	35	276	4	0	3	7
	%	9.1	9.4	11.4	9.3	1.9		6.1	2.5
	9–11 no.	595	15	70	680	56	1	13	70
	%	23.8	10.8	22.7	23.0	26.2	5.9	26.5	25.0
	12 no.	927	47	70	1,049	128	11	17	156
	%	37.1	33.8	22.7	35.5	59.8	64.7	34.7	55.7
	13 no.	203	17	12	234	20	2	5	27
	%	8.1	12.2	3.9	7.9	9.3	11.8	10.2	9.6
Percent with 12 or more years of school		45.2	46.0	26.6	43.4	69.2	76.5	44.9	65.4
Median years completed		11.4	10.8	8.9	11.1	12.3	12.4	11.3	12.3

Source: Author's calculations from the *1966 Urban Employment Survey*.
[a]The difference between the total and the sum of the three racial tallies is attributable to "Chinese, American-Indian, and others."

Table C–3

Years of School Completed—East Harlem, 1966

		Age 20+				Age 20–24			
		Black	White	Spanish-surname	Total[a]	Black	White	Spanish-surname	Total[a]
Number reporting		689	796	1,562	3,074	85	91	240	418
Years of school completed	0–7								
	no.	152	197	716	1,069	6	2	46	54
	%	22.1	24.7	45.8	34.8	7.1	2.2	19.2	12.9
	8								
	no.	77	131	188	399	6	3	22	31
	%	11.2	16.5	12.0	13.0	7.1	3.3	9.2	7.4
	9–11								
	no.	198	163	375	743	33	25	92	151
	%	28.7	20.5	24.0	24.2	38.8	27.5	38.3	36.1
	12								
	no.	234	221	257	717	37	36	68	142
	%	34.0	27.8	16.5	23.3	43.5	39.6	28.3	34.0
	13								
	no.	28	84	26	146	3	25	12	40
	%	4.1	10.6	1.7	4.7	3.5	27.5	5.0	9.6
Percent with 12 or more years of school		38.0	38.3	18.1	28.1	47.1	67.0	33.3	43.5
Median years completed		10.7	10.3	8.3	9.3	11.7	12.4	10.7	11.5

Source: Author's calculations from the *1966 Urban Employment Survey*.
[a]The difference between the total and the sum of the three racial tallies is attributable to "Chinese, American-Indian, and others."

Table C-4

Years of School Completed—Bedford-Stuyvesant, 1966

			Age 20+				Age 20–24		
		Black	White	Spanish-surname	Total[a]	Black	White	Spanish-surname	Total[a]
Number reporting		2,711	196	350	3,301	338	9	66	418
Years of school completed	0–7								
	no.	507	47	137	705	12	0	15	28
	%	18.7	24.0	39.1	21.4	3.6		22.7	6.7
	8								
	no.	265	21	52	343	9	1	8	21
	%	9.8	10.7	14.9	10.4	2.7	11.1	12.1	5.0
	9–11								
	no.	657	37	72	772	99	4	18	121
	%	24.2	18.9	20.6	23.4	29.3	44.4	27.3	28.9
	12								
	no.	1,092	72	77	1,255	191	3	24	219
	%	40.3	36.7	22.0	38.0	56.5	33.3	36.4	52.4
	13+								
	no.	190	19	12	226	27	1	1	29
	%	7.0	9.7	3.4	6.8	8.0	11.1	1.5	6.9
Percent with 12 or more years of school		47.3	46.4	25.4	44.9	64.5	44.4	37.9	59.3
Median years completed		11.7	11.4	8.7	11.3	12.3	11.2	10.7	12.2

Source: Author's calculations from the *1966 Urban Employment Survey.*
[a]The difference between the total and the sum of the three racial tallies is attributable to "Chinese, American-Indian, and others."

Table C–5

Years of School Completed—North Philadelphia, 1966

		Age 20+				Age 20–24			
		Black	White	Spanish-surname	Total[a]	Black	White	Spanish-surname	Total[a]
Number reporting		2,414	199	199	2,830	271	17	53	345
Years of school completed									
0–7	no.	599	40	94	739	10	1	21	32
	%	24.8	20.1	47.2	26.1	3.7	5.9	39.6	9.3
8	no.	210	26	39	275	5	0	9	14
	%	8.7	13.1	19.6	9.7	1.8		17.0	4.1
9–11	no.	790	37	38	870	111	5	16	132
	%	32.7	18.6	19.1	30.7	41.0	29.4	30.2	38.3
12	no.	720	57	22	804	130	6	5	143
	%	29.8	28.6	11.1	28.4	48.0	35.3	9.4	41.4
13	no.	95	39	6	142	15	5	2	24
	%	3.9	19.6	3.0	5.0	5.5	29.4	3.8	77.0
Percent with 12 or more years of school		33.8	48.2	14.1	33.4	53.5	64.7	13.2	48.4
Median years completed		10.5	11.7	8.1	10.4	12.1	12.3	8.6	11.9

Source: Author's calculations from the *1966 Urban Employment Survey.*
[a]The difference between the total and the sum of the three racial tallies is attributable to "Chinese, American-Indian, and others."

Table C-6

Years of School Completed—North Side, 1966

		Age 20+				Age 20–24			
		Black	White	Spanish-surname	Total[a]	Black	White	Spanish-surname	Total[a]
Number reporting		2,791	226	9	3,053	280	14	4	298
Years of school completed	0–7	no.	775	67	3	856	11	0	1	12
		%	27.8	29.6	33.3	28.0	3.9		25.0	4.0
	8	no.	448	60	1	514	17	2	1	20
		%	16.1	26.5	11.1	16.8	6.1	14.3	25.0	6.7
	9–11	no.	739	38	1	785	104	4	0	108
		%	26.5	16.8	11.1	25.7	37.1	28.6		36.2
	12	no.	616	47	1	666	114	6	0	120
		%	22.1	20.8	11.1	21.8	40.7	42.9		40.3
	13	no.	213	14	3	232	34	2	2	38
		%	7.6	6.2	33.3	7.6	12.1	14.3	50.0	12.8
Percent with 12 or more years of school		29.7	27.0	44.4	29.4	52.9	57.1	50.0	53.0
Median years completed		9.7	8.8	9.0	9.6	12.1	12.2	9.0	12.1

Source: Author's calculations from the *1966 Urban Employment Survey*.
[a]The difference between the total and the sum of the three racial tallies is attributable to "Chinese, American-Indian, and others."

Table C-7

Years of School Completed—Slums of San Antonio, 1966

		Age 20+				Age 20–24			
		Black	White	Spanish-surname	Total[a]	Black	White	Spanish-surname	Total[a]
Number reporting		320	157	1,849	2,328	31	15	290	336
Years of school completed									
0–7	no.	77	34	1,060	1,171	0	3	64	67
	%	24.1	21.7	57.3	50.3	0	20.0	22.1	19.9
8	no.	30	23	178	231	0	2	35	37
	%	9.4	14.6	9.6	9.9	0	13.3	12.1	11.0
9–11	no.	74	25	284	384	6	2	78	86
	%	23.1	15.9	15.4	16.5	19.4	13.3	26.9	25.6
12	no.	91	42	277	410	13	7	96	116
	%	28.4	26.8	15.0	17.6	41.9	46.7	33.1	34.5
13	no.	48	33	50	132	12	1	17	30
	%	15.0	21.0	2.7	5.7	38.7	6.7	5.9	8.9
Percent with 12 or more years of school		43.4	47.8	17.7	23.3	80.6	53.3	39.0	43.5
Median years completed		11.1	11.5	6.1	7.0	12.7	12.0	10.8	11.2

Source: Author's calculations from the *1966 Urban Employment Survey*.

[a]The difference between the total and the sum of the three racial tallies is attributable to "Chinese, American-Indian, and others."

Table C-8

Years of School Completed—Mission-Fillmore, 1966

		Age 20+				Age 20–24			
		Black	White	Spanish-surname	Total[a]	Black	White	Spanish-surname	Total[a]
Number reporting		720	881	267	1,954	113	123	38	281
Years of school completed									
0–7	no.	104	148	84	352	1	5	2	8
	%	14.4	16.8	31.5	18.0	.9	4.1	5.3	2.8
8	no.	43	115	28	194	0	3	5	9
	%	6.0	13.1	10.5	9.9		2.4	13.2	3.2
9–11	no.	195	140	55	401	31	17	9	58
	%	27.1	15.9	20.6	27.4	27.4	13.8	23.7	20.6
12	no.	235	268	76	614	51	38	20	111
	%	32.6	30.4	28.5	31.4	45.1	30.9	52.6	39.5
13	no.	143	210	24	393	30	60	2	95
	%	19.9	23.8	9.0	20.1	26.5	48.8	5.3	33.8
Percent with 12 or more years of school		52.5	54.3	37.5	51.5	71.7	79.7	57.9	73.3
Median years completed		12.1	12.1	10.1	12.0	12.5	12.9	12.1	12.6

Source: Author's calculations from the *1966 Urban Employment Survey*.
[a]The difference between the total and the sum of the three racial tallies is attributable to "Chinese, American-Indian, and others."

Table C-9

Years of School Completed—Salt River Bed, 1966

			Age 20+				Age 20–24		
		Black	White	Spanish-surname	Total[a]	Black	White	Spanish-surname	Total[a]
Number reporting		661	570	888	2,174	53	41	159	261
Years of school completed	0–7 no.	233	158	388	798	2	2	21	25
	%	35.2	27.7	43.7	36.7	3.8	4.9	13.2	9.6
	8 no.	98	120	192	415	4	0	40	45
	%	14.8	21.1	21.6	19.1	7.5		25.2	17.2
	9–11 no.	174	130	167	486	21	17	59	100
	%	26.3	22.8	18.8	22.4	39.6	41.5	37.1	38.3
	12 no.	94	120	114	340	14	17	28	62
	%	14.2	21.1	12.8	15.6	26.4	41.5	17.6	23.8
	13 no.	62	42	27	135	12	5	11	29
	%	9.4	7.4	3.0	6.2	22.6	12.2	6.9	11.1
Percent with 12 or more years of school		23.6	28.4	15.9	21.8	49.1	53.7	24.5	34.9
Median years completed		9.0	9.2	8.3	8.7	11.9	12.1	9.9	10.8

Source: Author's calculations from the *1966 Urban Employment Survey.*
[a]The difference between the total and the sum of the three racial tallies is attributable to "Chinese, American-Indian, and others."

Table C-10

Years of School Completed—Slums of New Orleans, 1966

		Age 20+				Age 20-24			
		Black	White	Spanish-surname	Total[a]	Black	White	Spanish-surname	Total[a]
Number reporting		2,047	593	29	2,691	266	55		328
Years of school completed									
0–7	no.	792	176	9	984	24	4		28
	%	38.7	29.7	31.0	36.6	9.0	7.3		8.5
8	no.	273	108	8	393	15	6		21
	%	13.3	18.2	27.6	14.6	5.6	10.9		6.4
9–11	no.	510	100	2	616	96	10	n.a.	108
	%	24.9	16.9	6.9	22.9	36.1	18.2		32.9
12	no.	345	150	9	510	87	24		114
	%	16.9	25.3	31.0	19.0	32.7	43.6		34.8
13	no.	127	59	1	188	44	11		57
	%	6.2	9.9	3.4	7.0	16.5	20.0		17.4
Percent with 12 or more years of school		23.1	35.2	34.5	25.9	49.2	63.6		52.1
Median years completed		8.8	9.4	8.6	8.9	11.9	12.3		12.1

Source: Author's calculations from the *1966 Urban Employment Survey*.   n.a. = not applicable.
[a]The difference between the total and the sum of the three racial tallies is attributable to "Chinese, American-Indian, and others."

SPECIFICATION OF THE REGRESSION MODELS

The formal wage models to be studied are:

$$(22) \quad w = \beta_0 + \beta_1 E + \beta_2 R + \beta_3 S + \sum_{i=4}^{7} \beta_i A_{i-3} + \sum_{i=8}^{15} \beta_i C_{i-7} + \epsilon$$

$$(23) \quad w = \beta_0 + \sum_{i=1}^{5} \beta_i E_i + \beta_6 R + \beta_7 S + \sum_{i=8}^{11} \beta_i A_{i-7} + \sum_{i=12}^{19} \beta_i C_{i-11} + \epsilon$$

where:

w	= hourly wages	
E	= years of school completed	

$E_1 = E_{0-7 \text{ years}} = \begin{cases} 1 \text{ if individual did not complete grade school} \\ 0 \text{ otherwise} \end{cases}$

$E_2 = E_{8 \text{ years}} = \begin{cases} 1 \text{ if individual completed exactly 8 years of school} \\ 0 \text{ otherwise} \end{cases}$

$E_3 = E_{9-11 \text{ years}} = \begin{cases} 1 \text{ if individual completed some but not all high} \\ \quad \text{school} \\ 0 \text{ otherwise} \end{cases}$

$E_4 = E_{12 \text{ years}} = \begin{cases} 1 \text{ if individual completed exactly 12 years of} \\ \quad \text{school} \\ 0 \text{ otherwise} \end{cases}$

$E_5 = E_{13+ \text{ years}} = \begin{cases} 1 \text{ if individual completed at least some college} \\ 0 \text{ otherwise} \end{cases}$

$R = \begin{cases} 1 \text{ if individual is white} \\ 0 \text{ otherwise} \end{cases}$

$S = \begin{cases} 1 \text{ if individual is male} \\ 0 \text{ otherwise} \end{cases}$

$A_1 = A_{20-24 \text{ years}} = \begin{cases} 1 \text{ if individual is aged 20–24} \\ 0 \text{ otherwise} \end{cases}$

$A_2 = A_{25-44 \text{ years}} = \begin{cases} 1 \text{ if individual is aged 25–44} \\ 0 \text{ otherwise} \end{cases}$

$$A_3 = A_{45-54 \text{ years}} = \begin{cases} 1 \text{ if individual is aged } 45-54 \\ 0 \text{ otherwise} \end{cases}$$

$$A_4 = A_{55+ \text{ years}} = \begin{cases} 1 \text{ if individual is older than 54 years of age} \\ 0 \text{ otherwise} \end{cases}$$

$$C_1 = \begin{cases} 1 \text{ if individual lives in Boston} \\ 0 \text{ otherwise} \end{cases}$$

$$C_2 = \begin{cases} 1 \text{ if individual lives in New York} \\ 0 \text{ otherwise} \end{cases}$$

$$C_3 = \begin{cases} 1 \text{ if individual lives in Philadelphia} \\ 0 \text{ otherwise} \end{cases}$$

$$C_4 = \begin{cases} 1 \text{ if individual lives in St. Louis} \\ 0 \text{ otherwise} \end{cases}$$

$$C_5 = \begin{cases} 1 \text{ if individual lives in San Antonio} \\ 0 \text{ otherwise} \end{cases}$$

$$C_6 = \begin{cases} 1 \text{ if individual lives in San Francisco} \\ 0 \text{ otherwise} \end{cases}$$

$$C_7 = \begin{cases} 1 \text{ if individual lives in Phoenix} \\ 0 \text{ otherwise} \end{cases}$$

$$C_8 = \begin{cases} 1 \text{ if individual lives in New Orleans} \\ 0 \text{ otherwise} \end{cases}$$

Variables (E_1), (A_4), and (C_8) were deleted in order to avoid singularity.

The interaction wage models are:

$$(24) \quad w = \beta_0 + \beta_1 ER + \beta_2 ES + \sum_{i=3}^{6} \beta_i EA_{i-2} + \sum_{i=7}^{14} \beta_i EC_{i-6} + \epsilon$$

$$(25) \quad w = \beta_0 + \sum_{i=1}^{5} \beta_i E_i R + \sum_{i=6}^{10} \beta_i E_{i-5} S + \sum_{i=11}^{30} \beta_i \sum_{j=1}^{5} \sum_{k=1}^{4} E_j A_k$$

$$+ \sum_{i=31}^{70} \beta_i \sum_{j=1}^{5} \sum_{k=1}^{8} E_j C_k + \epsilon$$

LEAST-SQUARES REGRESSION ANALYSIS WITH A DICHOTOMOUS DEPENDENT VARIABLE

A word is in order about the methodology for fitting a regression model when the dependent variable is dichotomous.[1] Given this condition, the residuals (ϵ) will be able to assume only the values $[-(\Sigma\beta_i X_i)]$ or $(1-\Sigma\beta_i X_i)$. It follows that the variance of the distribution of residuals will violate the least-squares assumption that it be constant. With a dichotomous dependent variable, the variance of the distribution of residuals will vary systematically with the explanatory variables. This condition—heteroskedasticity—reduces the efficiency of the regression estimates. When we minimize the sum of unequal squared residuals ($\Sigma\epsilon^2$; $\epsilon_m^2 \neq \epsilon_n^2$), we are weighting each of the $\{\epsilon_j\}$ equally, when they ought to be weighted unequally in order to restore the effect of constant variance.

In the case of a dichotomous dependent variable (y), and making use of another classical condition that the residuals be distributed with zero mean, we can show that, for the jth observation,

$$E(\epsilon_j^2) = (\Sigma\beta_i X_i)(1-\Sigma\beta_i X_i)$$

which we can estimate by

$$\sigma_{\epsilon j}^2 = (\hat{b}_i X_i)(1-\hat{b}_i X_i) = \hat{y}_j(1-\hat{y}_j)$$

A two-stage estimation procedure recommended by Goldberger is to fit the model $y_j = \sum_i \beta_{ij} X_{ij} + \epsilon_j$ by ordinary least-squares to obtain estimates of the $\{\hat{y}_j\}$, deflate each observation by the appropriate $\sqrt{(\hat{y}_j(1-\hat{y}_j))}$, and fit the OLS model again to the deflated data. The resulting weighted estimates are known as Aitken generalized least-squares estimates.

Nothing in this procedure guarantees that the final predictions will fall within the 0-1 interval required by the economic theory. If they do not, then a more complicated procedure of constrained estimation is required, based on a technique called probit analysis which has been adapted for econometric usage by Tobin.[2] Fortunately, in my own research with the UES, no more than 1.4 percent of the predicted unemployment probabilities $[p(u|E, A, R, S)]$ fell outside the interval 0-1. Therefore, it seemed unnecessary to go beyond the two-stage procedure described above. Instead, I arbitrarily set the outliers equal to 0 or 1.

---

1. The following discussion is based upon Arthur S. Goldberger, *Econometric Theory* (New York: Wiley, 1964), pp. 231–56.
2. James Tobin, "Estimation of Relationships for Limited Dependent Variables," *Econometrica*, 26 (1958).

APPENDIX **D.**

INTRAMETROPOLITAN
SEO
RESULTS

Table D-1

SEO Regression Results: Additive Models for Three Intrametropolitan Regions[a]

	Payoff Variable and Sample											
	Earnings ($/week)											
	Nonwhites						Whites					
	Central city poverty areas		Rest of central city		Ring		Central city poverty areas		Rest of central city		Ring	
Policy Variable	(b)	(c)	(b)	(c)	(b)	(c)	(b)	(c)	(b)	(c)	(b)	(c)
Education:												
E	1.81		3.61		26.4		4.05		5.82		8.75	
E_8								14.80		15.52		
E_{9-11}		8.33						24.88		20.22d		22.26
E_{12} (H.S. completion)										24.68		32.80
E_{13-15}		14.39				15.70		16.99d		38.04		52.76
E_{16}		41.36		53.50		38.87		61.36		76.30		98.12

252

Training:	(1)		(2)		(3)		(4)		(5)		(6)	
Institutional												
Completed	28.71	27.01										
Incompleted	12.51	11.26										
Apprenticeship												
Completed			17.78	18.13								
Incompleted												
Private OJT												
Completed					30.61	30.46						
Incompleted												
Armed Forces voc.												
Completed							30.09	33.79				
Incompleted												
Government program												
Completed									21.14	20.78		
Incompleted												
R^2	.352	.361	.367	.397	.306	.303	.280	.287	.268	.274	.282	.288
F	49.21	45.80	29.30	29.63	12.29	10.91	10.38	9.68	23.18	21.53	37.60	34.60
Sample sizes	2935	2935	1565	1565	845	845	821	821	2125	2125	3163	3163

Note: Footnotes are located at the end of the table.

Table D-1 (Continued)

Policy Variable	Payoff Variable and Sample											
	Unemployment (weeks unemployed last year as % of weeks in the labor force)											
	Nonwhites						Whites					
	Central city poverty areas		Rest of central city		Ring		Central city poverty areas		Rest of central city		Ring	
	(b)	(c)	(b)	(c)	(b)	(c)	(b)	(c)	(b)	(c)	(b)	(c)
Education:												
E	0.0		0.0		-0.5		-0.6		-0.4		-0.6	
E_8												
E_{9-11}				3.3								-3.5
E_{12} (H.S. completion)		-0.4						-3.5		-3.0		-6.1
E_{13-15}								-4.9		-3.3[d]		-6.1[d]
E_{16}								-5.4		-4.2		-6.4

Training:
Institutional
  Completed
  Incompleted
Apprenticeship
  Completed
  Incompleted
Private OJT
  Completed
  Incompleted
Armed Forces voc.
  Completed
  Incompleted
Government program
  Completed
  Incompleted

	7.9	7.8							6.1	6.2		
R^2	.221	.231	.240	.242	.205	.204	.129	.135	.133	.132	.112	.114
F	26.27	23.54	16.41	14.90	7.59	6.85	4.58	4.36	10.34	9.27	12.69	11.69
Sample sizes	2935	2935	1565	1565	845	845	821	821	2125	2125	3163	3163

Note: Footnotes are located at the end of the table.

Table D-1 (Continued)

Policy Variable	Nonwhites					Whites					
	Central city poverty areas (c)	Rest of central city (b)	(c)	Ring (b)	(c)	Central city poverty areas (b)	(c)	Rest of central city (b)	(c)	Ring (b)	(c)
Education:											
E	2.0	3.7		2.5		2.7		3.8		4.3	
E_8											5.2
E_{9-11}	2.9								11.6		10.4^d
E_{12} (H.S. completion)	10.2		11.9		8.5		15.8		20.6		21.0
E_{13-15}	17.4		20.7		18.8^d		24.1		28.5		31.2
E_{16+}	40.4		46.8		46.6		37.9		43.9		45.7

Payoff Variable and Sample

Occupational status (Duncan-NORC ordinal ranking of 0-96)

ıraınıng.

Training	b	c	b	c	b	c	b	c	b	c	b	c
Institutional												
Completed	3.3	3.0	4.3									
Incompleted												
Apprenticeship												
Completed				n.a.								
Incompleted												
Private OJT												
Completed						n.a.						
Incompleted												
Armed Forces voc.												
Completed							6.9	7.3				
Incompleted												
Government program												
Completed										n.a.	3.7	4.1
Incompleted												
R^2	.149	.203	.287	.363	.159	.265	.260	.309	.292	.304	.320	.325
F	26.67	32.19	35.98	41.57	9.38	14.26	15.42	16.24	44.71	39.67	75.51	64.36
Sample Sizes	2935	2935	1565	1565	845	845	821	821	2125	2125	3163	3163

[a] Only 95% significant coefficients are shown. All coefficients and standard errors are given in the dissertation.
[b] Additive model with continuous specification of E.
[c] Additive model with discontinuous specification of E.
[d] The difference between this and the preceding "step" is not significant at the .05 level.
n.a. = not applicable.

SELECTED
BIBLIOGRAPHY

Averitt, Robert. *The Dual Economy.* New York: W. W. Norton, 1968.

Becker, Gary S. *The Economics of Discrimination.* Chicago: University of Chicago Press, 1957.

_____. *Human Capital.* New York: Columbia University Press, 1964.

Berg, Ivar. *Education and Jobs: The Great Training Robbery.* New York: Praeger, 1970.

Blau, Peter M., and Duncan, Otis Dudley. *The American Occupational Structure.* New York: Wiley, 1967.

Cohn, Jules. *The Conscience of the Corporations.* Baltimore, Md.: Johns Hopkins Press, 1971.

Doeringer, Peter B., ed. *Programs to Employ the Disadvantaged.* Englewood Cliffs, N.J.: Prentice-Hall, 1969.

Doeringer, Peter B., and Piore, Michael J. *Internal Labor Markets and Manpower Analysis.* Lexington, Mass.: D. C. Heath, 1971.

Downs, Anthony. *Who Are the Urban Poor?* Supplementary Paper no. 26. New York: Committee for Economic Development, 1968.

Faux, Geoffrey. *CDC's: New Hope for the Inner City.* New York: Twentieth Century Fund, 1971.

Ferman, Louis A., *et al.,* eds. *Negroes and Jobs.* Ann Arbor, Mich.: University of Michigan Press, 1968.

Galbraith, John Kenneth. *The New Industrial State.* New York: Houghton Mifflin, 1967.

Gordon, David M., ed. *Problems in Political Economy: An Urban Perspective.* Lexington, Mass.: D. C. Heath, 1971.

_____. *Theories of Poverty and Underemployment.* Lexington, Mass.: Heath-Lexington Books, 1972.

Haddad, William F., and Pugh, G. Douglas, eds. *Black Economic Development.* Englewood Cliffs, N.J.: Prentice-Hall, 1969.

Harrison, Bennett. *Metropolitan Suburbanization and Minority Economic Opportunity.* Washington, D.C.: Urban Institute, 1973.

_____. *Public Employment and Urban Poverty.* Paper no. 113–43. Washington, D.C.: Urban Institute, 1971.

Hiestand, Dale. *Discrimination in Employment: An Appraisal of the Research.* Ann Arbor, Mich.: Institute of Labor and Industrial Relations, University of Michigan-Wayne State University, 1970.

Kain, John F., ed. *Race and Poverty.* Englewood Cliffs, N.J.: Prentice-Hall, 1970.

Levitan, Sar A.; Mangum, Garth L.; and Taggart, Robert, III. *Economic Opportunity in the Ghetto: The Partnership of Government and Business.* Baltimore, Md.: Johns Hopkins Press, 1970.

Lewis, Oscar. *A Study of Slum Culture: Backgrounds for La Vida.* New York: Random House, 1968.

Liebow, Elliot. *Talley's Corner.* Boston, Mass.: Little, Brown, 1967.

Malcolm X. *The Autobiography of Malcolm X.* New York: Grove Press, 1965.

National Industrial Conference Board. *Education, Training, and Employment of the Disadvantaged.* Studies in Public Affairs no. 4. New York: The Conference Board, 1969.

Piven, Frances Fox, and Cloward, Richard. *Regulating the Poor.* New York: Pantheon, 1971.

Ribich, Thomas. *Education and Poverty.* Washington, D.C.: Brookings Institution, 1968.

Scheer, Robert, ed. *Eldridge Cleaver: Post-Prison Writings and Speeches.* New York: Random House, 1969.

Schiller, Bradley R. *The Economics of Poverty and Discrimination.* Englewood Cliffs, N.J.: Prentice-Hall, 1972.

Sheppard, Harold L.; Harrison, Bennett; and Spring, William, eds. *The Political Economy of Public Service Employment.* Lexington, Mass.: Heath-Lexington Books, 1972.

Thurow, Lester C. *Investment in Human Capital.* Belmont, Cal.: Wadsworth, 1970.

―――. *Poverty and Discrimination.* Washington, D.C.: Brookings Institution, 1969.

U.S. Department of Labor. *Manpower Report of the President.* Washington, D.C.: Government Printing Office, annual.

Vietorisz, Thomas, and Harrison, Bennett. *The Economic Development of Harlem.* New York: Praeger, 1970.

INDEX

THE JOHNS HOPKINS UNIVERSITY PRESS

This book was composed in Press Roman Medium text and Melior display
by Jones Composition Company from a design by Edward Scott.
It was printed on 60–lb. Harmony Book Offset and bound in
Columbia Bayside linen cloth by Port City Press, Inc.

Library of Congress Cataloging in Publication Data

Harrison, Bennett.
    Education, training, and the urban ghetto.

    Includes bibliographical references.
    1. Negroes–Employment. 2. Negroes–Education.
I. Title.
E185.8.H3   331.6'3'96073   72-4023
ISBN 0–8018–1366–2